Apple Pro Training Series

Logic Pro 7
and Logic Express 7

Martin Sitter

Apple
Certified

Apple Pro Training Series: Logic Pro 7 and Logic Express 7
Martin Sitter
Copyright © 2005 by Martin Sitter

Published by Peachpit Press. For information on Peachpit Press books, contact:

Peachpit Press
1249 Eighth Street
Berkeley, CA 94710
(510) 524-2178
Fax: (510) 524-2221
http://www.peachpit.com
To report errors, please send a note to errata@peachpit.com.
Peachpit Press is a division of Pearson Education.

Series Editor: Serena Herr
Managing Editor: Kristin Kalning
Editor: Whitney Walker
Production Editor: Laurie Stewart, Happenstance Type-O-Rama
Technical Editor: Bill Burgess
Technical Reviewer: Victor Gavenda
Copy Editors: Karen Seriguchi, Elissa Rabellino
Compositor: Happenstance Type-O-Rama
Indexer: Joy Dean Lee
Interior and Cover Design: Frances Baca
Cover Illustration: Tolleson Design
Cover Production: George Mattingly
Coauthor, first edition: Robert Brock

ISBN 0-321-25614-X
9 8 7 6 5 4 3 2
Printed and bound in the United States of America

This book is dedicated to the memory of Brent Carmichael.

Brent DJ'd disco when disco was still king. He entertained thousands of people every month (sometimes every week) for decades. Brent taught me deep dark secrets about DJ'ing ... which at the end of the day is simply entertaining. In so many ways, Brent, I've done all of this for you.

Acknowledgments Special thanks to Patricia Montesion for providing the guidance that grew the Apple Pro Training Series. Thank you, Gerhard Lengeling, for supporting this book so strongly.

Kirk Paulsen, your guiding influence is felt, if not seen.

Serena Herr, thanks for understanding your author—you are the Queen of Cool. Would my editor, Whitney Walker, please stand up and take a bow. I must also thank my friends at Apple, the people that make this job not just fun, but also worth living: Vidas Neverauskas, Bob Hunt, Phil Jackson, David Dvorin, Jessica Steigerwald, Bill Forester, Brian Schmidt, Don Steele, Margaret Tinsley, and Victor Alexander.

Of course, my fellow lead trainers deserve immense recognition: Adam Green, Steve Martin, Abba Shapiro, Damian Allen, Mary Plummer, and Diana Weynand.

I'd like to thank DJ Drivetrain (Derrick Thompson), Donald Glaude, DJ Czech, and Tyler Stadius for their friendship over the years, and also for inspiring me through music.

And finally, for pushing me down the path that brought me here—for making me musically what I am today—I must thank DJ Rennie "Dubnut" Foster, Scott Newton, Matt Densham and Sally Malloy, Luca De Cotiis, David and Allison Meyer, Jay Lev, Jon V., Levi, Matty, David Tillson, James Boatman, Nigel Tasko, Barnabus Clark, German Mike, DJ Davie, Degree, Lori the Hi-Fi Process, Koosh, Tiger D'hula, Dimitri, Sherwood, Bill-e, and all the other DJ/producers that made Victoria the place to be ... way back in the mid-'90s.

Contents at a Glance

Table of Contents

Logic for Video Editors

Foreword

Through most of the decades since the founding of the first record label ("His Master's Voice") in 1900, the roles of composers, musicians, and recording engineers have stayed the same. To be sure, there were numerous improvements in technology, as studios moved from tubes to transistors and from analog to digital recording equipment, and the distribution medium changed from vinyl records to CDs, DVDs, and the Internet. Yet the workflow for recording and production remained largely unchanged. Musicians had to go to dedicated studios, filled with large and expensive equipment, to produce professional-quality recordings.

However, in the past few years, the arrival of extremely powerful personal computers has effected a revolution in the recording and production process, ushering in an exciting transition to an integrated, software-based system. This transition opens a world of possibilities for the recording musician, and it is unlikely that we'll see such a dramatic shift again in our lifetime.

Most recording studios have an array of hardware equipment, such as multitrack recorders, huge multichannel mixing boards, mastering devices, racks full of effects, and an army of keyboard and other instruments. All these devices and more can now be replaced by lines of code executed on a personal computer. A fast computer can provide extremely high sound quality, easily matching professional studios of just ten years ago at a fraction of the cost. This new development is profoundly changing the way we interact with the studio, giving us more power and possibilities, new types of effects and instruments, and tremendous versatility and ease of use. Not only is it now possible to produce projects on a portable Macintosh PowerBook, but that's actually become the norm.

These changes allow musical creativity to unfold unhindered by past economic constraints. Composing, performing, recording, mixing, and mastering can now all be accomplished in a home studio, at minimal cost, with amazing results. Needless to say, this has and will have a huge impact on music; and we have already begun to see the genesis of musical styles made possible only through these new means. Another result is a blurring between the creation, performance, and consumption of music, and the advent of computer artists joining musicians playing standard instruments onstage.

Logic started as a MIDI sequencer and notation package in 1993. With the addition of digital audio recording and DSP effects, Logic is now a complete software studio, with mixing and mastering capabilities and a wide array of software instruments. Logic has been used to produce many professional audio recordings and movie soundtracks, and it is recognized today as an industry standard.

Since 2004, Logic's audio engine and professional-level sound quality have been available to everyone in Apple's GarageBand consumer application. GarageBand is extremely easy to use but at the same time surprisingly powerful and versatile, and it comes with a "band" in the form of Apple Loops, a huge collection of prerecorded musical material that you can use in your own original songs.

Logic Pro 7 adds new software instruments including Sculpture and Ultrabeat, new effects including pitch correction, more mastering tools, and many workflow improvements in every area. Together, these additions enable you to realize your musical intentions with even greater ease and power. Some effects simply go beyond anything possible using analog hardware gear. Logic Pro 7 also supports Apple Loops and GarageBand Software Instruments and songs. You can "sketch" in GarageBand, then bring projects into Logic Pro 7 for finetuning and production. And with Apple's Jam Packs, you can add high-quality instruments and Apple Loops to your toolkit.

Logic Pro 7 gives users the best of both worlds—a top-notch professional software studio that is also easy to use and affordable. With this complete set of tools to make music anytime, anywhere, artists have the ability to realize their musical vision now more than ever. I am sure that this book will help you unlock that power.

Dr. Gerhard Lengeling
Senior Director, Lead Architect Audio/Music Applications
Apple Computer
December 2004

Getting Started

Computerized music production has undergone a revolution in the past several years. Where once you needed a studio filled with synthesizers and rackmount systems, mixing consoles, microphones, and of course, the high-priced talent that could afford all those expensive toys, now all it takes is a laptop and Logic 7.

Logic 7 is a true *studio in a box*. For less than half the price of a good hardware synthesizer, Logic 7 comes with everything you need to make professional music. There's a sampler, 33 software instruments, and 70 high-quality DSP effects (in Logic Pro). Everything you need to make awesome sound comes tightly wrapped and integrated into this one package. And with its updated interface and support for Apple Loops, Logic 7 is now easier to use (and more musical) than ever before. It has truly grown into a "killer app."

Apple Pro Training Series: Logic Pro 7 and Logic Express 7 is based on the premise that a technical book should be more than a tour of menus, commands, and windows—it should show you how to actually use the application. In this book, you will learn how to use Logic 7 by building a complete song from the ground up. If you've never used Logic before, you can follow the lessons to see how a song is made: importing audio, arranging audio and MIDI to create a composition, mixing volume levels and pan positions, and adding DSP effects that turn a good mix into a song that really shines. If you're an experienced audio professional, you'll appreciate the many tips and suggestions that will help you streamline your workflow in Logic and get the most out of the application.

The Methodology

This book is designed to be an introduction to Logic and is not meant for those who have a lot of experience using this program (experienced Logic users should read *Apple Pro Training Series: Advanced Logic Pro 7*). Video editors, audio hobbyists, and music producers switching to Logic from other sequencing programs will have the most to gain from reading this book.

This doesn't mean that the book's lessons are basic in nature. Logic is sophisticated software, and the lessons cover all its aspects. A lot goes into making a good song, so to cover it all the book is divided into four sections:

Logic Overview

▶ Lessons 1, 2, and 3 lay the groundwork by introducing you to Logic, its editing windows, and some basic functions such as setting up screensets, using the Transport to play and navigate through a song, and creating personalized key commands—skills you'll use throughout the book.

Creating a Song

▶ Lessons 4 through 10 build an actual song from the ground up. You start by importing MIDI and audio files, and then use Logic's editing windows to modify those imported files into an arrangement. Finally, you mix the song, add DSP effects to sweeten the sound, and also explore Logic's excellent automation features to breathe life into your songs by programming evolving ambiences through plug-in manipulation.

Customizing Your Setup

▶ Logic's Environment window is perhaps the single most intimidating window in the program, and it is arguably the one reason why some new users find the program difficult to learn. But this doesn't have to be the case. Lessons 11 and 12 break down these barriers by walking you through the process of customizing Logic to make it work in your studio. In the course of these two lessons you'll learn how to select synthesizers and use audio channels to get sound into and out of Logic. By the end of Lesson 12 you'll have created your own personalized Autoload Song that opens every time you launch Logic, and this Autoload Song will be perfectly config-ured to interact with your studio's MIDI devices.

Logic for Video Editors

▶ With the popularity of products like Final Cut Pro and DVD Studio Pro, there can be no doubt that video is an important part of Apple's Pro appli-cation line, and these days 5.1 surround sound is the hot-ticket item. If you're a video editor looking to add polish to your creations, Lesson 13 shows you how to score video in Logic 7, while Lesson 14 walks you through the intricacies of setting Logic up for 5.1 surround mixing that will help you create those immersive soundscapes you've been dreaming of.

About the Apple Pro Training Series

Apple Pro Training Series: Logic Pro 7 and Logic Express 7 is part of the official training series for Apple Pro applications developed by experts in the field. The lessons are designed to let you learn at your own pace. If you're new to Logic, you'll learn the fundamental concepts and features you'll need to master the program. If you've been using Logic for a while, you'll find that this book teaches many advanced features, including tips and techniques for using the latest version of Logic.

Although each lesson provides step-by-step instructions for creating a specific project, there's room for exploration and experimentation. It is recommended that you follow the book from start to finish or at least complete the first five chapters before skipping around. Each lesson concludes with a review section summarizing what you've covered.

System Requirements

Before beginning to use *Apple Pro Training Series: Logic Pro 7 and Logic Express 7,* you should have a working knowledge of your computer and its operating system. Make sure that you know how to use the mouse and standard menus and commands and also how to open, save, and close files. If you need to review these techniques, see the printed or online documentation included with your system.

Basic system requirements for Logic 7 include:

▶   Macintosh computer with PowerPC G4 or faster processor (G5 or dual G4 processors recommended)

▶   PowerPC G5 and Gigabit Ethernet connectivity for Logic Node applications

▶   Mac OS X 10.3 or later

▶   512 MB of RAM

▶   DVD drive for software installation

▶   Low-latency multi-I/O audio hardware and MIDI interface recommended

▶   4 GB of available hard-disk space

Installing Logic

The DVD-ROM that accompanies this book includes a full 30-day license of Logic Express 7, and no hardware key is necessary. To install your copy of the Logic Express 7 trial software, please follow the instructions listed in the Read Me document on the DVD-ROM.

Copying the Logic Lesson Files

The *Apple Pro Training Series: Logic Pro 7 and Logic Express 7* DVD-ROM includes folders containing the lesson files used in this course. Each lesson has its own folder, and you should copy these folders to your hard disk to use the files for the lessons. The companion disc also contains a folder called Song Files. Inside this folder you will find all the source audio and MIDI files used in the lessons.

To install the Logic Project Files:

1   Insert the *APTS_Logic_7* DVD-ROM into your DVD drive.

2   Create a folder on your hard disk and name it *APTS_Logic_7*.

3   Drag the Song Files folder from the DVD into the APTS_Logic_7 folder on your hard disk. You'll find the Project Files for each lesson within that Song Files folder.

Resources

Apple Pro Training Series: Logic Pro 7 and Logic Express 7 is not intended as a comprehensive reference manual, nor does it replace the documentation that comes with the Logic application. For more information about Logic's features, refer to these resources:

▶   The Reference Manual. Accessed through the Logic Help menu, the Reference Manual contains a complete description of all features.

▶   www.macProVideo.com. Watch online videos that walk you through all aspects of using Logic.

Apple Pro Certification Program

The Apple Pro Training and Certification Programs are designed to keep you at the forefront of Apple's digital media technology while giving you a competitive edge in today's ever-changing job market. Whether you're an editor, graphic designer, sound designer, special effects artist, or teacher, these training tools are meant to help you expand your skills.

Upon completing the course material in this book, you can become an Apple Pro by taking the certification exam at an Apple Authorized Training Center. Certification is offered in Final Cut Pro, DVD Studio Pro, Shake, and Logic. Successful certification as an Apple Pro gives you official recognition of your knowledge of Apple's professional applications while enabling you to market yourself to employers and clients as a skilled, pro-level user of Apple products.

To find an Authorized Training Center near you, go to www.apple.com/software/pro/training.

For those who prefer to learn in an instructor-led setting, Apple also offers training courses at Apple Authorized Training Centers worldwide. These courses, which use the Apple Pro Training Series books as their curriculum, are taught by Apple Certified Trainers and balance concepts and lectures with hands-on labs and exercises. Apple Authorized Training Centers for Pro products have been carefully selected and have met Apple's highest standards in all areas, including facilities, instructors, course delivery, and infrastructure. The goal of the program is to offer Apple customers, from beginners to the most seasoned professionals, the highest-quality training.

Logic Overview

1

Lesson Files	APTS_Logic_7 > Song Files > Lesson 1 Project Files > 01Begin.lso
	APTS_Logic_7 > Song Files > Lesson 1 Project Files > 01End.lso
Media	APTS_Logic_7 > Song Files > Lesson 1 Project Files
Time	This lesson takes approximately 1 hour to complete.
Goals	Launch Logic and open a song
	Learn to use the Arrange window
	Examine Logic's editing tools
	Use the Transport panel and the numeric keypad to control song playback
	Move the Song Position Line
	Adjust the tempo
	Insert and adjust DSP plug-ins
	Insert and play Logic's internal Audio Instruments
	Assign Channel Strip settings
	Bounce your song

Exploring the Workspace

This lesson serves as a primer to get you into the swing of using Logic's workspace. The exercises in this lesson lay the groundwork by covering common concepts used throughout the book. For example, you'll explore Logic's main editing window, the Arrange window, and also learn valuable techniques for setting the tempo and controlling the song playback as you edit. But it's not all theory—there's some time for fun, too! In the second half of the lesson you'll learn how to add DSP effects to change the sound of your song, and you'll explore playing and inserting Logic's internal Audio Instrument synthesizers to create new sounds for your songs. There's a lot to cover, so let's jump straight in.

Launching Logic

When you install Logic, a Logic application package is placed in your Startup Disk > Applications folder. It should be noted that this application package is more than just the Logic application itself. There is a whole bunch of stuff in the package, and all of it conspires to make Logic function. You can actually tunnel into the Logic application package by Ctrl-clicking (or right-clicking, if you have a multi-buttoned mouse) it and choosing Show Package Contents.

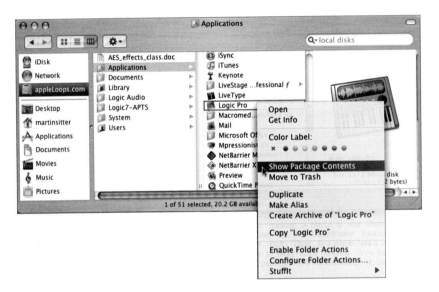

However, be warned: Don't move or change anything in the application package unless you know exactly what you are doing or are prepared to fully reinstall the program! Logic needs everything in the application package to remain exactly as it is or the program will not function correctly. With that in mind, let's launch Logic.

1   In a Finder window, navigate to the Startup Disk > Applications > Logic Pro or Logic Express, depending on which version of the program you are running.

   NOTE ▶ When this book asks you to navigate to the Startup Disk or User folder, please use your own startup disk and user folder.

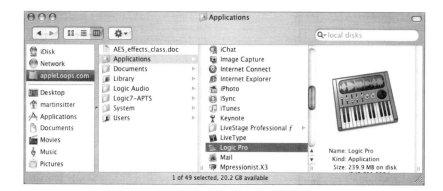

Let's make the Logic application easy to find by putting it in your computer's Dock.

2 Drag the Logic application icon to the Dock and drop it there.

3 Close the Finder window.

4 In the Dock, click the Logic icon.

Logic opens, and the default workspace appears on your computer's monitor.

NOTE ▶ The *workspace* is the name for all of Logic's editing windows combined. It's the *space* you *work* in as you make music.

Audio Instrument Tracks

Audio Tracks

GM MIDI Tracks

Logic's default workspace represents a *generic* studio with 8 audio tracks, 8 Audio Instrument tracks, and 16 MIDI tracks representing all the MIDI channels found on a General MIDI (GM) synthesizer. This is an adequate base for working in Logic, but it can be improved. For example, your studio probably has more than one synthesizer. You may also have a few digital-effects units and perhaps even a sampler or two. Logic's default workspace is not set up to communicate with these extra MIDI devices, so you need to change the workspace to better represent your studio. In the "Customizing Your Setup" section of the book you will do just that—take this generic workspace and customize it to reflect the exact setup of your studio, and then save that customized setup as an *Autoload Song* that opens every time you launch Logic.

NOTE ▶ *General MIDI* (GM) is a protocol developed by Roland (a manufacturer of electronic instruments and audio effects) that defines the type, name, and order of synthesizer sound programs.

Opening a Song File

There are several ways to open a Logic song file. For example, you can drag a song file and drop it onto the Logic application icon (in either the Finder or the Dock), or double-click a song file in any Finder window.

With Logic running, a common way to open a song file is to use the File > Open command located in Logic's main menu bar. To follow along with this lesson, use these steps to open the **01Begin.lso** song file:

1   Choose File > Open.

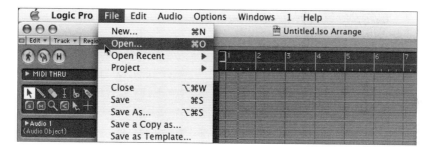

Logic's default song should still be open in the background, so a dialog appears asking if you'd like to close the currently open song before opening the new one.

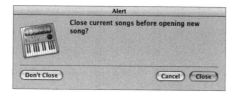

Logic lets you work on several songs at one time, which often comes in handy. For example, you can cut and paste MIDI or Audio Regions

between songs, or compare the DSP settings of a finished song against those of a song you're working on. But for now, let's concentrate on one song at a time.

2   Click the Alert dialog's Close button.

The default song closes, and an Open dialog appears.

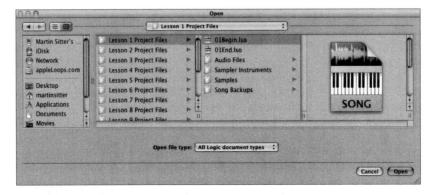

3   Navigate to APTS_Logic_7 > Song Files > Lesson 1 Project Files, and select the file named **01Begin.lso**, and click Open.

The **01Begin.lso** song opens.

TIP ▸ The File > Open Recent option offers a convenient way of opening songs you've recently been working on. If you select this option, a submenu of recently opened songs appears. You may now instantly open a song by clicking its name in this submenu, which saves you from having to locate the file on your hard disk(s).

Getting to Know the Arrange Window

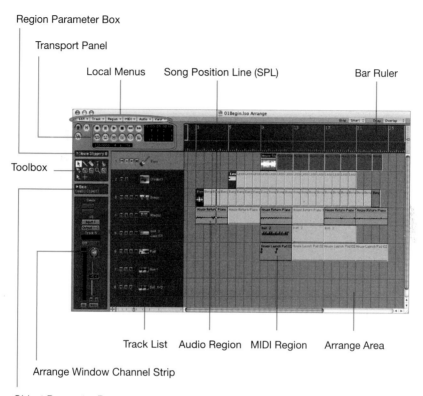

Region Parameter Box

Transport Panel

Local Menus Song Position Line (SPL) Bar Ruler

Toolbox

Track List Audio Region MIDI Region Arrange Area

Arrange Window Channel Strip

Object Parameter Box

Can you see sound? With Logic, you can. A soundscape is more or less an aural painting, filled with emotion and colored by experience in much the same way as a painting hung on the wall reflects the mood of the artist when she picked up her brush. In a painting, the artist arranges strokes and dabs of color across a canvas to make a visual picture. In Logic, you arrange strokes and dabs of sound across the Arrange window to make a song. The Arrange window is your sound canvas. It's also Logic's main editing window, and the majority of your time editing in Logic will be spent in this window.

Let's take a brief look at the various parts of the Arrange window.

The Arrange Area

The heart of the Arrange window is the Arrange area. This large rectangular space occupies most of the Arrange window, and it has one function only: It's used to arrange MIDI Regions and Audio Regions to make a song.

The Song Position Line

The Song Position Line (SPL) is Logic's playhead. As a song plays, the SPL moves across the Arrange area to let you see which part of the song you are hearing.

The Bar Ruler

The Bar Ruler is divided into bars and beats. It's your song's timeline. As the song plays, the Bar Ruler works in conjunction with the SPL to help you determine the current playback position in your song.

The Transport Panel

The Transport panel holds buttons used to control Logic's playback and recording functions.

MIDI Regions

MIDI Regions are little boxes that contain MIDI data. A MIDI Region is a tightly wrapped package, and if you open one up by double-clicking it, you'll see a collection of note-on and note-off messages; volume, pan, and continuous controller data; and other information (such as SysEx messages) that tell a synthesizer how to play notes.

It's important to note that MIDI Regions do not contain sounds. The sounds all sit in your synthesizers. Think of a player piano in an Old West saloon. In this device, a roll of paper with holes punched in it cycles through the piano. The punched-out holes represent note information that tells the player piano which keys to press and when to press them. If your synthesizer is a player piano, MIDI Regions are the rolls of punched paper that tell it which keys to press.

Audio Regions

An Audio Region is a selected area of an audio file. Like MIDI Regions in the Arrange window, Audio Regions look like horizontal boxes. But there's a difference: While MIDI Regions hold MIDI data that plays your MIDI devices, Audio Regions point to digital audio files stored on your hard disks. This can be audio recorded directly into Logic through your sound card, audio imported from a folder on your hard disk or a CD, or even converted MP3 files downloaded from the Internet.

The Track List

In Logic, all MIDI Regions and Audio Regions are recorded and arranged on horizontal lines called *tracks*. These tracks are listed vertically, from the top of the Arrange window toward the bottom. Toward the left edge of the Arrange window there is a column displaying the names of your song's tracks—this is called the Track List.

The Region Parameter Box and the Object Parameter Box

These boxes update to show you information about MIDI Regions and Audio Regions selected in the Arrange area. There are a lot of settings in these boxes, each with a unique purpose, so let's defer the discussion of them until the appropriate lessons later in this book.

The Toolbox

MIDI Regions and Audio Regions sometimes need to be erased, cut, or combined. The tools for these jobs can be found in the Arrange window's toolbox. There are many tools in this box, and each is designed for a specific purpose. The functions of most of these tools are obvious from their icons, and you'll discover how to use each one as you work through this book's lessons. In this lesson, we'll stick to some general tips about selecting tools quickly and efficiently.

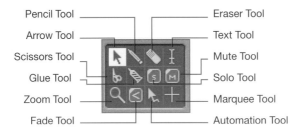

NOTE ▶ The Marquee and Automation tools are not available in Logic Express.

Selecting Tools

Selecting tools from the toolbox is every bit as easy as you'd expect—just move the pointer over the tool and click it! But still, there are some tricks you can use to make selecting tools quicker. Let's explore a few of them now.

NOTE ▶ The following tricks work in all editing windows that have a toolbox.

1   In the toolbox, click the Pencil tool, and then move its pointer over the Arrange area.

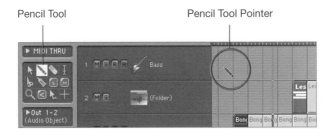

Toolbox tools are designed to work on Arrange area Regions, so the selected tool does not appear until you move its pointer into the Arrange area.

Using the Secondary Tool

Logic gives you access to both a main tool and a secondary, or alternative, tool. The main tool is the one currently selected and highlighted in the toolbox. The secondary tool is reserved for any function you use often. It is accessed by holding down the Command key. For example, if you're constantly returning to the toolbox to grab the Glue tool, save yourself some time by making the Glue tool your secondary tool, and it will become available each time you press the Command key. Let's assign the Glue tool to the Command key now.

> **NOTE** ▶ Pressing the Control key always enables Logic's Magnifying Glass (Zoom) tool. This cannot be changed.

1   Hold down the Command key and select the Glue tool.

2   Move the mouse pointer over the Arrange area.

   The pointer still shows the Pencil tool.

3   Press Command.

   While you hold down the Command key, the pointer turns into the Glue tool.

Using the Floating Toolbox

Instead of moving the mouse pointer all the way over to the toolbox, you can open the toolbox right under the pointer's current position in the Arrange area by holding down the Escape key.

1   With the mouse pointer over the Arrange area, press the Escape key.

   The toolbox opens under the pointer.

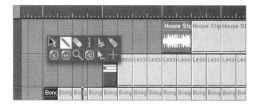

You can select a tool from this floating toolbox by either clicking it or pressing a number key.

2   Press the 3 key.

The floating toolbox disappears, and the pointer turns into the Eraser tool.

3   To return to the Arrow tool, press the Escape key twice in a row.

The floating toolbox appears, and then quickly disappears, and the Arrow tool is activated. You will need the Arrow tool for the rest of this lesson's exercises, so leave it selected.

NOTE ▶ For the sake of simplicity, we're going to call this arrow-shaped tool the *Arrow tool*, but you will run across occasions when Logic calls it the *Pointer tool*.

Exploring the Transport Panel

The Transport panel contains buttons that control Logic's playback and record functions. These buttons look similar to the control buttons on a cassette deck or recordable audio CD player, and indeed, they work exactly the same way. The Transport panel's other displays are used to edit your song's tempo, move the SPL, or set up loop boundaries for cycle Playback and Record modes.

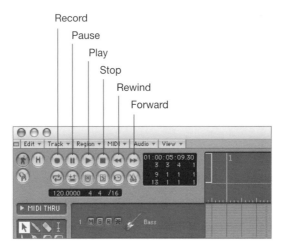
Record
Pause
Play
Stop
Rewind
Forward

Let's use the Transport panel controls to start and stop the playback of your song.

1   Click the Transport's Play button to begin playing back the song.

The song plays.

2   Click the Stop button to stop playback.

The song stops.

You can also start and stop playback by pressing the spacebar.

3   Press the spacebar once.

The song starts playing.

4   Press the spacebar a second time.

The song stops playing.

Controlling Playback Using the Number Pad

If your computer keyboard has a number pad, you can also start and stop playback using the Enter and 0 keys.

1   Press the Enter key on your computer's number pad (PowerBook or iBook users can press the Enter key to the right of the spacebar).

The song starts playing.

2   Press the 0 key on your computer's number pad (PowerBook or iBook users can press Function-M).

The song stops playing. If you press the 0 key while the song is stopped, the SPL jumps to the beginning of the song.

3   Press the 0 key a second time.

The SPL jumps to the beginning of the song.

Feel free to play and stop the song at any time as you explore the various sections of this lesson. After all, Logic is meant to make music, and hearing the song is a big part of the process!

NOTE ▶ If you have the Cycle mode enabled, pressing the 0 key while the song is stopped causes the SPL to jump to the beginning of the Cycle range, and not the beginning of the song. The Cycle mode is discussed in Lesson 3, "Understanding Workflow Techniques."

Moving the Song Position Line

As you've seen above, the SPL is a thin vertical line that travels across the Arrange window as your song plays. The SPL has one function only: It shows you the current playback position of your song. As you audition various parts of your song, such as intros, choruses, and breakdowns, you will need to move the SPL to the area you want to hear. This is an interactive process—move the SPL, listen, move the SPL, listen again. In fact, basic as it may seem, moving the SPL is an important editing technique, and Logic provides you with several ways to do it.

Using the SMPTE/Bar Position Display

The Transport's SMPTE/Bar Position display offers the most precise method of moving the SPL, because it lets you type in an exact song position for the SPL to jump to. Available in both the Transport panel and Transport window, this display is made of two separate sets of numbers: the Bar Position display and the SMPTE display.

Exploring the Bar Position Display

Songs are measured in bars and beats. Obligingly, the Bar Position display shows your current song position in bars and beats, and also allows a greater degree of resolution by breaking bars into divisions and ticks.

While bars and beats are basic music concepts, divisions and ticks are a bit more confusing. To show how the Division and Tick settings work, we need to open the Transport window.

1   Choose Windows > Transport (Cmd-7).

The Transport window opens. This window contains all of the same settings as the Transport panel, and a few extras as well. For now, however, let's focus on the Bar Position display.

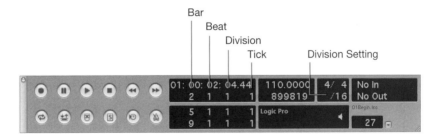

The Bar Position display's division number is governed by the Transport's Division setting, and the Division setting tells Logic to divide each bar a certain number of times. For example, with a Division setting of 16, each bar is divided into 16 parts, which are equivalent to sixteenth notes. Each beat is a quarter note, and there are four sixteenth notes in a quarter note, so each beat in the Bar Position display is further divided into four parts. These four parts are reflected in the Bar Position display's division number. With a Division setting of 32, the Bar Position display's division value can be used to divide each quarter note into eight parts, and so on. (Don't worry if you find this confusing, because you won't often have to enter division values into the Bar Position display.)

If the Division setting doesn't offer a fine enough degree of resolution, you can also dial a tick number into the Bar Position display. At $\frac{1}{3840}$ of a bar, ticks are the smallest bar subdivision offered by Logic.

2   Leave the Transport window open.

Using the Bar Position Display to Move the SPL

Now that you're familiar with how the Bar Position display works, let's use it to move the SPL.

1   In either the Transport window or the Arrange window's Transport panel—it doesn't matter which—double-click the Bar Position display.

A text field appears. Let's move the SPL to the beginning of the song, at bar 1.

2   Type *1 1 1 1* (that is, type four 1s with spaces in between), and press Return.

The SPL jumps to bar 1, beat 1, division 1, tick 1, which is the very beginning of bar 1 (make sure to insert a space between the numbers; otherwise the SPL will jump to bar 1111 instead of the beginning of bar 1).

To save time while moving the SPL, Logic lets you avoid typing in all four position numbers. If you only want to jump to the beginning of bar 7, for example, you don't need to type *7 1 1 1* into the Bar Position display—just type *7* and press Return. Similarly, to jump to bar 7, beat 2, you can type *7*, press the spacebar, type *2*, and press Return.

3 Double-click the Bar Position display, type *7*, and press Return.

The SPL jumps to the beginning of bar 7.

4 In the Transport, click and hold the Bar Position display's beat value, and then drag up or down to change the value.

As you drag, the beat value changes and the SPL moves back and forth across the Arrange window.

About the SMPTE Display

The SMPTE display shows the SPL's position in minutes and seconds. The SMPTE display is really designed for Logic users who are spotting sound to video, because this display shows SMPTE time code.

SMPTE (Society of Motion Picture and Television Engineers) time code is used for determining time points and frame positions in a video stream. Video displays a series of still pictures over time. Each picture is called a *frame*, and as the frames flip by, they create the effect of motion. Because video is a frame-based medium, its smallest degree of resolution is a single frame. Consequently, the SMPTE display shows hours, minutes, seconds, frames, and subframes.

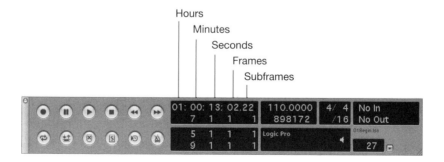

NOTE ▶ Broadcast video has two major competing standards: NTSC (National Television Standards Committee) and PAL (phase alternating line). The standard you use is dependent on the country you live in. In NTSC countries, video progresses at a frame rate of 29.97 frames per second (fps), while PAL countries use a frame rate of 25 fps. Keep this difference in mind when reading the frame portion of the SMPTE display.

1   In either the Transport window or the Arrange window's Transport panel, double-click the SMPTE display.

A text field appears. Let's move the SPL to 15 seconds into the song.

2   Type *01:00:15:00.00* and press return.

The SPL moves to 15 seconds into the song.

Using the Bar Ruler

A common way to move the SPL is to drag it along the Arrange window's Bar Ruler. The Bar Ruler has a horizontal line that divides it into two parts. The section under the line is used for moving the SPL.

1   Click in the lower section of the Bar Ruler at bar 5.

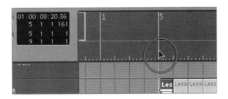

The SPL jumps to bar 5.

2   In the lower third of the Bar Ruler, click and drag left and right.

The SPL moves back and forth across the Arrange area.

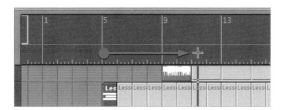

TIP ▸ Double-click the lower portion of the Bar Ruler to start playback from the clicked position.

You might notice that the SPL's movement is jerky. This is because it's snapping along Logic's internal time grid. Let's disable this snapping in the next step.

3   Hold down the Control key while dragging along the bottom section of the Bar Ruler.

NOTE ▸ Pressing the Control key engages a finer resolution mode (which becomes more precise the more you're zoomed in).

Using the Transport's Position Slider

The Transport window's position slider provides a further method of dragging the SPL forward or backward through your song. The position slider represents the length of your song, and it provides a very intuitive method for quickly navigating your arrangement.

1 From the Transport window's pop-up menu, choose Position Slider.

The position slider appears along the bottom of the Transport window.

NOTE ▶ Logic Express users will not have the same Transport menu choices listed in the figure above, which was taken from Logic Pro.

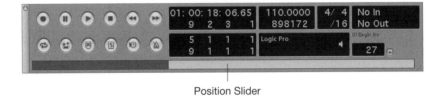

Position Slider

2 Drag the right end of the gray area to move the position slider.

The SPL moves through your song.

NOTE ▶ The position slider is available only in the Transport window and not in the Arrange window's Transport panel.

3 Close the Transport window.

Setting a Tempo

Ever since our ancestors learned to beat sticks on logs to make rhythms, music has had tempo. Tempo gives music its pace and is in part responsible for the way the music feels. Songs using a fast tempo, such as jungle, samba, or hard house, have a certain sense of urgency not found in music of a slower tempo like jazz, trip-hop, or deep house.

Tempo is measured in beats per minute (bpm). Sometimes you'll set the tempo based on the style of music or mood you're trying to create, while other times you'll choose a bpm that matches the tempo of the samples or drum loops you intend to use. In any case, Logic's metronome clicks along to the bpm you set for your song, and Arrange window Audio Regions snap to a grid with the timing determined by the song's tempo, so setting the tempo is one of the first things you'll do when creating a new song.

1   Play the song.

A quick glance at the Transport panel's Tempo display shows that the song plays at 120 bpm. Let's take a moment to experiment with bpm settings and see how they affect the sound of the song.

Tempo Display

2   Double-click the Tempo display.

A text box appears.

3 Type in *60,* and press Return.

The song plays at half speed.

4 Click and hold the Transport's Tempo display (on the numbers before the decimal point) and drag up *slowly,* until the tempo reaches 110.

The song changes tempo in real time, which can make it a lot easier to find that perfect bpm.

TIP ▶ Dragging the Tempo display before the decimal point adjusts the bpm in whole beats, while dragging behind the decimal adjusts the bpm in partial beats.

5 Press the spacebar to stop playback.

About the Arrange Window Channel Strip

The Arrange window channel strip sits in the bottom left corner of the Arrange window. It looks like a software emulation of the channel strip you'd see on a classic analog mixing console. The Arrange window channel strip always updates to display the channel strip for the track currently selected in the

Arrange window's Track List. This makes it easy to both arrange and mix your songs right in the Arrange window.

Arrange Window Channel Strip

1   In the Track List, select the Bass track.

The channel strip updates to show the Bass track's settings.

2 In the Track List, select the Pad track.

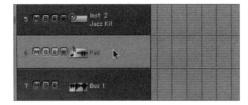

The channel strip updates to show the Pad track's settings.

Viewing the Arrange Window Channel Strip

The channel strip is big, and it takes up a significant portion of the Arrange window's left edge. In fact, in the song you're looking at, the Region Parameter box, toolbox, Object Parameter box, and channel strip are all fighting for real estate. By default, the top of the channel strip is hidden so you can see the other display boxes. To see more of the channel strip you can either stretch the Arrange window vertically to make it taller, or use the following trick.

1 From the Arrange window's local menus, choose View > Channel Strip Only.

The Region Parameter box, toolbox, and Object Parameter box are hidden, allowing the channel strip to fully display.

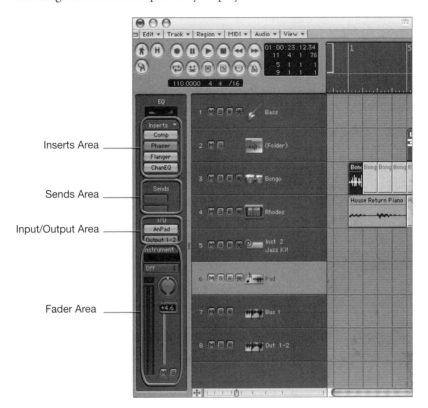

Using DSP Plug-ins

Plug-ins are power! These essential tools can turn an OK mix into a chart topper by taking good sounds and making them truly sparkle. Logic Pro comes with 70 high-quality DSP plug-ins, while Logic Express users have access to 37 plug-ins. If Logic's stock plug-ins don't provide exactly the sound you're after, not to worry—there are dozens of third-party plug-in manufacturers that make every type of sound-processing plug-in imaginable. However, keep this in mind: Logic 7 supports *only* Audio Units plug-ins, the standard audio plug-in format for Mac OS X.

TIP ▶ While plug-ins can take a good sound and make it better, they are only marginally successful at making bad sounds good. For this reason, always start your songs with the best possible source sounds.

Inserting Plug-ins

You insert plug-ins into the Insert slots at the top of the channel strip. By default the channel strip displays only two Insert slots. But you're not limited to two—as you insert plug-ins, new Insert slots appear. Depending on your version of Logic and the speed of your computer, you can insert up to 15 DSP plug-ins on each channel! Let's insert one into the Rhodes channel to see how the process works.

NOTE ▶ Logic Pro provides 15 inserts per channel, while Logic Express provides 4.

1   In the Arrange window make sure the Rhodes track is selected.

With the Rhodes track selected, the channel strip displays the Rhodes track's settings.

2   In the channel strip, click and hold the top Insert slot.

The Inserts menu appears and shows all of Logic's available DSP plug-ins.

3 From the Inserts menu, choose Stereo > Logic > Modulation > Modulation Delay.

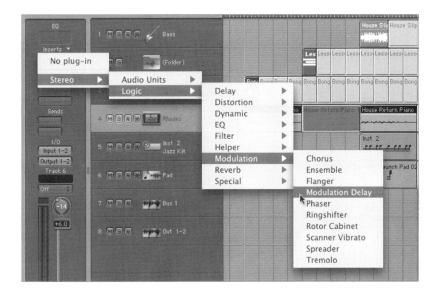

The Modulation Delay opens in a plug-in window. Leave this plug-in open for a bit, because you are going to work with it through the next several exercises.

Bypassing Plug-ins

Bypassing a plug-in turns it off so that you no longer hear its effect. Bypassed plug-ins do not drain system resources, and toggling the Bypass button lets you perform a simple A-B test to compare the affected audio against the channel's nonaffected sound, which in turn lets you make sure the plug-in is actually having the effect you want.

1   Move the SPL to bar 9.

2   Press the spacebar to start playback.

3   In the Modulation Delay plug-in window, click the Bypass button.

The Modulation Delay stops affecting the Rhodes track. In the channel strip, the Modulation Delay Insert slot is now colored gray, which indicates that it's bypassed.

4   In the channel strip, hold down the Option key and click the Modulation Delay's Insert slot.

The Modulation Delay is un-bypassed, and it turns back on. Back in the Modulation Delay plug-in window, the Bypass button is no longer activated. Pressing the Option key while clicking an Insert slot toggles the insert's Bypass status. This is a great shortcut to keep in mind, because it allows you to quickly bypass a plug-in without opening the plug-in window.

Using Plug-in Presets

Almost all plug-ins come with presets stored in the Settings menu, which is accessed by clicking the Arrow button below the Bypass button. Presets are named for their intended use. For example, the Modulation Delay has a preset called Slow Panning Chorus that sounds excellent on the Rhodes track. As you might expect, the Slow Panning Chorus preset is the one you are going to choose. From there you can change the plug-in to suit your sound, and then save the preset for future use.

1   In the Modulation Delay plug-in window, click and hold the Arrow button to open the Settings menu.

The Settings menu appears.

2 Choose the Slow Panning Chorus preset.

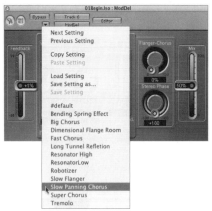

Listen to how the Slow Panning Chorus preset affects the Rhodes track.

MORE INFO ▶ Key commands come in handy for skipping through plug-in presets. In Lesson 3 you'll learn to assign Next and Previous Plug-in Setting key commands to Option-Cmd-N and Option-Cmd-B.

3 Adjust the Slow Panning Chorus's sliders until the Rhodes track sounds the way you want it to.

4 Choose Settings Menu > Save Setting as.

The "Save Setting as" dialog opens, and Logic has automatically selected a destination folder to save your custom preset into. Do not navigate to a new folder—Logic has picked the proper folder for this preset. You need only type in a name for your custom preset.

5   Type a name for your preset setting, and click Save.

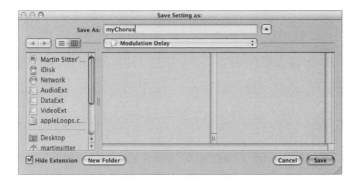

By saving your custom preset in the folder that Logic suggests, you ensure that it will always be available from the Settings menu.

6   Click and hold the Modulation Delay's Settings menu.

Your custom plug-in setting is now listed as a preset!

NOTE ▶ To help you keep your settings organized, the Modulation Delay's default settings have been moved to the Factory menu option below your custom setting. In the Finder you can also organize your custom settings into folders, and the folders will appear as hierarchical menu options in the Settings menu. When you navigate to the folder, the settings inside will appear.

The custom plug-in setting is stored in your User > Library > Application Support > Logic > Plug-In Settings > (name of plug-in type folder). Logic needs all custom Plug-In Settings files (or aliases to those files) to be located in this folder, or it will not see them. If you want the plug-in setting to be available to all of the computer's users, store it in the Startup Disk > Library > Application Support > Logic > Plug-In Settings > (name of plug-in type folder).

Opening Multiple Plug-in Windows

Right now, each time you open a plug-in, it opens in its own plug-in window. This makes it easy to, for example, compare settings between two plug-ins, or adjust the parameters of several plug-ins at one time. However, with multiple plug-in windows open, your screen quickly fills up and the Arrange window becomes hard to see. To conserve screen real estate you can tell Logic to open all new plug-ins in the same plug-in window by activating the window's Link button.

1   In the top left corner of the Modulation Delay plug-in window, click the
    Link button to turn it on (the Link button is the one with a chain on it).

Link Button

    With the Link button activated (it turns violet), each time you open a new
    plug-in, it replaces the old plug-in in the currently open plug-in window.
    Deactivating the Link button changes this behavior, and each new plug-in
    opens in its very own plug-in window.

2   In the Arrange window channel strip, click and hold the second Insert slot,
    and choose Stereo > Logic > EQ > Channel EQ.

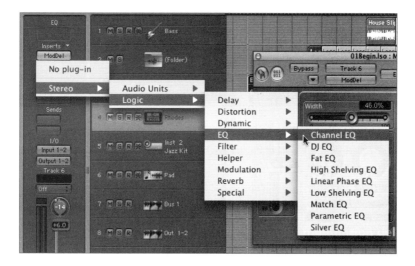

    The Channel EQ replaces the Modulation Delay in the plug-in window.

3   In the top left corner of the plug-in window, click the Link button to disable it.

The Link button turns gray.

4   In the Arrange window channel strip, double-click the Modulation Delay insert.

The Modulation Delay opens in its very own plug-in window.

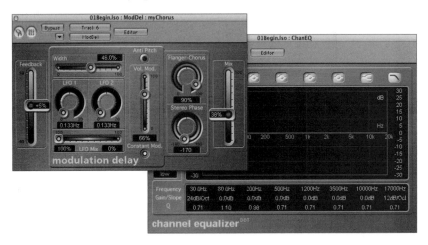

5   Close both plug-in windows.

Using Audio Instruments

Logic 7 has become a virtual production studio, complete with many software instruments (called Audio Instruments) that generate nothing short of awesome sounds. Indeed, with 32-bit floating-point internal processing and support for sampling rates of up to 192 kHz (hardware permitting), Logic's internal instruments sound as good as, or better than, most of the hardware synthesizers on the market. These days you need little more than a laptop, a MIDI controller keyboard, and Logic to create songs of the highest caliber.

Logic's Audio Instruments are assigned as inputs to a special type of track, called an *Audio Instrument track*. A hybrid between MIDI and audio tracks, Audio Instrument tracks use MIDI to trigger sounds from the inserted instrument. If you take a quick look at the Arrange window, you'll notice that two of the song's tracks use MIDI Regions instead of Audio Regions. These are Audio Instrument tracks.

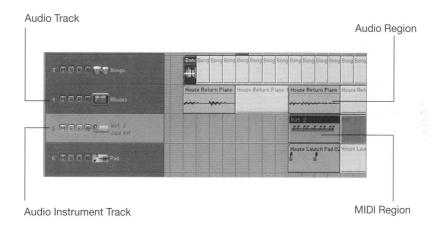

Audio Track

Audio Region

Audio Instrument Track

MIDI Region

Playing Audio Instruments

The song you are currently working on uses two Audio Instruments. One is a Drum Kit instrument, while the second is an Analog Pad instrument. Let's play them now to hear what they sound like.

1   In the Arrange window's Track List, select the Inst 2 (Jazz Kit) track.

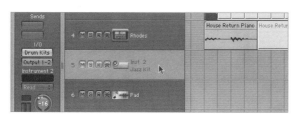

The Arrange window channel strip updates to show the track's settings. Furthermore, in Logic Pro, the R button to the left of the track's name turns red. This is the track's Record Enable button. When this button is activated, all incoming MIDI signals are passed to the track's instrument, which in turn allows you to play the track's instrument from an external MIDI controller. However, Audio Instrument tracks in Logic Express do not have Record Enable buttons; to prepare a track for recording, simply select it.

▶ Playing the Caps Lock Keyboard

If you don't have a MIDI controller keyboard, Logic 7 has a great new feature for you: *the Caps Lock Keyboard.* If you press the Caps Lock key on your computer's keyboard, a small MIDI controller appears on your screen. You can now play your computer keyboard as if you had a MIDI controller attached to your system. The Caps Lock Keyboard is polyphonic (you can play more than one note at a time) and you can select different velocity values using the letter keys on the keyboard's bottom row. You can even adjust the transparency of the Caps Lock Keyboard using the slider in its top right corner. Now doesn't that come in handy for those times when you need to program beats on the bus ride home?

2   Play your MIDI controller.

   You hear a drum kit.

3   In the Arrange window Track List, select the Pad track.

4   Play your MIDI controller.

   You hear a pad sound.

5   In the Arrange window channel strip's I/O area, double-click the Insert
   slot (the slot that says AnPad).

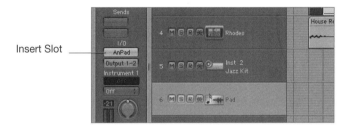

The analog pad Audio Instrument opens in a plug-in window.

6   From the plug-in window's Settings menu, choose a new setting.

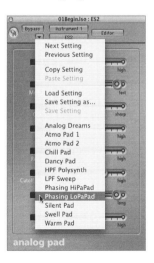

7 Play your MIDI controller.

The Audio Instrument's sound changes. As you can see, the Settings menu in Audio Instruments is used to select new sounds (also called patches) for the instrument. This is a very valuable concept to understand, because all of Logic's instruments come with preset sounds—some Audio Instruments, like the ES2, have hundreds of them!

8 Close the Analog Pad instrument.

9 Play your song, and use the Arrange window channel strip's volume fader and pan control to adjust the Pad track's sound so it properly sits in the mix.

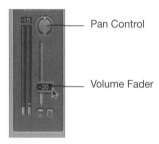
— Pan Control

— Volume Fader

Creating a New Audio Instrument Track
To play a different Audio Instrument, you must first create a new Audio Instrument track. Here's the technique:

1 Under the Out 1-2 track at the bottom of Logic's Track List, double-click the empty track slot.

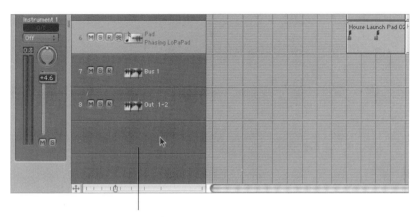

Empty Track Slot

A new track is created. By default, this track is assigned to the same instrument as the last track selected in the Track List.

2 Click and hold the new track's name.

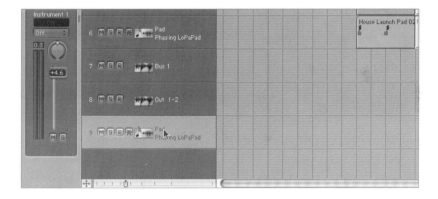

A hierarchical menu appears.

3 Choose Audio > Audio Instrument > Inst 3.

The track is now assigned to Audio Instrument 3.

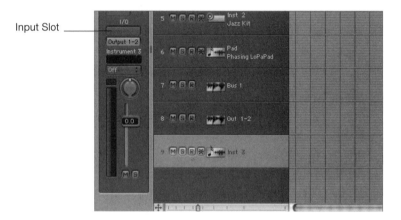

However, it does not make sound yet. This is because the channel's Input slot is empty. Read on to the next section to find out how to assign an Audio Instrument as the channel's input.

Inserting Audio Instruments

Audio Instruments are always inserted into the Input slot of an Audio Instrument track. In essence, the Audio Instrument is creating the sound that *goes into* the track, so it just makes sense to insert it via the Input.

1 Click and hold the Arrange window channel strip's Input slot.

A hierarchical menu appears.

2   Choose Stereo > Logic > EFM1.

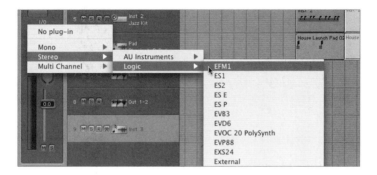

NOTE ▸   If you have any Audio Units–compatible third-party software instruments installed on your computer, they are accessible from the Stereo > AU Instruments submenu.

The EFM synthesizer opens.

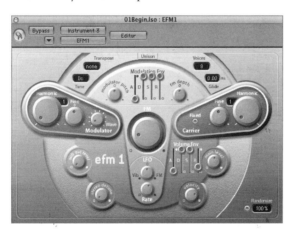

3   Play your MIDI controller.

You hear the EFM.

4   Experiment with the preset sounds contained in the EFM's Settings menu.

Want to hear some of Logic's other Audio Instruments? Bet you do . . .

5   In the Arrange window channel strip, click and hold the Input slot and assign a new instrument.

6   When you're done experimenting, close the plug-in window.

Using Channel Strip Settings

Channel Strip settings are a new Logic 7 feature that make it incredibly easy to create finished sounds. It's a fact of audio production: Raw sounds usually need to be processed with DSP effects. For example, drum tracks like Bongo often benefit from a touch of equalization and compression. You could insert your own effects and then adjust them to create the sound you're after, or you could add a Channel Strip setting that is suited to your sound. The Channel Strip setting will load all of the necessary effects, and also load the effect settings you want.

Channel Strip settings work a bit differently for audio tracks than for Audio Instrument tracks, so you'll explore both in the following section.

NOTE ▶ Logic Pro comes with more than 1300 Channel Strip settings.

Using Audio Track Channel Strip Settings

Let's experiment with Channel Strip settings by assigning one to the Bongo track.

1   In the Track List, select the Bongo track.

The Arrange window channel strip updates to display the settings for the Bongo track. Notice that the Insert slots are all currently empty. At the top of the Inserts area, the word *Inserts* has a small downward-pointing triangle to its right. This triangle indicates there is a menu available.

2 At the top of the channel strip's Inserts area, click and hold the word *Inserts.*

The Channel Strip Settings menu appears.

3 Choose 02 Drums > Percussion > Bongos.

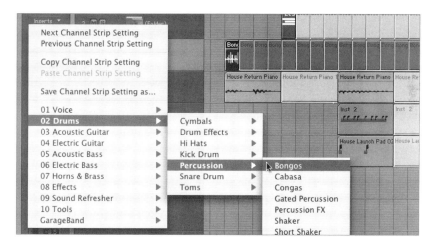

Several DSP plug-ins are loaded into the Bongo channel's Insert slots. Furthermore, each of these plug-ins has been preconfigured with settings that work well with bongo sounds.

NOTE ▶ The Fat EQ is not available to Logic Express users and will be disabled in the channel strip.

4 Play the song and listen to how the Channel Strip setting has affected the Bongo track's sound.

Of course, you just picked a Channel Strip setting that was designed for a Bongo track. But half the fun of Channel Strip settings is mixing and matching effects with sounds. Let's experiment with some different Channel Strip settings and see how they affect the Bongo track.

5 On the channel strip, click and hold the word *Inserts* and pick a new Channel Strip setting.

The Bongo track's sound changes again.

6 Continue experimenting with Channel Strip settings until you find one that affects the Bongo track in a way you like.

7 Use the Arrange window channel strip's volume fader and pan control to adjust the Bongo track's sound so it properly sits in the mix.

Using Audio Instrument Channel Strip Settings

Audio Instrument Channel Strip settings work similarly to audio track Channel Strip settings, except they also load an Audio Instrument to produce sound! This is a fantastic way to find almost any sound you're after, so let's give it a shot.

1   In the Track List, select the Audio Instrument track at the bottom of the arrangement (the one named Inst 3).

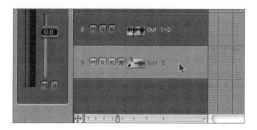

The Arrange window channel strip updates to display the track's settings.

2   At the top of the channel strips Inserts area, click and hold the word *Inserts*.

A hierarchical menu appears.

3   Choose 06 Bass > Delay Synth Bass > Reso Tubed Delay Bass.

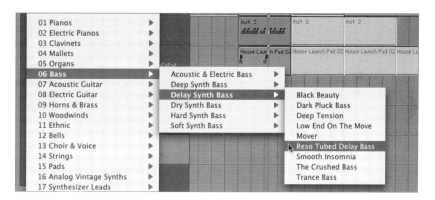

Several DSP plug-ins are loaded into the channel's Insert slots. But even more exciting, an ES1 Audio Instrument is loaded into the channel's Input slot.

Inserted DSP Effects

Inserted Audio Instrument

4   Play your MIDI controller keyboard.

You hear a delayed bass sound.

5   Experiment with a few more Audio Instrument Channel Strip settings.

Bouncing a Song

Bouncing is the process of turning your song into a finished audio file. Logic 7 comes with several new bounce options. For example, not only do you now have the option to bounce a song to AIFF, WAV, or SDII, but you can also directly encode MP3 and AAC file formats from Logic. In fact, Logic 7's brand-new Bounce dialog even lets you burn an audio CD of your bounced song! Let's open the Bounce dialog and take a look around.

1 Choose File > Bounce.

The Bounce dialog opens.

2 In the Bounce dialog's Destination area, make sure that PCM is selected.

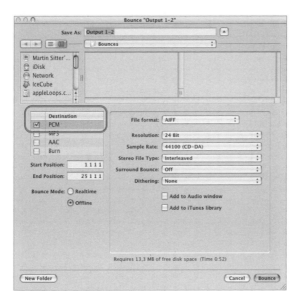

PCM stands for pulse-code modulated audio. This is simply uncompressed digital audio, including AIFFs, WAVs, and SDII files. Logic can bounce any of those formats.

3   From the File format menu, make sure AIFF is selected.

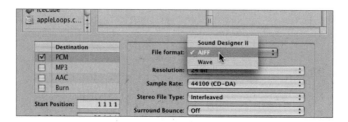

4   From the Resolution menu, choose 16 Bit.

The Resolution setting determines the bit resolution of the bounced file. With higher resolutions, the digital data reproduces the audio waveform more accurately, the dynamic range of the audio is expanded, and the signal-to-noise ratio is increased. However, recording at higher resolutions increases a file size dramatically—and not all audio hardware can handle 24-bit files. A setting of 16-Bit is appropriate for files you want to burn to an audio CD.

5   From the Sample Rate menu, choose 44100 (CD-DA), which translates to
44.1 kHz.

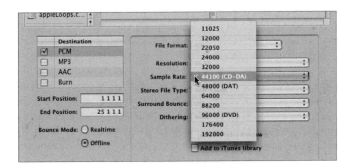

This is the sampling rate commonly used for CD-Audio. Logic also
enables you to bounce to other all other common digital audio
sampling rates.

6   From the Stereo File Type menu, choose Interleaved.

Since you are bouncing a stereo file, the resulting bounce can end up
either as two mono files (one for the left channel and one for the right)
or in a single interleaved file that contains both audio channels. Most
CD-burning programs require interleaved files for stereo playback.

7 Leave Surround Bounce set to Off (Logic Pro only).

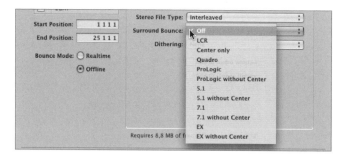

Surround Bounce should always be off, unless you're working in surround sound. You can learn how to create and bounce a surround sound mix in Lesson 14, "Surround Mixing."

8 From the Dithering menu, choose a dithering algorithm.

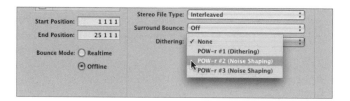

Dithering is a process of reducing an audio signal from a higher-bit resolution to a lower one. All audio processed within Logic is done at a 32-bit resolution. A CD can only play files saved in 16-bit resolution. Different types of dithering, and noise shaping, can produce subtle differences in how the audio sounds once the bit resolution is reduced. Choosing among these differences is mostly a matter of personal preference. You may want to experiment with dither settings, but keep in mind that the sonic differences are minute.

9   Set the Start Position to 1 1 1 1 (bar 1) and the End Position to 27 1 1 1 (bar 27).

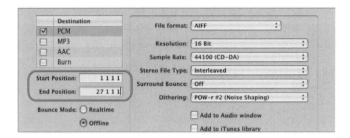

The Start Position and End Position settings determine which area of the song is bounced. The song you're working on has Regions that end at bar 25. However, you have told Logic to stop bouncing at bar 27. The reason is simple: Leaving two more bars at the end provides a bit of extra time to catch reverb and delay tails, as well as Audio Instruments that have a long release time. (The *release time* is the time it takes for the instrument to stop making sound after a note ends.)

10 Choose Offline.

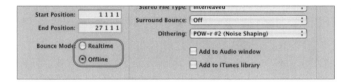

The Bounce Mode setting affects whether the bounce is done in real time or offline. Real-time bouncing will cause Logic to play the song just as you've been playing it. You will hear the song play, and Logic will record the audio you are hearing to the bounce file on the hard disk. Offline bouncing allows the computer to process the file as fast as it can. The faster your computer, the faster the bounce will happen. However, you will not hear the song play.

11 Navigate to a folder on your hard disk where you want to save the bounced song.

12 Enter a name for your bounced song.

13 In the bottom right corner of the Bounce dialog, click the Bounce button.

A Progress dialog appears.

When Logic is finished bouncing, you are left with a 16-bit stereo AIFF at 44.1 kHz.

14 Find the bounced file on your hard disk, open it in QuickTime Player or iTunes, and have a listen.

What You've Learned

▶ To open a floating toolbox directly under a pointer, press the Escape key.

▶ Pressing the Command key gives you access to a secondary tool. To set the secondary tool, press Command and select a tool from the toolbox.

▶ The Transport's Bar Position display let's you enter bar, beat, division, and tick values that control precise placement of the SPL.

▶ The Transport's position slider offers a fast way to move the SPL around your song.

▶ DSP plug-ins are added to the channel strip's Insert slots.

▶ Channel Strip settings are plug-ins that combine to make a certain sound.

▶ The plug-in window's Channel Strip Settings menu holds default plug-in settings.

▶   Audio Instrument tracks are special tracks that let you play Logic's internal synthesizers (called Audio Instruments).

▶   Audio Instruments are inserted via the Input slot of an Audio Instrument channel.

▶   Logic can directly bounce AIFF, WAV, and SDII files at 16 or 24 bits, and at any common sampling rate.

2

Lesson Files   APTS_Logic_7 > Song Files > Lesson 2 Project Files > 02Begin.lso

APTS_Logic_7 > Song Files > Lesson 2 Project Files > 02End.lso

Media   APTS_Logic_7 > Song Files > Lesson 2 Project Files

Time   This lesson takes approximately 30 minutes to complete.

Goals   Get to know Logic's editing windows and their relationships to each other

Learn about floating windows

Use and create screensets that store custom window layouts

Exploring the Editing Windows

In the following lesson you'll explore all of the windows that make up Logic, and along the way you'll learn a few important tricks and techniques that make working with Logic easier. Even if you have a bit of experience with the program, take the time to work through the exercises. Many of the concepts in the early parts of this book are vital to later lessons, so you should not miss a step. With that in mind, let's explore the editing windows that combine to give Logic its immense power over sound.

Getting to Know the Editing Windows

In the last lesson you explored the Arrange window, your doorway into Logic. It's the center of this program, and the window from which all editing decisions are initiated. The rest of Logic's editing windows are all used to either add MIDI and Audio Regions to this window, or to affect them. Since you've already seen what the Arrange window's various parts do, we can now turn our attention to Logic's other editing windows.

A First Look at the Track Mixer

The Track Mixer is a virtual mixing console used to position Logic's tracks "in the mix," or give tracks their own unique place in the aural picture you're painting. Using this window, you can change a track's volume or panorama (pan) position, insert DSP effects like reverb or dynamic range compression, or mute and solo individual channels. The Track Mixer is explored in detail in Lesson 9, "Mixing," but let's take a quick look now.

1   Open the file named **02Begin.lso**, or continue working on your song from the last lesson.

2   To open the Track Mixer, choose Windows > Track Mixer (Cmd-2).

The Track Mixer opens.

The Track Mixer is used to mix the sound of audio and MIDI tracks together. It's an adaptive window that mirrors the number and order of tracks in the Arrange window. For example, the Track Mixer currently has several channels, each corresponding to an Arrange window track. Each time you add a track to the Arrange window, it automatically appears in the Track Mixer. If you delete a track from the Arrange window, it also disappears from the Track Mixer.

3 Click the red Close button in the top left corner of the Track Mixer to close it.

A First Look at the Event List

The Event List presents a catalog of song events, such as MIDI note events or Region start events. This editor replaces the graphic interface of the other editors with a straightforward list displaying a progression of song events over time, and it's covered in Lesson 7, "Editing MIDI in the Hyper Editor and Event List."

1   To open the Event List, choose Windows > Event List.

The Event List opens.

The Event List's display area currently shows the start times of all the Arrange window's MIDI and Audio Regions.

2   Position the Event List so you can clearly see it and the Arrange window at the same time.

3   In the Event List, click the first House Return Piano event.

The House Return Piano event is selected—and the first House Return Piano MIDI Region is also selected back in the Arrange window, as you can tell by the black highlight across its top. This demonstrates an important feature of Logic: When you select an event in one window, the same event is selected in all the other open editing windows. This feature really helps you keep track of what you're editing and where, when the workspace gets crowded with several open editors.

4   Select a few other events, and watch as the corresponding Regions are selected in the Arrange area.

5   Close the Event List.

A First Look at the Score Editor

If you're coming to Logic from a formal music background, you'll feel right at home in the Score Editor. This window uses traditional music notation (staves and notes) as an interface for programming and editing MIDI Regions. Using Logic's Print function, you can even print out complete musical scores of the MIDI Regions you program in Logic (including Regions created with any of Logic's other MIDI editing windows).

Due to its reliance on music notation, the Score Editor is suited to a small subset of Logic users—those who can read music. If you can't read music, don't let this scare you, because *you don't need to!* Logic's other editors graphically display notes and note events, so there's no need to ever get into music theory. In the next few steps you'll open the Score Editor and take a look around, but this will be one of the few times you'll see the Score Editor in these lessons. For more detailed information on the Score Editor, see the *Apple Pro Training Series: Advanced Logic Pro 7*.

1   In the Arrange area, select the House Launch Pad MIDI Region.

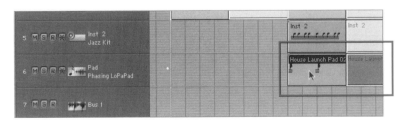

The Score Editor is a MIDI editor. Before you open it, it helps to have a MIDI Region selected so that Logic knows what MIDI data to display.

2   Choose Windows > Score (Cmd-3).

The Score Editor opens to display the House Launch Pad's MIDI data as notes in a musical score.

3   Close the Score Editor, and click the Arrange area's background to make sure that no objects are selected in the Arrange area.

4   Once again, choose Windows > Score (Cmd-3).

The Score Editor reopens, but this time it displays two lines of notes. These lines represent the notes from each of the song's two MIDI tracks. This demonstrates another important point about Logic's MIDI editors: If no MIDI Region is selected when you open a MIDI editor, the editor shows the MIDI data of *all* the song's MIDI Regions, together (the exception to this rule is the Hyper Editor, as you'll see in a moment). This is a great technique to keep in mind, because it allows you to compare or edit the MIDI data of more than one Region at the same time.

5   Close the Score Editor.

A First Look at the Hyper Editor

The Hyper Editor is a very specialized editor that displays control-change messages, but it can also be used to program drum sequences. This editor is covered in Lesson 7.

1   Once again, in the Arrange window select the House Launch Pad MIDI Region.

Unlike the other MIDI editors, the Hyper Editor will not open unless a MIDI Region is selected in the Arrange area, so this is an important step.

2   Choose Windows > Hyper Edit (Cmd-5).

The Hyper Editor opens.

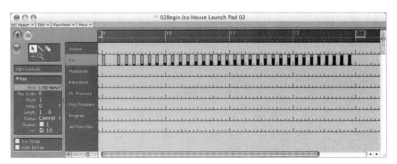

In the Hyper Editor, control-change events are displayed as vertical beams with a black bottom and a gray top. The line dividing the top and bottom sections determines the value of the event.

3 Close the Hyper Editor.

A First Look at the Matrix Editor

The Matrix Editor displays notes as rectangles along a piano keyboard. Unless you're coming to Logic from a traditional music background (in which case you might prefer the Score Editor), the Matrix Editor will be your primary MIDI editing window. The Matrix Editor is examined in detail in Lesson 6, "Editing MIDI in the Matrix Editor."

1 Make sure the House Launch Pad MIDI Region is selected.

2 Choose Windows > Matrix Edit (Cmd-6).

The Matrix Editor opens.

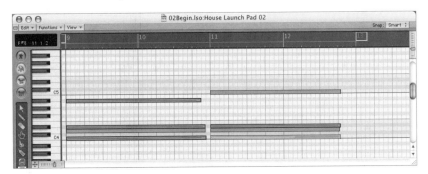

A MIDI controller keyboard provides the most common way of entering notes into Logic, and the Matrix Editor obligingly provides a keyboard along its left edge. In the Matrix Editor's display area, note events (notes) look like colored rectangles, and their positions along the keyboard show you exactly which notes they represent.

3 Close the Matrix Editor.

NOTE ▸ As with the Score Editor, if no MIDI Region is displayed when you open the Matrix Editor, it defaults to show the note events for all of your song's MIDI Regions.

A First Look at the Environment

The Environment is a virtual representation of your recording studio. When properly configured, Logic's Environment contains a separate Instrument Object to represent each MIDI device in your studio. Recording studios can be very complex places with lots of equipment that all conspires to make sound, and because of this the Environment is one of Logic's deepest windows. By the time you're done with this book, you'll feel right at home in this awesome and powerful editing window. In the "Customizing Your Setup" section of this book you will strip the Environment down to its bare essentials, then build it back up again. But for now, this quick first look is just to whet your appetite.

1   Choose Windows > Environment (Cmd-8).

The Environment window opens to display a mapped MIDI instrument.

The Environment primarily acts as Logic's ears and mouth: It listens for incoming audio and MIDI information, which it then transmits into Logic's sequencer, and it also speaks, or sends audio and MIDI information back out to your synthesizers, samplers, and sound card. It's extremely important to understand that the Environment is Logic's link to the outside world, because without the Environment, Logic could not communicate with your studio's external devices.

The Environment itself is organized into layers, much the same as the Hyper Editor. Layers are selected using the Environment's Layer box, which is located directly under the toolbox in the top left corner. You can switch layers by making a selection from the Environment's Layer menu.

2 Click and hold the Environment's Layer box.

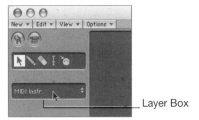

Layer Box

3 From the Layer menu, choose Audio.

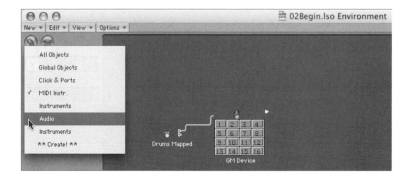

The Audio layer appears in the Environment window. This layer holds Audio Objects for all of the audio channels available to Logic, including Audio Instruments, audio tracks, busses, inputs, and outputs. It's a very complex layer, but also essential to the way Logic works, as you'll come to see in Lesson 11, "Setting up the MIDI Environment," and Lesson 12, "Setting up the Audio Environment."

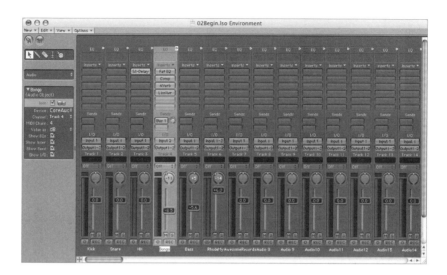

4 Close the Environment window.

A First Look at the Audio Window

The Audio window holds and organizes all of your song's audio files. You can also use this window to rename audio files and Regions, to optimize files by deleting unused portions, to move files from one hard disk to another, and to change your song's sampling rate. But most important of all, the Audio window is used to add audio files from your hard disks to your song, a process that's fully covered in Lesson 4, "Editing Audio Regions."

Let's look at how this window displays information about audio tracks.

1 Choose Audio > Audio Window (Cmd-9).

The Audio window opens. As mentioned above, the Audio window displays your song's audio files. These files are represented by thin horizontal rectangles that have a disclosure triangle on their left edge. If you click the triangle, it twirls down and the Audio file expands to show its Audio Regions.

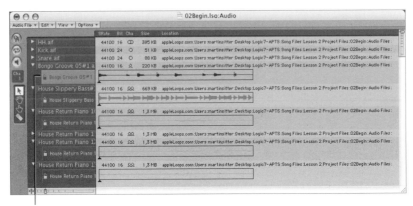

Selected Region

2   Position the Arrange window and the Audio window so you can clearly see both.

3   In the Audio Window, click the House Slippery Bass Region.

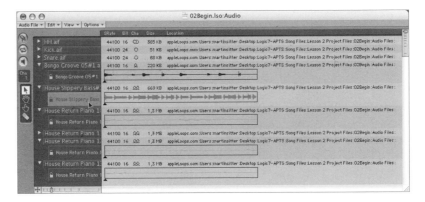

The Region is selected, and back in the Arrange window the first Region in the Bass track is also selected. As you might have guessed, this is exactly the same Region in both windows. You saw this interconnection between Logic's editing windows a few exercises ago when selecting events in the Event List. As your songs become more complex, with dozens or even hundreds of Regions crowding the song, you'll find this interconnectivity an invaluable way to locate Regions in Logic's various editing windows.

4   Close the Audio window.

A First Look at the Sample Editor

The Sample Editor is used to adjust the length and anchor points of your song's Audio Regions. This window lets you make sample-accurate edits to audio files, giving you such precise control that you can edit the individual samples that make up your audio files.

Let's open the Sample Editor and take a look.

1   An Audio Region must be selected before the Sample Editor will open, so in the Arrange window select the first Audio Region in the Bass track.

2   Choose Audio > Sample Editor (or simply double-click on the selected Region).

The Sample Editor opens. You'll notice right away that this window provides a very accurate view of the Region's waveform—and indeed, that's its purpose! It's the Sample Editor, and it lets you zoom right down to the individual sample level of any Audio Region in your song.

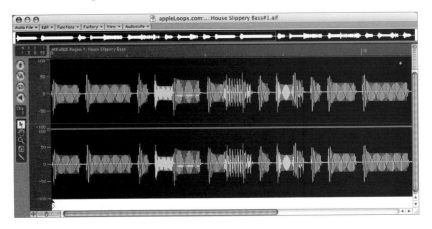

NOTE ▶ Logic is capable of a sample-accurate display of waveforms right in the Arrange window. (Sample-accurate means you can edit the individual samples that make up the audio file.) However, it's often much more convenient to use the Sample Editor to make precise edits to Audio Regions, because it saves you from having to zoom in on Objects in the Arrange window and then zoom back out after you've made your edits.

3   Close the Sample Editor.

Working with Windows

Why is real estate such a good investment? Because land is the only thing they're not making more of. The same holds true for screen real estate, or the amount of space you have available on your computer monitor. While you can increase your screen real estate by using multiple monitors, if you're like most of us, you have only a single screen at your disposal, and this screen is capable of displaying only a limited number of windows at any one time. Juggling editing windows is a fact of life in Logic, so let's explore a few basic window-management techniques.

Making Windows Active

The active window is the window that's ready to receive input from the mouse or keyboard—it's the one you are going to interact with.

> **NOTE ▶** The active window is not necessarily the top window. Logic uses floating windows to keep important windows on the surface at all times. The Transport window is an example of a floating window, as is a plug-in window.

1   First choose Windows > Event List, then choose Windows > Score (Cmd-3).

The Event List opens on top of the Arrange window, and then the Score Editor opens on top of the Event List. Your screen currently shows three windows, with the Score Editor being the *active* window.

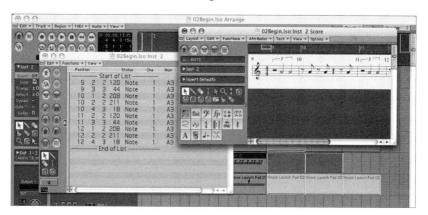

2 Click anywhere in the Arrange window.

The Arrange window is brought to the surface and made active. But more important, the Arrange window is now hiding the Event List and Score Editor. Without moving the Arrange window out of the way, you can't click the Event List or Score Editor to make them active. Here's a trick to help you solve this problem:

3 Click and hold the Windows menu.

Near the bottom of the Windows menu is a list of Logic's currently open windows. This is the *windows list*. Look closely at this windows list and you'll see a check mark next to the Arrange window, indicating that the Arrange window is active.

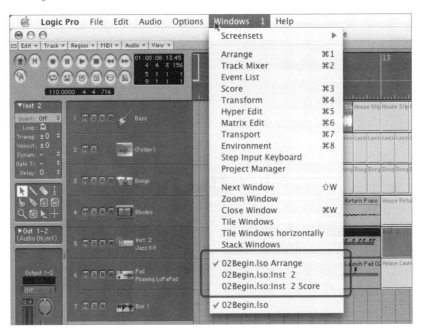

Of course, you don't need the windows list to show you which window is active—you can just look at the screen to see that. The windows list's primary function is to help you quickly locate windows, such as the Score Editor, that are buried under other windows on your screen.

4   From the list of open windows, select the option with *Score* at the end.

   The Score Editor jumps to your screen's surface and becomes the active window.

5   Use the trick you've just learned to make the Event List the active window.

6   Close the Event List, but leave the Score Editor open for the next exercise.

Using Floating Windows

Floating windows always remain above other windows. In previous exercises you might have noticed that the Transport window is always visible. That's because it's a floating window, and as such it cannot be hidden behind other windows (however, a floating window *can* be covered by another floating window). Other examples of floating windows include Logic's software instruments and plug-in windows.

You can distinguish a floating window from a normal window by looking at its title bar. Normal windows have a thicker title bar with rounded corners, while floating windows have a thinner title bar with square corners. Incidentally, floating windows are not unique to Logic. For example, Adobe Photoshop's palettes are floating windows, and Microsoft Word's toolbars are also floating windows—in fact, any window that can't be hidden under other windows is a floating window, regardless of the software program.

   NOTE ▶ Another interesting fact about floating windows is that switching to a different application causes them to disappear, while the normal document windows remain visible.

While Logic is not unique in its use of floating windows, it does have one special feature not found in most other programs: Logic lets you, the user, turn any window into a floating window. Any window at all! For example, if you're making important edits in the Matrix Editor and you want to ensure that the window doesn't get lost behind others, hold down the Option key while you open the window.

Let's practice making floating windows and moving them around.

1 Press Option and choose Windows > Event List.

The Event List opens as a floating window. Note how the Event List's title bar is now thinner than normal, with square corners.

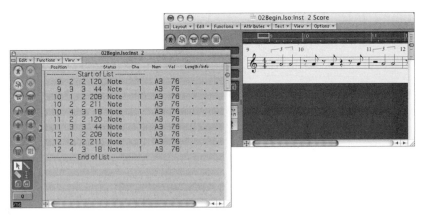

2 Click the Score Editor to make it the active window.

The Score Editor becomes the active window, but it does not jump above the floating Event List.

3 Close the Score Editor.

4 In the Arrange window, select the Inst 2 MIDI Region.

5   Now, hold down Option and choose Windows > Matrix Edit.

The Matrix Editor opens as a floating window.

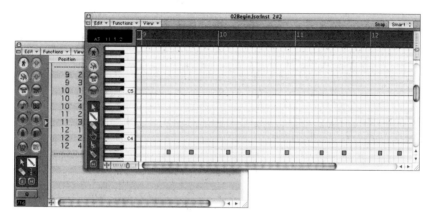

6   Click the floating Event List, and drag it over the floating Matrix Editor.

Aha! The floating Event List can be moved over the floating Matrix Editor, showing that floating windows can be moved above other floating windows.

Before moving on, let's set up the screen so that it's prepared for the next exercise.

7   Close the floating Event List, but leave the floating Matrix Editor open.

Linking Windows

In the top left corner of most editing windows is a button with a chain-link icon. This is called the Link button, and activating it links Logic's editing windows together. There are two ways to link windows together; the first is called *Link mode*, and the second is called *Content Link mode*.

▸   In Link mode, the Link button is violet. With the Link mode enabled, all newly opened objects always open into the linked window.

▸   In Content Link mode, the Link button is yellow, and the editors show the *contents* of any object selected in the active window.

These may seem like esoteric features at first glance, but they are very useful. The best way to see the differences between these two modes is to try them out.

1 Position the floating Matrix Editor so you can clearly see it and the Regions in the Arrange window.

2 In the Matrix Editor, click the Link button to turn it off (gray).

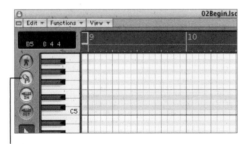

Link Button Off

3 In the Arrange window, double-click the House Launch Pad MIDI Region.

The Region opens in a second Matrix Editor under the floating Matrix Editor that displays the Inst 2 MIDI Region. Because the Link buttons are not activated each time you open a new Matrix Editor, the editor opens in its own window. This is great if you need to work on the MIDI events of two or more MIDI Regions at the same time, but all these open Matrix Editors can quickly fill your screen. Let's see how linking windows solves this problem.

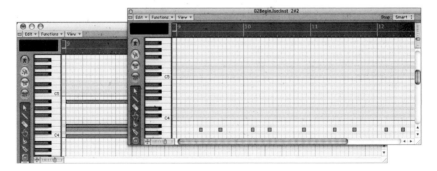

4 Close the Matrix Editor that just opened.

5 In the floating Matrix Editor, click the Link button once to turn it purple.

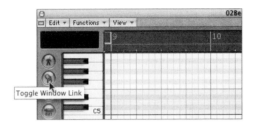

6 In the Arrange window, once again double-click the House Launch Pad MIDI Region.

This time, the MIDI Region opens in the floating Matrix Editor, replacing the events it previously displayed! With the Link button on, any time you open a Region into a Matrix Editor, it will always open in the linked Matrix Editor.

The Content Link mode works in a similar fashion, except you only have to select the MIDI Region in the Arrange window. Logic then prints the content of the selected Region into the content-linked window.

7 In the floating Matrix Editor, double-click the Link button.

The Link button turns yellow.

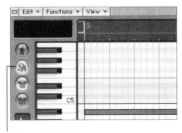

Yellow Link Button

8   In the Arrange window, single-click the Inst 2 MIDI Region to select it.

The Region's events—or rather, the *content* of the Region—appears in the floating Matrix Editor.

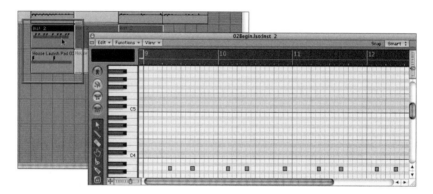

9   Close the floating Matrix Editor.

Using Screensets

Screensets are customized window combinations you create and assign to your keyboard's number keys. Screensets exactly recall the screen positions of windows, their zoom values, and even the selected tools. Using screensets efficiently is one secret to mastering Logic.

You may ask yourself, isn't it just as easy to open windows as needed and close them when you're done? The short answer is no. As a simple example, Screenset 6 could show the Matrix Editor with the Pencil tool enabled, while Screenset 16 shows the same Matrix Editor but with the Velocity tool enabled. By switching between Screensets 6 and 16, you can flip back and forth between tools, editing notes and velocities without returning the pointer to the Matrix Editor's tool-box to select the next tool. Add in different zoom values, and you've unleashed some true screenset power.

Time is money, and screensets save you time. So do screensets save you money? Well, only if you use them! Let's check out some screensets that are already set up in the song you are working on.

1   Press the 2 key.

The Track Mixer appears on your screen. If you look in the main menu bar, you'll notice the number 2 to the right of the Windows menu option. This indicates that you are currently looking at Screenset 2.

2   Press the number keys in order, from 3 to 9, and check out each screenset.

These first nine screensets match the order of the editing windows as listed in the Windows menu, with one extra—Screenset 9 is the Audio window.

Creating a Screenset

As you saw above, the first nine screensets are used to open Logic's individual editing windows, providing a fast way to call up those windows when you need them. Of course, this means that any custom screensets you create will need to be saved to the double-digit numbers, starting at 11.

There are a few things to keep in mind when creating screensets. First, a value of 0 is not allowed, which means that screensets 0, 10, 20, 30, and so on are not available. Second, to call screensets above 9, you must hold down the Control key as you type in the number. But other than that, using double-digit screensets is just as easy as using the first nine. Let's practice now by creating a custom screenset and assigning it to Screenset 11.

NOTE ▶ Logic lets you store up to 90 screensets per song.

1 Hold down the Control key and press 1 and then 1 again.

Screenset 11 appears on your screen—sort of! Screenset 11 is currently empty, but if you look next to the Windows menu option, you'll see the number 11, so you know you're in the right place.

Screenset 11

2 Choose Audio > Audio Window (Cmd-9).

3 Choose Windows > Arrange (Cmd-1).

You should now have both the Audio and Arrange windows open in Screenset 11.

4 Choose Windows > Tile Windows horizontally.

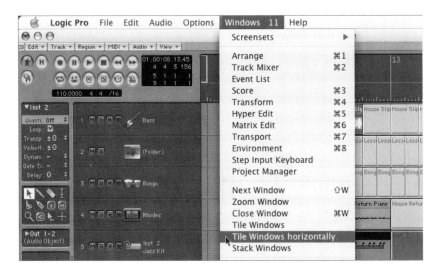

The Windows are tiled, with the Arrange window on top and the Audio window on the bottom. This is a common screenset used for adding audio to the Arrange window.

Congratulations! You've just created a screenset.

5   Press the 1 key.

Screenset 1 opens to show just the Arrange window.

6   Hold down Control, and press 1 and then 1 again.

Screenset 11 reappears just as you left it, with the Arrange window tiled above the Audio window.

Copying a Screenset

As you edit in Logic, from time to time you'll create a window layout that is really useful. To save it for later use, copy the window layout to its own screenset by following the steps in this exercise.

1   Press 1 to select Screenset 1.

The Arrange window opens.

2   Choose Windows > Matrix Edit.

The Matrix Editor opens.

3   Position the Arrange window and Matrix Editor so that you can clearly see both.

4   Choose Windows > Screensets > Copy Screenset.

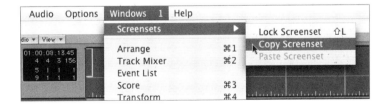

A copy of your current screenset is stored in the Clipboard.

5   Hold down Control, and press 1 and then 2 to open Screenset 12.

6   Choose Windows > Screensets > Paste Screenset.

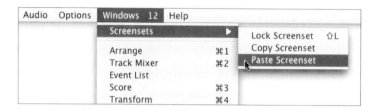

Screenset 1 is pasted into Screenset 12.

7   Press 1 to open Screenset 1, and close the Matrix Editor.

Now, Screenset 1 returns to showing just the Arrange window.

8   Hold down Control, and press 1 and then 2.

Screenset 12 opens to show the Arrange window and Matrix Editor.

NOTE ▶ You can also copy screensets by holding down Ctrl-Shift and pressing the screenset number. Two-digit screensets are copied by holding down Ctrl-Shift and typing 11 through 99 (except numbers ending in 0).

Locking a Screenset

Locking a screenset ensures that it can't be permanently altered. Under normal conditions, if you change the layout of a screenset, the changes are automatically stored. By locking the screenset, you can make changes to the layout, but each time you return to that screenset, you'll return to the original and not the altered layout.

To try out this feature, let's lock Screenset 12.

1   Hold down Control, and press 1 and then 2 again to go to Screenset 12.

The Arrange window and Matrix Editor appear.

2   Choose Windows > Screensets > Lock Screenset (Shift-L).

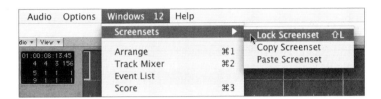

In Logic's main menu bar, a dot appears before the screenset number (beside the Windows menu option). This indicates that this screenset is locked.

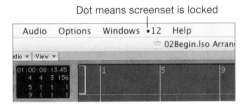

Dot means screenset is locked

3 While still in Screenset 12, choose Windows > Tile Windows (not "Tile Windows horizontally").

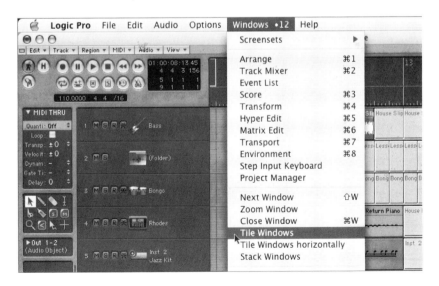

The Arrange window and Matrix Editor tile vertically on the screen. Oops! The Arrange window displays tracks, which by their very nature are wide and short. This screen layout makes it hard to see the Arrange window's tracks, and consequently it's not that useful. Thank goodness you locked Screenset 12.

4   Hold down Control and press 1 and then 2 to recall the locked Screenset 12.

The windows revert to the way Screenset 12 was when you locked it.

NOTE ▶ To unlock the screenset, choose Windows > Screensets > Lock Screenset (Shift-L) again.

5   Press 1 to return to Screenset 1.

What You've Learned

▶   Use the Windows menu to open all but two of Logic's editing windows. The Audio window and Sample Editor are located in the Audio menu.

▶   The Track Mixer is a virtual mixing console used to position Logic's tracks "in the mix." Using this window, you can change a track's volume or panorama (pan) position, insert DSP effects like reverb or dynamic range compression, and mute and solo individual tracks.

▶   The Event List presents a catalog of song events, such as MIDI note events or Region start events. This editor replaces the graphic interface of the other editors with a straightforward list displaying a progression of song events over time.

▶   The Score Editor uses traditional music notation (staves and notes) as an interface for programming and editing MIDI Regions.

▶   The Hyper Editor displays control-change messages, but it can also be used to program drum sequences.

- ▶ The Matrix Editor displays notes as beams stretched across a piano keyboard, and it shows the length, position, and velocity of each note in a MIDI Region.

- ▶ The Environment is a virtual representation of your recording studio. When properly configured, Logic's Environment contains a separate Instrument Object to represent each MIDI device in your studio.

- ▶ The Audio window holds and organizes all of your song's audio files.

- ▶ The Sample Editor is used to adjust the lengths and anchor points of your song's Audio Regions.

- ▶ Screensets are customized window combinations assigned to your keyboard's number keys.

3

Lesson Files	APTS_Logic_7 > Song Files > Lesson 3 Project Files > 03End.lso
Media	APTS_Logic_7 > Song Files > Lesson 3 Project Files
Time	This lesson takes approximately 1 hour to complete.
Goals	Create a project folder to hold the song file, along with all of its audio files
	Import audio into the Arrange window
	Learn common selection techniques
	Use the Cycle mode
	Name Regions
	Experiment with Logic's Catch and Scroll in Play functions
	Set up custom key commands

Understanding Workflow Techniques

You're now at home in the workspace, you've seen how Logic's editing windows interrelate, and you've explored the Transport's playback functions. It's time to get a bit deeper into editing songs. This lesson explores some basic functions you'll use throughout this book, such as zooming in and out on an editing window's display, making selections with Logic's unique selection techniques, hiding tracks, and creating custom key commands to control Logic's editing functions. Just because these functions are basic doesn't mean they are any less important than the things you'll learn later in this book. In fact, the techniques in this lesson provide a good foundation of skills you'll constantly use while making music in Logic. So with no further ado, let's jump straight in and learn some workflow techniques.

Creating a New Song

No two songs start from the same inspiration. Indeed, Logic is a program that wears many hats. For example, you can use it to master music, score video, create basic arrangements, or mix surround audio (Logic Pro only). Depending on your purpose, the number and configuration of Arrange window tracks will vary. Happily, Logic 7 comes with several song templates that let you start making music with an Arrange window tailored to your specific music-making needs.

Using Song Templates

Logic's song templates are just empty song files that have no media in them. They provide a great launch pad for making music because they are preconfigured with a set of empty tracks designed for a specific purpose. For example, Logic comes with a default song template designed for mastering, another for 24-track recording, and still others for surround mixing. By choosing a song template, you immediately start with a set of Arrange window tracks that match your needs, and this saves you time, because you don't need to set up or configure the tracks before making music.

> **NOTE** ▶ All song templates are stored in either the Startup Disk > Library > Application Support > Logic > Song Templates folder, or the User > Library > Application Support > Logic > Song Templates folder. You can create your own song templates by saving customized song files and storing them in either of those locations.

1   Choose File > New (Cmd-N).

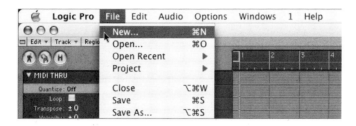

The New dialog appears with two check boxes: "Use song template" and "Create project folder." We'll return to the "Create project folder" option in a minute. For now, let's concentrate on the "Use song template" option.

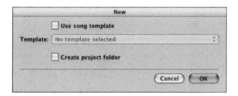

2   In the New dialog, select the "Use song template" check box.

3   From the Template menu, choose Cinema Display 20" > Basic Production.

NOTE ▶   If your monitor is not a 20-inch Apple Cinema Display, don't worry—Logic automatically resizes the Arrange window so it fits your screen. Logic Express users must choose Logic Express > Cinema Display 20" > Basic Production.

4 In the bottom right corner of the New dialog, click OK.

An Alert dialog opens and asks if you'd like to close the song you are working on.

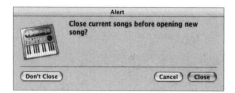

5 Choose Close.

The old song closes and a new one opens onscreen. Notice that the new song has exactly 12 audio tracks, 12 Audio Instrument tracks, and Click, Bus, and Stereo Output tracks.

6 Explore some of Logic's other song templates to see what they offer.

Creating a Project Folder

Logic 7 will now create a project folder to hold the song file, along with all the audio files, EXS instruments and samples, and Space Designer impulse response files (Logic Pro only) used in the song. A project folder ensures that all of the audio needed to produce your song is stored in one easy-to-find location, and this in turn makes it a simple matter to back your song up to a DVD-ROM or transfer it between computers.

1 Choose File > New (Cmd-N).

The New dialog appears.

2 In the New dialog, make sure the "Use song template" check box is deselected.

3   Next, select the "Create project folder" check box.

The New dialog expands to include several additional options.

Copy external audio files to project folder All audio files added to the song are copied to the Audio Files folder that will be created in the project folder.

Convert audio file sampling rate when importing Imported audio files that use a different sampling rate than the song does will be converted to the song's sampling rate before they are added to the project's Audio Files folder.

Copy EXS instruments to project folder The EXS24 sampler uses instrument files that tell it which samples to load and how to play them. Without the instrument files, the EXS24 does not know how to make its sounds. Selecting this option ensures the instruments are saved in the project folder along with your song file.

Copy EXS samples to project folder The EXS24 sampler generates sound based on digital audio samples stored on your hard disk(s). This option ensures that all samples used are saved in the project folder along with your song file.

Copy impulse response files to project folder All Space Designer impulse response files will be saved in the project folder along with your song file. (This step applies to Logic Pro files only.)

4 In the New dialog, make sure all of the remaining check boxes are selected (except for the "Use song template" check box—leave that one unselected).

Next, you need to name your song and also tell Logic where to create the song's project folder.

5 Directly under the Location text box, click the Set button.

A Save dialog drops down from the New dialog's title bar.

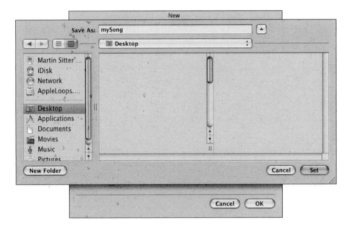

6 In the Save dialog's Save As text box, enter a name for your song.

7 In the Save dialog, navigate to your computer's desktop.

Saving the song on the desktop makes it easy to find and delete after you've finished this lesson.

8 Click the Set button.

The Save dialog closes.

9 In the New dialog, make sure all the remaining check boxes are selected.

10 In the bottom right corner of the New dialog, click OK.

An Alert dialog opens and asks if you'd like to close the song you are working on.

11 Choose Close.

The old song closes and the new one opens onscreen.

12 Open a Finder window and navigate to the new project folder that Logic has created on your desktop.

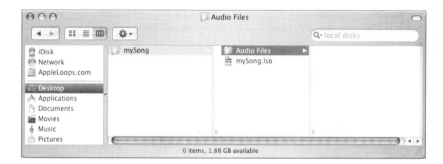

The project folder currently contains the song file, along with an empty Audio Files folder. When you import audio into the song a bit later in this lesson, the imported audio files will be copied into this Audio Files folder. There are currently no folders to hold EXS24 instruments or samples, even though you selected the appropriate check boxes back in the New dialog. The reason? Logic is smart and does not create these folders until they are required. Let me prove it to you.

13 In the Arrange window, select the first Audio Instrument track.

The Arrange window channel strip updates to display the track's settings.

14 Add the following Channel Strip setting to the track: Inserts > 06 Bass > Deep Synth Bass > Deep House. (For more information on Channel Strip settings, see Lesson 1, "Exploring the Workspace.")

NOTE ▸ Logic Express users should choose Logic Express > Bass > Finger Lickin.

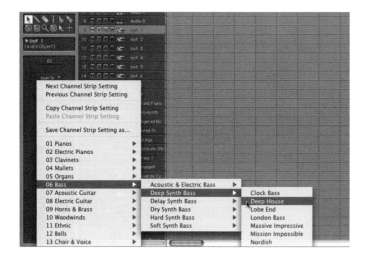

The EXS24 is inserted as the Audio Instrument and a sampler instrument with its corresponding set of samples is loaded into it.

15 Press Cmd-S to save your song.

A Progress dialog pops open and tells you that Logic is copying audio files. In fact, Logic is copying the samples used for the Deep House sampler instrument to the project folder saved on your desktop.

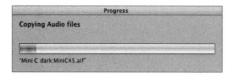

16 In the Finder, navigate once again to the new project folder that Logic has created on your desktop.

Notice that Logic has created new folders to hold the sampler instrument settings and samples!

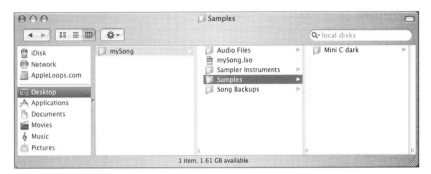

17 Close the Finder window.

Setting the Sampling Rate

The song's *sampling rate* determines how many samples per second Logic uses when working with digital audio files. Conceptually, the sampling rate is similar to the number of frames per second used in video. For example, most of Europe uses the PAL video standard, in which frames cycle by at the rate of 25 per second (North America uses NTSC video at 29.97 frames per second). Each frame is a picture in a longer sequence. When these individual pictures flick quickly by, the illusion of motion is created.

In a digital audio file, the sound of the file is stored in discrete samples in much the same way that the picture content of a video is stored in frames— except there are a lot more samples per second in an audio file than there are frames per second in a video. In fact, as computers get faster it is becoming common to use sampling rates of 48,000, 96,000, and even 192,000 samples per second. The higher the sampling rate, the better the sound, because there are more individual samples racing by in each and every second!

For our purposes here, we will set the song to a sampling rate of 44,100 samples per second. That's 44.1 kHz, which is the same sampling rate used in CD-Audio discs.

1   Choose Audio > Sample Rate > 44100.

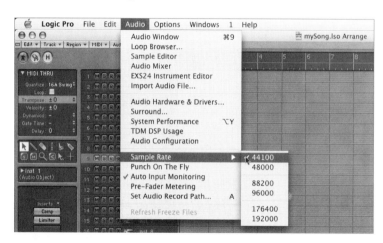

Importing Audio into the Arrange Window

Importing audio into the Arrange window is easily accomplished using either the Audio > Import Audio File option, or even dragging and dropping audio files from a Finder window directly into the Arrange area. Of the two techniques, drag and drop is perhaps the easiest. Additionally, you can drag and drop multiple files into the Arrange area at one time. Let's explore both techniques now.

1   In the Arrange window's Track List, select the first audio track (the one at the top of the Track List).

2   Make sure the SPL is at 1 1 1 1.

In the next step you will import an audio file using Logic's Audio menu. It's important to note that when you import audio files this way, they always drop into the selected track at the SPL's current position.

3 From Logic's main menu bar, choose Audio > Import Audio File.

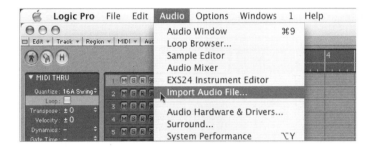

The Open file dialog appears.

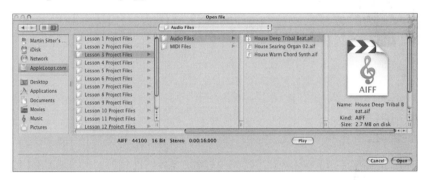

4 Navigate to APTS_Logic_7 > Song Files > Lesson 3 Project Files > Audio Files, and select and **House Deep Tribal Beat.aif**.

5 In the bottom right corner of the Open file dialog, click the Open button.

The audio file is imported into the arrangement and placed at bar 1 of Track 1.

6   Open a Finder window over your arrangement and navigate to the
APTS_Logic_7 > Song Files > Lesson 3 Project Files > Audio Files folder.

7   Hold down the Shift key and select both the **House Searing Organ.aif** and
the **House Warm Chord Synth.aif** files.

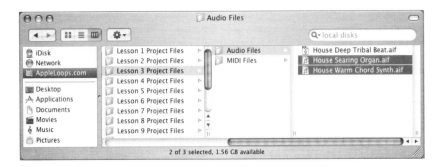

8   Drag both files into the Arrange window, and drop them when the pointer
is directly over 1 1 1 1 (the first beat of bar 1) of the Audio 2 track.

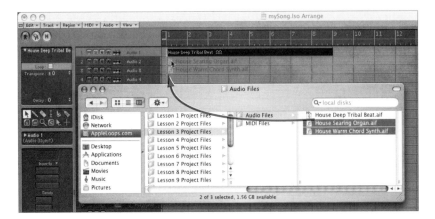

9 Close the Finder window.

In Logic, the Add Selected Files to Arrange dialog appears.

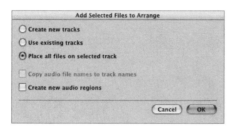

This dialog controls how Logic adds multiple files to Arrange window tracks. The options on offer include:

Create new tracks Logic creates new tracks for each added audio file. Additionally, the new tracks are named the same as the added audio files.

Use existing tracks Logic adds each audio file to a different, preexisting track in the Arrange window.

Place all files on selected track Logic imports the files and places them end to end on the same track.

10 Click the "Use existing tracks" radio button.

When you select this option, the ghosted "Copy audio file names to track names" check box becomes available. This is a great option to use because it automatically names the tracks the same thing as the audio files you are importing.

11 Select the "Copy audio file names to track names" check box.

12 In the bottom right corner of the Add Selected Files to Arrange dialog, click OK.

Each file is added to a separate track in Logic's Arrange window. However, at the moment the track names may not have updated. Here's a little trick to ensure they do.

13 Deselect both of the imported files.

14 Reselect one of the imported files.

The track names update to reflect the names of the imported audio files.

TIP ▸ By default, all Logic tracks are mono, so when you import a stereo audio file (as you just did in the steps above) you need to click the Stereo/Mono button to make the audio track stereo. Working with stereo tracks is fully explored in Lesson 4, "Editing Audio Regions."

Stereo/Mono Button

Importing MIDI into the Arrange Window

Importing MIDI files into Logic is just as easy as importing audio files—you simply drag them from the Finder and drop them onto any Arrange window MIDI or Audio Instrument track.

Earlier in this chapter you applied the House Bass channel strip to the first Audio Instrument track in the arrangement. The track is ready to make sound; all it needs is a MIDI Region to trigger it. Let's drag a MIDI file into the Arrange window now.

1   Open a Finder Window over your arrangement and navigate to the
    APTS_Logic_7 > Song Files > Lesson 3 Project Files > MIDI Files folder.

    Inside this folder you will find a file called **Bass Line.mid**.

2   From the Finder, drag the **Bass Line.mid** file over the first Audio
    Instrument track, and drop it at bar 1.

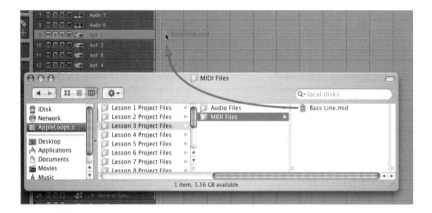

The MIDI file is added to Audio Instrument track.

Depending on how your version of Logic is configured, you might see a
dialog that says, "New SMPTE Frame rate recognized! Use it?" *SMPTE*
denotes a measurement of time in video, but you are not using video in
this project, so if you get this dialog, click Cancel to dismiss it.

Zooming and Magnifying

Songs in Logic can be made up of elaborate combinations of audio recordings and MIDI Regions. When you display a song in Logic's Arrange window, you have to balance the need to see all the tracks at once with the need to see the details in individual Regions. Logic provides controls that let you zoom in to see more detail in your song, or zoom out to see more of your song at once. The first situation is called *zooming in*, and the second is *zooming out*.

You activate Logic's zoom functions using the vertical zoom control in the top right corner of Logic's editing windows, and the horizontal zoom control in the bottom left corner. You can also use Logic's Magnifying Glass tool (Zoom tool) to zoom in and out on individual Regions.

Vertical Zoom Control

Horizontal Zoom Control

Let's experiment with Logic's zoom controls and the Magnifying Glass tool.

1   In the Arrange window's top right corner, drag the vertical zoom control down.

As you drag down, you vertically zoom in on Logic's tracks. The tracks become taller and you can now see the audio waveforms and MIDI notes in the tracks' Regions.

TIP ▶ The following key commands have the same functions as Logic's zoom controls: Ctrl–Left Arrow zooms out horizontally, Ctrl–Right Arrow zooms in horizontally, Ctrl–Up Arrow zooms out vertically, and Ctrl–Down Arrow zooms in vertically.

Next you'll use Logic's Magnifying Glass tool to zoom in on a certain area of a window. Logic will then expand the selected area to fill the window.

2   Select the Magnifying Glass tool and drag a rectangle around the House Searing Organ Region.

TIP ▶ If you press the Control key, the pointer turns into the Magnifying Glass tool.

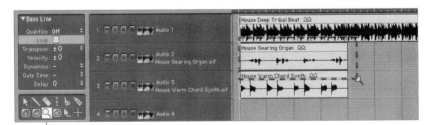

Magnifying Glass Tool

The House Searing Organ Region fills the Arrange area.

3 To revert to the premagnified state, click with the Magnifying Glass tool anywhere on the Arrange area.

The Arrange window reverts to its premagnified state.

TIP ▶ The Magnifying Glass tool remembers multiple magnification states. If you magnify a section of the Arrange area, and then zoom in on that section, you can click the Arrange area twice to restore the Arrange area to its premagnified state.

Using Auto Track Zoom

Auto Track Zoom is a method for zooming in or out on the track selected in the Arrange window. When your arrangements grow to include dozens of tracks, Auto Track Zoom really comes in handy because it lets you focus in on the track you're editing while still allowing you to see all the tracks in your arrangement at one time.

1 From the toolbox, select the Arrow tool.

2 Position the Arrow pointer over the bottom left corner of the House Searing Organ track.

The pointer turns into a pointing hand.

3 Drag down.

The track zooms vertically, while all other tracks remain unchanged.

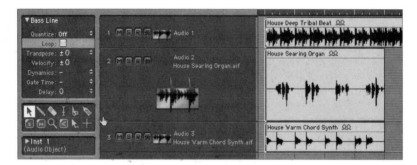

4 Make sure the House Searing Organ track is selected in the Track List.

5 From the Arrange window's local menu bar, choose View > Auto Track Zoom.

6 In the Arrange window's Track List, select a different track.

The newly selected track automatically zooms to an increased height.

Selecting with the Arrow Tool

Whether you're selecting notes in the Matrix Editor, MIDI Regions in the Arrange window, or Regions in the Environment, Logic's selection techniques always function the same way. You can select any Region by simply grabbing the Arrow tool and clicking the Region, but there are also a few other selection techniques you should be aware of. A good understanding of these techniques greatly speeds song editing, so work carefully through the following steps, and make sure you try each one.

1   From the toolbox, select the Arrow tool and click the House Searing Organ Region.

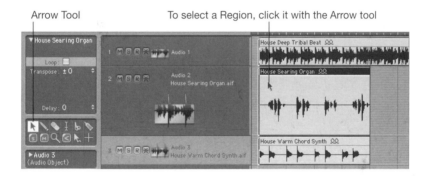

Arrow Tool   To select a Region, click it with the Arrow tool

The Region is selected.

2   In the Arrange window's Track List, click the Audio 1 track's name.

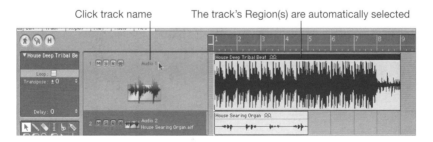

Click track name   The track's Region(s) are automatically selected

Clicking the track name selects all Regions in that track.

TIP ▶ With the Cycle mode enabled, clicking the track name selects only events falling within the cycle Region.

3 Click the Arrange window's background to deselect all Regions in the Arrange area.

Shift-clicking lets you select noncontiguous Regions (Regions that are not beside each other).

4 Hold down the Shift key and click several Regions.

The Regions are added to a selection range. You can continue to add Regions to the selection by Shift-clicking more Regions.

Rubber-Band Selecting

Rubber-band selecting refers to the process of dragging a selection range around one or more Regions at the same time.

1 Click the pointer in an empty part of the Arrange area under the House Warm Chord Synth Region and drag up and over the other three Audio Regions.

A rectangular outline is traced behind the pointer, and all Regions touched or enclosed by the rubber-band outline are selected.

2 Hold down the Shift key and drag a rubber band over *all* the Arrange area's Regions.

This reverses the selection! Holding down Shift while rubber-banding Regions causes previously selected Regions to be deselected, while unselected Regions are added to the selection range.

3 From the Arrange window's local menus, choose Edit > Toggle Selection (Shift-T).

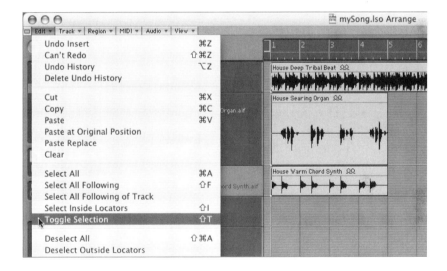

The selection range inverts, or toggles, so that all unselected Regions are selected, and selected ones are deselected. The Toggle Selection command comes in handy if you have to select all but a few Regions in the Arrange area, because it's often easier to first select the few Regions and then toggle the selection.

> **MORE INFO ▶** You might have noticed that the Edit menu contains several selection options. There are too many here to go over individually, but they all have specific functions that are immediately identifiable by their names. Pay particular attention to Select Inside Locators (Shift-I), which is a good way to select all the Regions that make up a particular verse or chorus, and Select Muted Regions (Shift-M), which offers a great way to select all muted Regions for deletion.

4   Click the Arrange area's background to deselect all Regions.

Using the Cycle Mode

The Cycle mode causes a specified section of your song to repeat over and over again. The Cycle mode is particularly useful for practicing MIDI Regions before recording, editing song events as you listen to them, or driving your roommates and neighbors crazy with a continuously looping beat.

But seriously, the Cycle mode lets you focus on a small section of your song as you practice or home in on exact edits—and this makes it an extremely important editing technique. For example, if you're using the Hyper Editor to program a MIDI drum Region, the Cycle mode lets you hear that Region over and over while you arrange its drum hits.

The Cycle mode uses the Transport's Cycle button in conjunction with the Locator display to set the left and right locators for the cycle. (The Locator display is found in both the Transport window and Arrange window Transport panel.)

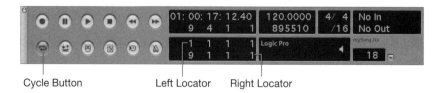

Cycle Button   Left Locator   Right Locator

The Cycle mode is a feature you'll use often while working through this book's lessons, so pay particular attention to the exercises in this section!

Setting the Locators

Let's change the locators to create a new cycle Region in your song.

1   In the Transport window, click the Cycle button to engage the Cycle mode.

2   In the Transport's Locator display, double-click the left locator, type *5*, and press Return.

This sets the first locator to 5 1 1 1, which defines the beginning of your cycle.

3   In the Transport's Locator display, double-click the right locator, type *9*, and press Return.

This sets the cycle's end locator to 9 1 1 1. You may have noticed that changing the locator positions changed the length of the highlighted section in the top of the Bar Ruler. This highlighted section shows you the length of the cycle, and it's called the *cycle Region*.

Cycle Region

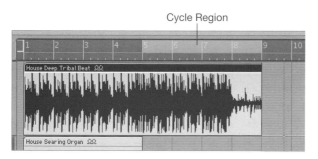

4   Press the spacebar to play your song.

The SPL begins playing from the left locator. When it hits the right locator, it jumps back to the left locator and begins playing the cycle again. The transition between locators is seamless, and you hear a continuous loop.

5   In the Transport, click Stop to halt playback.

6   Click the Transport's Cycle button to turn the Cycle mode off. (The slash [/] key also toggles the Cycle mode on and off.)

Defining a Cycle Region from the Bar Ruler

In the last exercise you saw that the cycle Region is displayed as a highlight in the top portion of the Bar Ruler. Guess what? You don't have to use the left and right locators to set the Cycle mode's boundaries. A much quicker technique is just to drag a cycle Region right into the top portion of the Bar Ruler!

1   In the Bar Ruler's top portion (above the dividing line) click and hold at bar 1, and drag to the right until you hit bar 5.

As you drag out this cycle Region, a few things happen. First, the pointer turns into a Finger tool. Second, a help tag opens to display the start point of the cycle Region, as well as its duration.

2   Press the spacebar to play the cycle Region.

The song cycles between bar 1 and bar 5.

3   Click and hold the center of the cycle Region, and drag right.

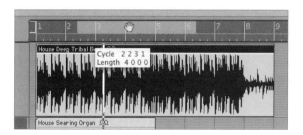

The pointer turns into the Move tool, and the entire four-bar cycle Region drags right.

4   Release the cycle Region when it covers the four bars from bar 5 to bar 9.

You can adjust the boundaries of a cycle Region by grabbing its lower left or lower right corner and dragging. But note that you must drag the lower portion of the corner, because dragging anywhere else moves the entire cycle Region, not just the Region's boundary.

5   Click the lower left corner of the cycle Region, and drag left until you get to bar 1.

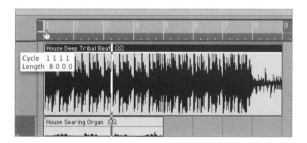

Using the Skip Cycle Mode

The Skip Cycle mode is like the Cycle mode inverted: Instead of cycling continuously through the cycle Region, the Skip Cycle mode jumps right over the Region specified in the Locator display. In fact, to set up the Skip Cycle mode, you enter the left and right locator positions in reverse! In Cycle mode, the left locator is always earlier in the song than the right locator. In Skip Cycle mode, the left locator is always *later* in the song than the right one.

Think of it this way: In both Cycle and Skip Cycle modes, the SPL jumps from the right locator to the left one. In Cycle mode the right locator comes after the left, so the SPL jumps from the right locator *back* to the left locator *earlier* in the song. In Skip Cycle mode, the right locator comes before the left, so the SPL jumps from the right locator *forward* to the left locator *later* in the song. By jumping forward in the song, you skip a section of the song's content. Clear as mud? Let's do a little practice to drive this concept home.

1   In the Transport's Locator display, double-click the left locator, type 9, and press Return.

The left locator is set to the beginning of bar 9.

2   In the Transport's Locator display, double-click the right locator, type 5, and press Return.

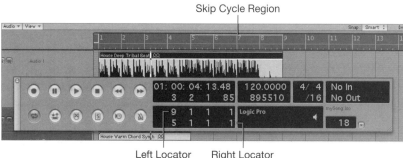

Skip Cycle Region

Left Locator   Right Locator

The right locator is set to the beginning of bar 5, which is *earlier* in the song than the left locator. In the Bar Ruler, notice how the cycle Region's thick highlight has been replaced by thin one. This thin Region defines a Skip Cycle Region.

> **TIP** ▶ To quickly create a Skip Cycle Region, drag from right to left in the top portion of the Bar Ruler.

3   Play the song from bar 1.

The song plays, but skips right over bars 5 through 9!

4   Press the spacebar to stop the song.

5   To turn off the Skip Cycle mode, click once in the middle of the cycle Region (this does exactly the same thing as clicking the Cycle button or pressing /).

The cycle Region's highlight disappears, and the Skip Cycle mode is turned off. A quick glance at the Transport's Cycle button shows that it is no longer activated.

> **TIP** ▶ To turn the Cycle mode back on, click the top section of the Bar Ruler. The Cycle mode will automatically turn on, and a cycle Region will be created between the left and right locators defined by the Transport's Locator display.

Dividing Regions

In the Arrange window, dividing Regions is the act of splitting one Region into two, and for this Logic provides the Scissors tool. This tool is one of the few that operate differently for MIDI Regions and Audio Regions, so you'll look at Audio Regions first, then move on to MIDI Regions.

Dividing Audio Regions

Dividing Audio Regions is a straight-ahead affair—just grab the Scissors tool and cut. Regions divide where you click the Scissors tool.

1   From the Arrange window's toolbox, select the Scissors tool.

2   On the Audio 1 track's House Deep Tribal Beat Region, click and hold at the beginning of bar 5 (5 1 1 1), but don't release the mouse.

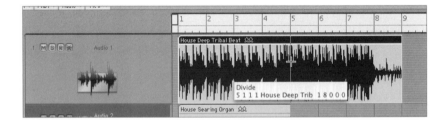

An indicator line extends vertically down the Arrange area to show you the position of your divide. Additionally, a help tag pops up to show the position of the indicator line, which in turn displays the position where the divide will occur if you release the mouse.

3   Drag the crosshair along the House Deep Tribal Beat Region.

As you drag, Logic enters Solo mode and plays a preview of the sound under the crosshair, and the indicator line snaps along behind the crosshair. The degree of this snapping is determined by the Arrange window's zoom setting, so using the telescopes to zoom in causes the indicator line

to snap with a finer degree of resolution. This is an important considera-
tion, because all Regions divide at the position of the indicator line, not
at the position of the Scissors tool.

TIP ▶ To temporarily disable snapping, hold down the Control key as
you divide Regions. The indicator line will now precisely follow the
pointer, enabling you to divide Regions between grid points.

4 Drag the pointer back to the beginning of bar 5, and then release the mouse.

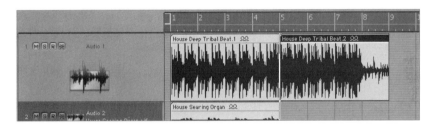

The House Deep Tribal Beat Region divides at the start of bar 5, cutting
the old Region into two new ones.

Dividing MIDI Regions

For the most part, dividing MIDI Regions works exactly the same as dividing
Audio Regions, but with one difference: It's possible for MIDI notes to overlap
the point where you are dividing the Region. When this happens, Logic asks if
you'd like to keep, shorten, or split the overlapping notes.

Keep Leaves all the notes unaltered. The Region is divided, but the new Region
on the left of the division will have a note, or notes, that extend beyond the
end of the Region. These notes will play in their entirety. Keep is the default
action.

Shorten Truncates all overlapping notes at the point where the Region is
divided.

Split Divides the overlapping notes. Two notes are created with the same pitch
and velocity; together, their lengths equal the total length of the original note.

Now that you know the theory, let's put it into action by dividing the Bass Line Region. But before doing so, select the Bass Line Region and open up the Matrix Editor so you can see the effect that dividing a MIDI Region has on the MIDI events it contains.

1   From the toolbox, select the Arrow tool.

2   Select the Bass Line MIDI Region and choose Windows > Matrix Edit (Cmd-6).

The Matrix Editor opens.

3   Horizontally scroll the Matrix Editor until you can see the beginning of bar 9 (9 1 1 1).

Notice that a single MIDI note crosses from bar 8 into bar 9. Let's now see what happens when you divide the Bass Line Region at bar 9.

Note crosses from bar 8 to bar 9

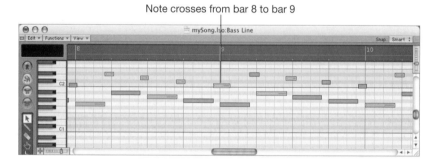

4   Position the Matrix Editor and Arrange window so that you can see both.

5   In the Arrange window, select the Scissors tool, then click the Bass Line
Region at bar 9 1 1 1.

An Alert pops up to tell you that overlapping notes have been found. This
means at least one MIDI note crosses the boundary between bar 8 and bar 9.

At this point you are presented with the three choices detailed above:
Keep, Shorten, or Split. These choices are a result of that single note span-
ning the transition between bar 8 and bar 9—right where you're cutting
the Region!

6   Choose Shorten.

The Region is divided in two, and the overlapping MIDI note is shortened
to fit within the new Region on the left, as you can see by taking a quick
look at the Matrix Editor.

Overlapping note is shortened

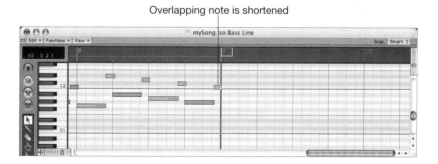

NOTE ▶ The decision to select Keep, Shorten, or Split is based entirely on the MIDI Region and the type of sound it triggers. If this were a long synth sweep, or a note triggering a long sample, you would instead choose to keep the note so that the synth swell or sample finished playing in its entirety.

7 Close the Matrix Editor.

Dividing Regions by Locators (Logic Pro Only)

Dividing Regions by locators provides a quick way to create Regions that are the same size as a cycle Region.

1 In the top portion of the Bar Ruler, drag from 3 1 1 1 to 5 1 1 1 to create a two-bar cycle Region.

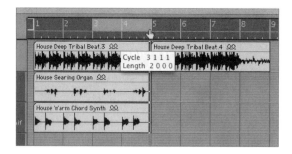

2 In the Track List, select the Audio Instrument 1 track that contains the Bass Line MIDI Regions.

3 From the Arrange window's local menus, choose Region > Split/Demix > Split Regions by Locators (Cmd-Y).

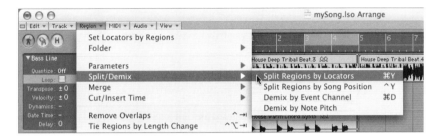

The Bass Line Region is divided at bar 3 and bar 5.

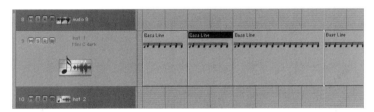

4 Click the top portion of the Bar Ruler to disable the Cycle mode.

The cycle Region disappears.

NOTE ▶ A cycle Region does not have to be enabled to split Regions by locators—this function merely looks at the position of the left and right locators and isn't concerned with whether the Cycle mode is enabled. However, setting a cycle Region is the fastest way to set the locators, so you'll often end up creating a cycle Region before activating the Split Regions by Locators function.

Moving and Copying Regions

Moving and copying Regions is a basic part of creating an arrangement, so take a moment to familiarize yourself with the following techniques.

1 From the Arrange window's toolbox select the Arrow tool, and then select the House Searing Organ Region.

2 Drag the House Searing Organ Region to 9 1 1 1.

3 Next, hold down the Option key and drag the House Warm Chord Synth Region to 5 1 1 1.

NOTE ▶ In Logic, or any other Apple program, Option-dragging always copies the dragged object.

A copy of the House Warm Chord Synth Region is created.

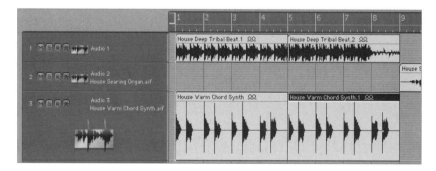

4 In the Track List, select the House Warm Chord Synth track.

Both of the track's Regions are selected. This is an important step, because when you paste a Region into the Arrange area, it always pastes into the track selected in the Track List.

5 Press Cmd-C.

Logic copies the Regions from the Arrange area and to the Clipboard. Let's paste these Regions back in at bar 9.

6 Click the Transport's Bar Position text box and type in *9 1 1 1;* then press Return.

TIP You can also just click the Bar Ruler at bar 9 to move the SPL. However, this is an important edit, and positioning the SPL by entering a value for the Transport's bar position is much more accurate.

7 Press Cmd-V to paste the cut Regions from the Clipboard back into the Arrange area.

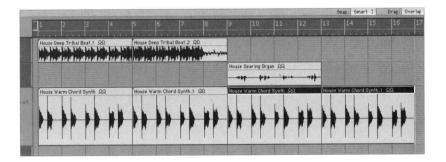

The cut Regions are pasted back in at bar 9 1 1 1.

Naming Regions

The toolbox has a special tool for naming MIDI Regions and Audio—the Text tool.

1 From the Arrange window's toolbox, select the Text tool.

2 Click the House Searing Organ Region.

A text box opens.

3 Type *myOrgan,* and press Return.

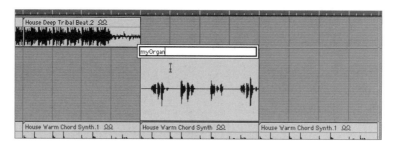

The Audio Region is named myOrgan.

Transferring Track Names to Regions

Logic provides a great method for naming Regions after the tracks they are arranged in.

1 In the Track List, hold down the Command key and double-click the name of the House Warm Chord Synth.

A text box opens. When you hold down Command and double-click a track in the Track List, Logic lets you change the name of the track!

2   Type *Synth Chords* into the text box, and press Return.

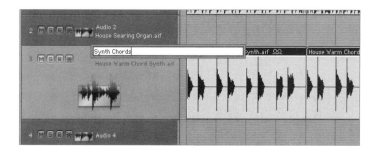

The Track is named Synth Chords.

3   From the Arrange window's local menu bar, choose Region > Track Names To Regions.

The track's name is applied to its Audio Region.

Naming Sequential Regions

You can also use the Text tool to name several Regions at the same time.

1   Using the Text tool, rubber-band select all of the Bass Line MIDI Regions in the Audio Instrument 1 track.

> **NOTE** ▸ Logic Express users will only have two Regions in the Audio Instrument 1 track.

2   With the Text tool, click the first Audio Region, name it *Bass 1*, and press Return.

The first Region is given the name Bass 1, while the second is given the name Bass 2, the third is Bass 3, and so on. Logic has automatically recognized the number at the end of the name and incremented it in the following Audio Region. This works with as many Regions as are sequentially selected.

If you don't want selected Regions to be given sequentially numbered names, use the following trick:

3   With the Text tool, click the first Audio Region, name it *Bass 1* followed by a space (that's a spacebar space), and press Return.

All of the selected Audio Regions are named exactly the same thing— Bass 1!

Hiding Tracks (Logic Pro Only)

Logic projects can get large, and it's common to have dozens of MIDI and audio tracks populating the Arrange window. With so many tracks competing for valuable screen real estate, you will sometimes want to hide certain tracks temporarily to get them out of the way. You'll still hear the hidden tracks, but they won't be visible in the Arrange window.

1   In the Arrange window's upper left corner, click the Toggle Hide Edit button (sometimes also called the Hide View button).

Toggle Hide Edit Button   Hide button appears on each track

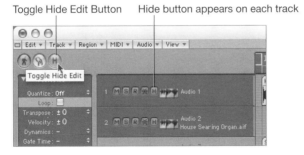

The Toggle Hide Edit button turns from gray to teal green. In the Track List, an individual Hide button appears beside each track's name.

2 Select the Hide buttons on all of the Arrange window's top three audio tracks.

As you select these Hide buttons, they turn green to match the color of the Toggle Hide Edit button, but the tracks are not yet hidden.

3 In the Arrange window's upper left corner, click the Toggle Hide Edit button one more time.

The three audio tracks disappear from view, and the Toggle Hide Edit button turns orange. The orange color is important to note, because this is your visual clue that some Arrange window tracks are hidden.

The Toggle Hide Edit button is orange, indicating tracks are hidden

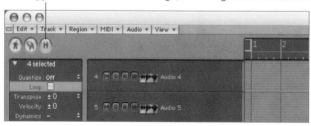

MORE INFO ▶ The Toggle Hide Edit button has three color states: Gray indicates that no tracks are hidden; green shows the setup mode and displays the Hide buttons for all the tracks; and orange means that one or more tracks are hidden.

To unhide tracks (show them again), just reverse the process.

4   Click the Toggle Hide Edit button once again.

The hidden tracks reappear.

5   Deselect the tracks' Hide buttons.

6   Click the Toggle Hide Edit button one last time to turn off Logic's Hide Tracks feature.

Using the Catch Function

In the Arrange window's top-left corner, the button with the little running man enables Logic's Catch function. This button is called the Catch button, and when it's activated, the Arrange area's visible section follows the SPL as the song plays.

NOTE ▶ The Catch mode is available to all windows that show a progression of song events, such as the Matrix Editor, Event List, and Score Editor.

1   Use the Arrange window's horizontal zoom control to zoom in until bars 1 to 5 fill the Arrange area.

NOTE ▶ The song you're working on isn't very long. To see the Catch mode in action, the Arrange area's Regions must stretch beyond the Arrange area's right edge, so you need to zoom in.

2   Make sure that the Arrange window's Catch button is blue, which means it's activated. If the Catch button is not blue, click it.

Catch Button

3   Press the spacebar to play the song.

The SPL plays to the right edge of the Arrange area. When the SPL hits the right edge, the Arrange area jumps forward and the SPL commences playing from the left to right edges once more.

4   Without stopping the playback, at the bottom of the Arrange window, grab the scroll bar and scroll so that bars 1 to 5 are once again centered in the Arrange area.

The song continues to play, but notice that the Catch function has been disabled, and the Catch button is now gray (off). This demonstrates an important point: If you manually change the displayed area of a song (by either moving the scroll bar along the Arrange window's bottom edge or using the Magnifying Glass tool), the Catch function is automatically disabled, so the newly selected display area does not disappear.

5   Your song should still be playing. With the Catch function remaining off, single-click the Bar Ruler's lower portion at bar 1.

The SPL jumps back to bar 1 and the song starts playing from that point. But more important, the Catch function is turned back on. This is an example of Logic's *automatic Catch function,* which activates the Catch mode each time the Play or Pause buttons are clicked, or whenever a playback command is initiated. Typically, you will want to keep the automatic Catch on, but you can disable it by choosing Logic > Preferences > Global Preferences pane > Catch tab and deselecting the "Catch when sequencer starts" and "Catch when moving song position" check boxes.

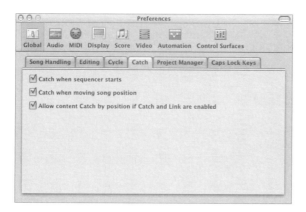

Using Scroll in Play

Scroll in Play works in a similar way as the Catch mode, but instead of having the SPL play across the Arrange area's Regions, the Arrange area's Regions scroll past a stationary SPL.

1   From the Arrange window's local menu bar, choose View > Scroll in Play.

2   Play from the beginning of the song.

The SPL plays to the middle of the Arrange window, at which point it stops and the Arrange area's Regions start scrolling left past the SPL.

3   To turn Scroll in Play off, choose View > Scroll in Play once again.

Using Key Commands

While the mouse remains your primary source of interaction with Logic, key commands provide an alternative way for you to control the program. Key commands give you access to most of Logic's functions directly from the keyboard, which saves you having to search through Logic's menus to look for the function you're after. Becoming familiar with Logic's key commands—and using them—will save you time as you arrange your songs. In fact, there are many key command functions that just plain aren't available from Logic's menus—if you don't know these key commands, you can't use the functions! (You'll learn several of these secret key commands over the course of this book's lessons.)

> **TIP** ▶ For you to become a true Logic commander, your hand on the keyboard is just as important as your hand on the mouse. By default, Logic comes preconfigured with several key commands, many of which you've already seen and used. A word of advice: As you work through this book, pay attention to all discussed key commands, and be sure to try them out.

Restoring the Default Key Commands

To make sure you are working from the same page as the steps in this book, it's a good idea to restore Logic's default key command set before continuing. This is particularly true if you've upgraded to Logic 7 from an older version of the program, because installing Logic 7 may automatically load the older version's key commands.

> **NOTE ▶** Key commands are saved with your Logic preferences and are available to all songs. Additionally, you can back up your key commands by saving a copy of your Logic preferences file.

1   Choose Logic > Preferences > Key Commands (in Logic Pro, you can press Option-K).

The Key Commands window opens, and you are presented with a large list of key commands, along with their functions.

The Key Commands window breaks Logic's key commands into several sections. Global key commands (the ones that affect all of Logic's editing windows) are listed first, with subsequent sections listing key commands unique to each type of editing window.

2   From the Key Commands window's Options menu, choose Initialize all
Key Commands.

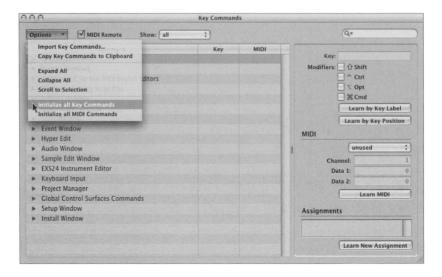

Logic 7's default key command set is loaded, and you can now be sure
your key commands match the ones used in this book.

Changing Key Commands

Logic lets you assign any function you want to any key or combination of keys.
If you don't like Logic's default key commands, feel free to change them. But
keep in mind that this book uses Logic's default key command set, so if you
change any of these commands, you may experience some differences between
this book's results and your own.

Bearing this warning in mind, let's go ahead and assign some new key commands—the important word here is *new*, because we are not changing any
of the default commands. Instead, the following exercise adds a few new key
commands to the *Next Plug-In Setting* and *Previous Plug-In Setting* key commands—two functions that come in handy when you want to audition Logic's
plug-in presets without constantly visiting the plug-in's Settings menu.

NOTE ▶ The functions whose names are preceded by a bullet (•) are available only via key commands.

1   In the search field in the top right corner of the Key Commands window, type *Plug-In Setting*.

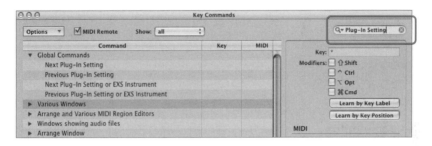

The Key Commands window updates to list only the key commands that have the words *Plug-In Setting* in their function names. In the Global Commands list, the Next Plug-In Setting and Previous Plug-In Setting functions are now listed.

2   Click the Next Plug-In Setting function to select it.

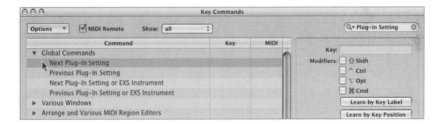

The Next Plug-In Setting function currently has no key command assigned. Let's change that now.

3   Click the Learn by Key Label button.

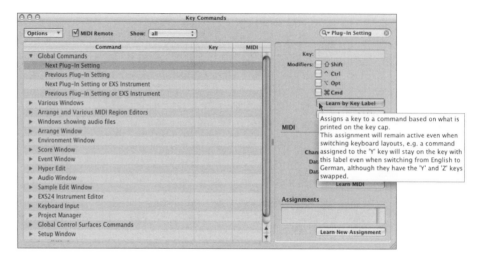

4   Press Option-Cmd-N (think of it as Option-Cmd-<u>N</u>ext).

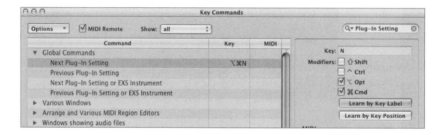

Option-Cmd-N appears to the left of the Next Plug-In Setting function, alerting you that the key command has been assigned and is now ready for use.

5   Repeat steps 2 to 4 to assign Option-Cmd-B to the Previous Plug-In
Setting function (think of it as Option-Cmd-<u>B</u>ack):

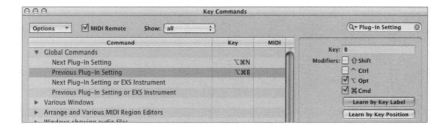

6   Close the Key Commands window.

7   In the Arrange window, select the Audio Instrument 1 track (the one playing the bass line).

The Arrange window channel strip updates to show the track's settings.
There are a couple of plug-ins inserted into this track.

8   Double-click the Comp plug-in to open the Compressor.

9   Press Option-Cmd-N.

The next plug-in setting is loaded into the compressor.

10   Press Option-Cmd-B.

The previous plug-in setting is loaded into the compressor. Keep these key
commands in mind, because they are not only handy but also invaluable!

TIP ▶ For quick reference, print out your key commands. First, visit the
Key Commands window's Show menu and select the Used option. The Key
Commands window will now show only those key commands that have
been assigned. Then, in the Key Commands local menu, select Option >
Copy Key Commands to Clipboard. Paste the list into any text-editing
software. You should be able to print your key commands.

What You've Learned

▶ Song templates are preconfigured song files that contain an Arrange window set up for certain types of music production.

▶ When you create a project folder, all audio files added to the song will be copied into the project folder. This makes it easy to back up your song when you're finished making music.

▶ Rubber-banding lets you drag a selection range around multiple adjacent Regions. All Regions enclosed or touched by the rubber band are selected.

▶ The Cycle mode, when enabled, defines an area of your song that will play over and over again. To create a cycle, drag from left to right in the top portion of the Bar Ruler.

▶ Skip Cycle mode defines an area of your song that Logic jumps over, or skips. To create a skip cycle, drag from right to left in the top portion of the Bar Ruler.

▶ The Scissors tool is used to divide Regions.

▶ Hiding tracks removes them from the Arrange window's display, but the tracks are still part of the arrangement and they continue to play (Logic Pro only).

▶ The running man button in the top left corner of an editing window activates Logic's Catch mode. With this button enabled, the window's display area follows the SPL as the song plays.

▶ To disable the Catch mode, move the scroll bar at the bottom of the editing window.

▶ The Scroll in Play function causes Arrange area Regions to scroll past the SPL like tape scrolling past a playhead.

▶ Key commands give you access to most of Logic's functions direct from the keyboard. You create them using the Key Commands window. Choose Logic > Preferences > Key Commands (Option-K) to open the Key Commands window.

Creating a Song

4

Lesson Files   APTS_Logic_7 > Song Files > Lesson 4 Project Files > 04Begin.lso

APTS_Logic_7 > Song Files > Lesson 4 Project Files > 04End.lso

Media   APTS_Logic_7 > Song Files > Lesson 4 Project Files

Time   This lesson takes approximately 90 minutes to complete.

Goals   Produce a finished beat out of kick, snare, and hi-hat samples

Import audio files into the Audio window

Edit Audio Regions in the Audio and Arrange windows

Set Region Anchors

Convert sampling rates

Adjust audio files to match the tempo of a song

Editing Audio Regions

It's no secret in the music-production world (particularly at higher levels) that Logic is the best *MIDI sequencer* on the market. But its audio side is equally well developed, and there are features in Logic that you just plain won't find anywhere else. You'll appreciate the little things, like the Region Anchor (the point in the Region that ties it to Logic's time grid) and simple functions that match an audio loop's tempo to that of a song. You even have the ability to audition audio loops through any set of effects applied to any audio track in the Arrange window before you add the loops to your arrangement. These are the sorts of features that make Logic a quick and intuitive audio editor.

This lesson focuses on Logic's audio side, specifically. You will learn how to use the Audio window to organize and add Audio Regions to an arrangement. Along the way you will learn how to adjust Region boundaries, set Region Anchors, and also explore some interesting ways to work with tempo while editing audio in the Arrange window.

Exploring the Audio Window

The Audio window acts as your song's audio library. All of the audio files you record or import into Logic are listed in this window, along with information about the files' sampling rates, bit depths, channel configurations (stereo/mono), sizes, and locations.

The main draw of the Audio window is that it catalogs not only audio files but also any *Regions* that have been created from particular files. Audio files themselves are displayed as thin horizontal beams, while Regions are a bit taller and show actual waveform overviews of the audio in the files. The difference between audio files and Regions is that audio files represent the actual audio file on your hard disk, while a Region is just a pointer that Logic uses to reference a certain part of an audio file. (In the Arrange window, you edit and arrange Regions, not audio files.) Because Regions act as pointers to the original audio files on your hard drive, and because Logic never actually changes those original audio files, Logic is classified as a *nondestructive* audio editor.

> **NOTE ▶** The Sample Editor, which you will explore a bit later in this lesson, is Logic's only destructive audio editing window—it will change your source files! But other than the Sample Editor, Logic is a completely nondestructive audio editor; happily, no source audio files are ever harmed or injured in the course of audio production.

As you'll come to see in the following exercise, you can edit audio files and Audio Regions right here in the Audio window, either before you add an audio file to the project, or after it's already in the arrangement (in which case the edits you make will ripple into the arrangement, changing any affected Audio Regions). The Audio window is a powerful tool, so let's open it and take a closer look.

> **NOTE ▶** The Audio window's Channel Configuration menu displays a single circle for mono files, and two interlocked circles for stereo files.

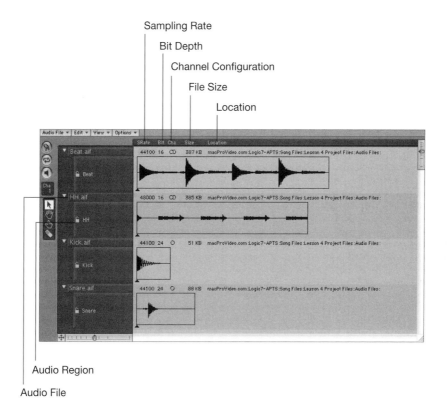

Sampling Rate

Bit Depth

Channel Configuration

File Size

Location

Audio Region

Audio File

1   In this book's companion files, which you have already downloaded as
     APTS_Logic_7 > Song Files, select the Lesson 4 Project Files folder and
     open the project named **04Begin.lso**.

     An empty Arrange window appears on your screen. To save time later, this
     file has been preconfigured with four audio tracks and four Audio Instru-
     ment tracks. The first three audio tracks have been named for you, and a
     Stereo Delay DSP effect has been inserted on the HH track (Track 3).

2 Press the Option key and choose Audio > Audio Window.

The Audio window opens. As you saw in Lesson 2 "Exploring the Editing Windows," pressing the Option key as you open an editor causes the editor to open in a floating window. This is denoted by a narrower gray title bar. Working with the Audio window in this way is particularly convenient because you will often need to drag audio files and Regions from the Audio window into the Arrange window. If the Audio window is behind the Arrange window, that becomes very hard to do!

Title Bar   Audio Window

NOTE ▶ You can also open the Audio window by pressing Cmd-9, but then it will not open in a floating window.

Importing Audio into the Audio Window

In Lesson 1, "Exploring the Workspace," you learned how to import audio files directly into the Arrange window. In that situation, audio files were imported into your project and automatically added to Arrange window tracks. Importing audio files into the Audio window follows a similar process, but in this case the files are not automatically added to the arrangement. Instead, they patiently sit in the Audio window waiting for you to add them when the time is right. Let's import a few audio files now in preparation for beginning our arrangement.

1   In the Audio window, choose Audio File > Add Audio File.

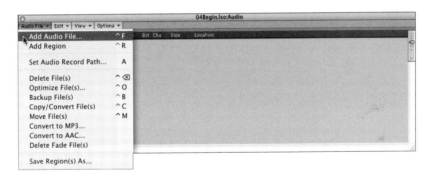

The Open file dialog appears.

TIP ▶ You can also drag audio files straight from a Finder window into the Audio window to add them to your project.

2 Use the Open file dialog to navigate to the Audio Files folder for
04Begin.lso (the song file you opened in the previous set of steps).

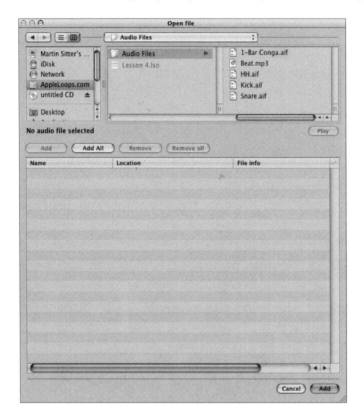

The Audio Files folder has five files in it. Four are AIFFs and the fifth is an
MP3 file. Ignore the MP3 file for a moment—you'll import that one later.
Additionally, we'll leave the **1-Bar Conga.aif** for a bit later in the lesson. For
now, let's concentrate on the **HH.aif**, **Kick.aif**, and **Snare.aif** files.

3 Select the **HH.aif** file.

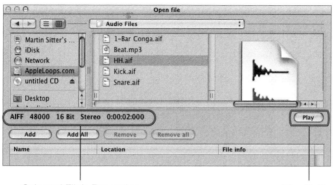

Selected File's Properties   Play Button

Below the file browser, the selected file's properties are displayed, and the Play button is activated.

4 Check out the **HH.aif** file's properties and click the Play button to audition the file.

The Play button turns into a Stop button and the **HH.aif** file plays.

5 Click the Stop button to halt the playback.

6 Repeat steps 3 to 5 while auditioning the other three files.

7 Press Shift and click all three AIFF files (**HH.aif**, **Kick.aif**, and **Snare.aif**).

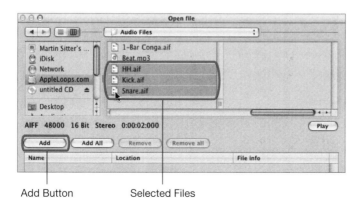

Add Button   Selected Files

8   Click the Add button.

The files are added to the import file list.

9   In the bottom right corner of the Open file dialog, click the Done button.

The files are added to the Audio window.

Importing MP3 Files

MP3 files import just as easily as audio files, but with one catch: All MP3 files must be converted to PCM (pulse code modulated) files before Logic can use or edit them.

> **NOTE** ▶ PCM files are simply uncompressed digital audio. AIFF, WAV, and SDII files are all examples of PCM files.

Logic automatically converts MP3 files to 16-bit AIFFs at the same sampling rate as the song you are working on. So let's take a quick digression to see exactly what that sampling rate is, and then import the **Beat.mp3** file.

1   Choose Audio > Sample Rate.

As you can see, this song is set to a sampling rate of 44,100, or 44.1 kHz. Although you could change the sampling rate to 48 kHz using this menu, most of the audio files you imported in the previous step use a sampling rate of 44.1 kHz, so let's leave this setting right where it is and import the MP3 file.

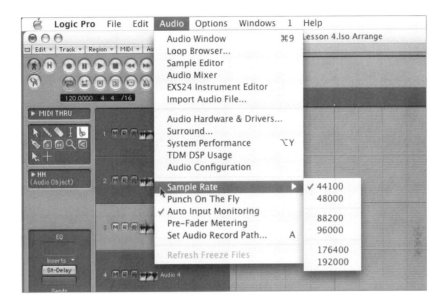

2   In the Audio window, choose Audio File > Add Audio File and add the
Beat.mp3 file to your project.

A few things happen next, and they happen quickly! Depending on the
speed of your computer, you may not even notice it, but in the background
Logic first converts the **Beat.mp3** file into a 16-bit, 44.1 kHz AIFF, and
then adds the new AIFF file to the Audio window. In fact, if you take a
quick look at the information listed to the right of the newly imported
Beat file in the Audio window, you'll see the imported file is in fact an
AIFF, at 16 bits and 44.1 kHz.

3   Open a Finder window and navigate to **04Begin.lso**'s Audio Files folder.

Converted AIFF

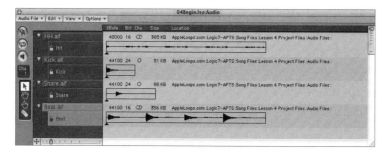

The converted AIFF file is there with the original MP3 file, and it is this converted file that Logic uses in your song.

4   Close the Finder window.

Selecting Audio Files vs. Audio Regions

The Audio window displays audio files along with all Audio Regions associated with each file. Currently, the Audio window just displays thin horizontal beams representing audio files. Directly to the left of each horizontal beam is a disclosure triangle that you can click to view each file's Audio Region(s). By default, one Audio Region is created for each file imported into the song.

1   In the Audio window, click the disclosure triangle to the left of each audio file.

The file's default Audio Region is displayed, along with a waveform overview of the file's audio.

TIP ▸ As a general rule of thumb, when choosing operations from the Audio window's *Audio File* menu, you must first select an audio file, and not an Audio Region. Audio Region waveforms can be seen in the display window, but the original audio file can only be selected by using the thin horizontal beam with the disclosure triangle.

Using the Sample Editor

The Sample Editor wears its name for a reason: Using this editing window you can zoom in until individual samples are visible. Because the Sample Editor gives you such exact control over audio edits, it's classified as a *sample-accurate* editor. This contrasts to the Audio window, which allows edits accurate only to within 256 samples.

NOTE ▸ The Arrange window is also a sample-accurate editing window.

Navigating the Sample Editor

When editing in the Sample Editor, you will often be zoomed closely in on the waveform. Consequently, navigating the Sample Editor becomes a major concern. You could use the scroll bar at the bottom of the window to zip around the file, but when you're zoomed in close, this becomes a difficult and time-consuming process. Fortunately, Logic provides great techniques for navigating in this window.

1   In the Audio window, double-click the Kick Region.

The Sample Editor opens.

TIP ▸ You can double-click a Region in either the Audio window or the Arrange window to open the Region in the Sample Editor.

As you can see, the Sample Editor already gives you a much closer view of the Region's waveform than either of the other windows.

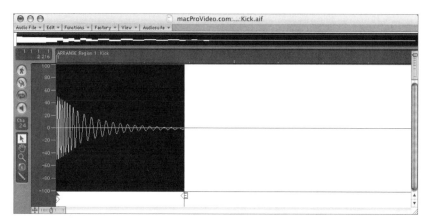

2 Drag the Sample Editor's horizontal zoom control all the way to the right.

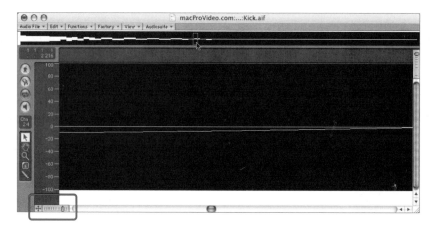

You are now looking at the Kick Region's individual samples.

NOTE ▶ You can edit individual samples in a waveform with the Sample Editor's Pencil tool. This comes in very handy when you need to edit pops and clicks out of an audio file—just grab the Pencil tool and draw them out. But be careful: Making this type of edit permanently changes the audio file on your hard drive!

Along the top of the Sample Editor is a waveform overview that shows the Region's entire audio file. At the front of this overview, a dotted box shows you the area of the waveform that's currently in the Sample Editor's main display area. To quickly jump to other points along the audio file, click the waveform overview.

3   In the waveform overview at the top of the Sample Editor, click somewhere close to the middle (this is just for practice, so it doesn't matter exactly where you click).

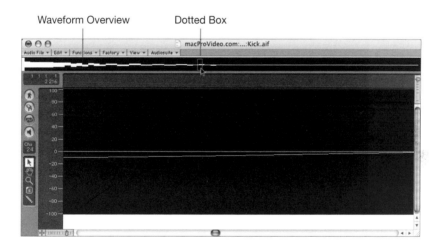

The dotted box moves to the clicked area of the waveform, and the Sample Editor's display area updates to show the portion of the waveform outlined by the dotted box.

In the Sample Editor's main display area, Regions are defined by the start and end playback indicators. The start playback indicator looks like a right-pointing arrow with an *S* on it, while the end playback indicator is a left-pointing arrow labeled with an *E*. Somewhere between those icons you'll find the Region's Anchor, which looks like an upward-pointing triangle. (You'll explore Anchor points a bit later in this lesson.) When you're zoomed in close on a waveform, these three things are a bit hard to find. You can click the waveform overview to get close, but the following key commands are much more precise:

4   Press the right arrow key on your computer keyboard.

The Sample Editor jumps to display the Region's end boundary indicator.

5   Press the down arrow key.

The Sample Editor jumps to display the Region's Anchor.

6   Press the left arrow key.

The Sample Editor jumps to the Region's start boundary indicator.

Remember these three key commands: Using the arrow keys provides a convenient way for you to quickly jump between Region boundary indicators and the Anchor without having to zoom out and find the part you're looking for.

7   Close the Sample Editor.

Auditioning Audio

Before adding audio to your arrangement, it's often helpful to listen to the audio file first so you know exactly what it is! Indeed, songs can get complex, sometimes using dozens or even hundreds of separate audio files. With that many files to juggle, you'll be forgiven if you forget which file sounds like what. Thankfully, you can easily audition audio files and Regions directly in the Audio window before adding them to your song. To do so, you'll use the Audio window's monitoring feature.

1   Position the Arrow tool above the Beat waveform.

The pointer turns into a speaker icon.

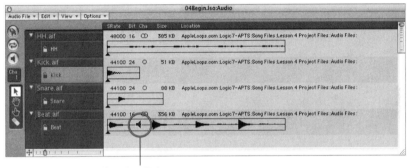

Speaker Pointer

2   Click and hold the Beat waveform.

The Audio Region plays from the exact point where you click.

3   Select the **Beat.aif** file. (Alternatively, you can select the Region instead. For the sake of this example, it makes no difference because there is currently only one Region associated with this file.)

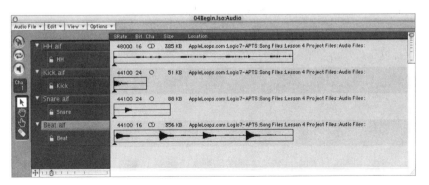

4   Along the left edge of the Audio window, click the Audition button (the one that looks like a speaker).

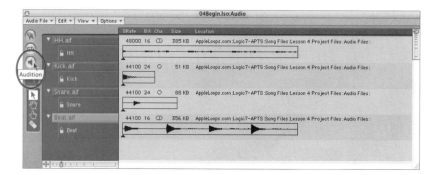

The **Beat.aif** file plays once and then stops. If you should so choose, you can also tell Logic to loop the file as you audition it.

5   Along the left edge of the Audio window, click the Toggle Cycle button, then click the Audition button to begin playback.

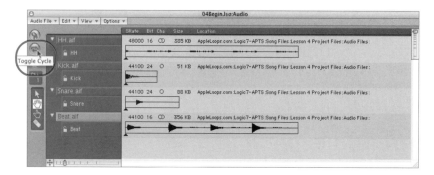

The Cycle mode is enabled in the Audio window and the **Beat.aif** file loops continuously.

6   Click the Audition button or press the spacebar to halt playback.

Auditioning Audio in the Sample Editor

Many of the same auditioning features you just saw in the Audio window are also available in the Sample Editor. Let's open the Sample Editor and explore its auditioning features.

1   In the Audio window, double-click the HH Region.

The HH audio file opens in the Sample Editor.

2   At the top of the Sample Editor, click and hold the Arrow tool above the waveform overview.

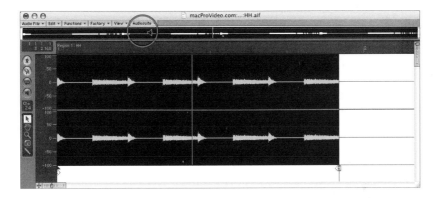

The pointer turns into a speaker icon and Logic plays the waveform from the Arrow tool's position.

3   On the Sample Editor's left edge, click the Audition button.

The selection loops. Why? The Sample Editor's Cycle mode is permanently linked to the Audio window's Cycle mode. Consequently, if you activate it in one window, it is automatically activated in the other window.

To demonstrate the point, do the following:

4   Position the Sample Editor so you can see it and the Audio window at the
    same time on your screen.

5   On the left edge of the Sample Editor, click the Toggle Cycle button to
    disable it.

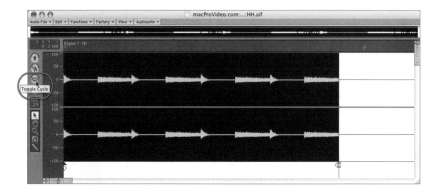

The Audio window's Toggle Cycle button is also disabled (this works even
if the window's link buttons are disabled).

6   Click the Toggle Cycle button again to turn it back on.

7   Press the spacebar.

    The Sample Editor's Audition button is activated and the loop in the
    Sample Editor plays.

8   Click the Sample Editor's Audition button to halt playback.

Scrubbing Audio in the Sample Editor

You can also use the Sample Editor's Solo tool to scrub the audio file in forward or reverse.

> **TIP** Scrubbing in the Sample Editor while recording your system's audio outputs is a great way to make sound effects!

1   From the Sample Editor's toolbox, grab the Solo tool (the square with an *S* on it).

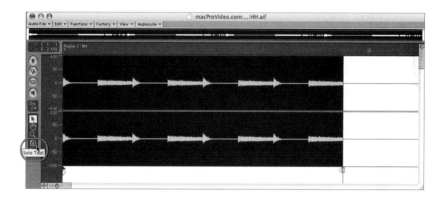

2   Click and drag the Solo tool back and forth along the waveform in the Sample Editor's display area.

The sound scrubs back and forth, following the Solo tool.

3   Close the Sample Editor.

Setting an Audition Channel

As you audition audio in the Audio window or Sample Editor, you may want to hear it through the effects of the Arrange window track to which you will eventually add the audio. To facilitate this, Logic employs a cool little trick: Along the left edge of the both the Audio window and Sample Editor is a channel setting. This setting determines which of Logic's *audio track channels* you will audition through—and this includes the channel's inserted DSP effects. The channel setting works the same way in both the Audio window and Sample Editor, so the following steps show you how to set the channel in the Audio window only. Once you understand this method, you'll be able to set it in the Sample Editor just as easily.

1   In the Arrange window, select the HH track (Track 3).

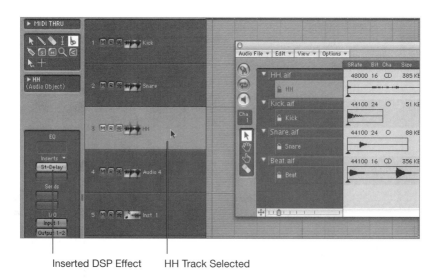

Inserted DSP Effect   HH Track Selected

In Lesson 1 you learned that the Arrange window's channel strip always updates to display the channel strip for the selected track. With the HH track selected, the Arrange Window channel displays an inserted Stereo Delay effect. As you can see, a stereo delay has been applied to the HH track.

2   Back in the Audio window, select the HH Region and then click the Audition button.

The HH Region plays. The Audio window's Toggle Cycle button should still be activated, so the HH Region will continue to loop as you go through the next few steps.

3   On the left edge of the Audio window, double-click the channel setting.

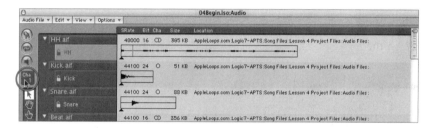

A text box appears. Let's set the Audio window to audition through channel 3, the same channel as the HH track with the inserted Stereo Delay effect.

4   In the text box, type *3* and press Return.

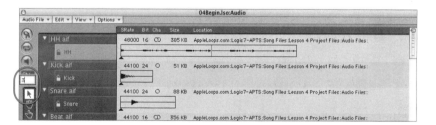

The sound of the auditioned file changes. It is now playing through channel 3 and thus through channel 3's inserted Stereo Delay effect. In fact, if you take a close look at the Arrange window's channel strip, you can even see the level meter pulsing along to display the HH file's level.

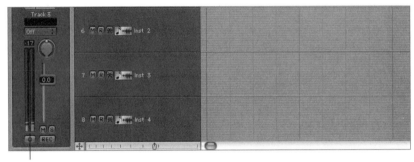

Level Display

5   Position the Arrow tool above the Audio window's channel setting and drag up until the channel is set to 24.

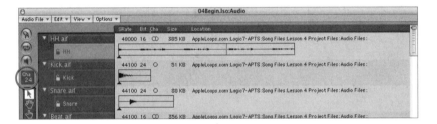

6   Stop playback.

You probably don't want to audition all of your audio through the Stereo Delay effect. In fact, in most situations it's best to audition audio files dry (without effects) so you can hear what the source file sounds like. If you set the Audio window's channel setting back to 1, any effects you insert into the Kick track in the Arrange window (channel 1) will be applied to all auditioned audio. By setting the channel to a very high number, such as 24, you are less likely to accidentally audition audio through a channel with any effects inserted, because it's less likely you will use that channel in your song. (But it can still happen if you add 24 audio tracks to your song, so watch out!)

> **NOTE** ▶ The channel setting refers to the *audio track channel* that the Arrange window track plays through, and not the track number or order in the Arrange window itself. In Lesson 12, "Setting Up the Audio Environment" you will explore audio channels in detail, but as a quick heads-up you can see the selected audio track's channel number in the Object Parameter box, next to the channel setting. This is the actual channel you are choosing in the Audio window's channel setting.

Adding Audio Files to the Arrangement

All right, enough with the background info—let's have some fun by beginning the arrangement!

Adding audio to the Arrange window is a simple matter of dragging Audio Regions out of the Audio window and dropping them onto Arrange window tracks. However, if you drag more than one Audio Region at the same time, you should be aware of some extra options. We'll start by dragging a single file into the Arrange window, then look at the differences that occur when you drag multiple files all at one time.

1   From the Audio window, drag the HH Region and drop it onto the Arrange window's HH track at exactly 1 1 1 1.

> **TIP** ▶ As you drag the file into the Arrange window, watch the info box under the Arrow tool. The display in the bottom left corner of this box tells you the exact bar, beat, division, and tick at which the Region will drop.

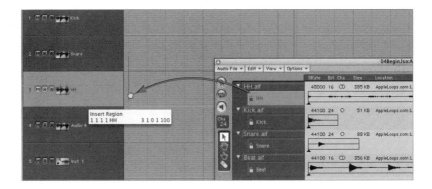

Dragging a single Region into the Arrange window operates exactly as you'd expect, so what happens if you drag in two or more Regions at once?

2   In the Audio window, press the Shift key and select both the Kick and Snare *audio files*.

For this trick to work, it is very important that you select the thin horizontal beams representing the audio files, and not the Regions.

3 In one fell swoop, drag both audio files over the Arrange window and drop them on the Kick track at 1 1 1 1.

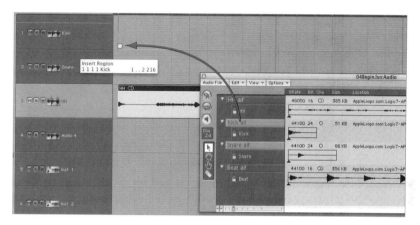

The Add Selected Files to Arrange dialog appears.

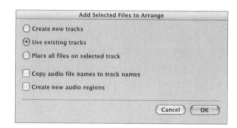

This dialog controls how multiple files are added to Arrange window tracks. You saw this dialog first in Lesson 3, "Understanding Workflow Techniques," when you used Logic's Multiple File Import function with the Arrange window. Well, here it is again, and it works exactly the same way.

MORE INFO ▶ If you need more information about the Add Selected Files to Arrange dialog options, refer back to Lesson 3.

4   The target tracks already exist as named tracks in the Arrange window, so from the Add Selected Files to Arrange dialog, select the "Use existing tracks" option and click OK.

An Alert dialog pops up to tell you two files will be added to the arrangement.

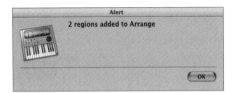

5   Click OK.

The Kick Region is added to the Kick track, and the Snare Region is added to the Snare track. Now that's a real time saver!

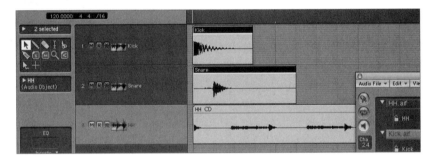

Editing Audio Regions

In Lesson 3 you learned how to trim Audio Regions using the Scissors tool, and that's a great way to make rhythmic cuts that conform to Logic's time grid while you're editing in the Arrange window. But you can also change the duration of an Audio Region by simply dragging the Region's bottom corners—in either the Arrange window or the Audio window. In fact, when you edit an Audio Region in one window, that edit is mirrored in the other one. As you proceed through the following steps, watch how your edits affect the Regions in both windows.

1   Position the Audio window so you can see the Regions in both the Arrange and Audio windows at the same time.

2   In the Audio window, increase the vertical zoom setting so that you can clearly see the Snare Region's waveform.

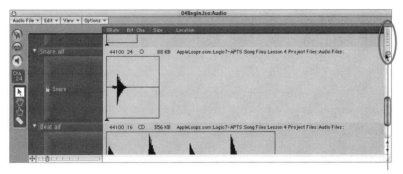

Vertical Zoom Slider

This sample has a bit of sound before the peak hit. It is important you don't accidentally trim the sound off, so make sure you increase the vertical zoom accordingly.

3   Click somewhere in the background of the Arrange window to deselect the newly added regions.

4   In the Arrange window, position the Arrow tool over the bottom right corner of the Snare Region.

The pointer turns into a Region-resize pointer.

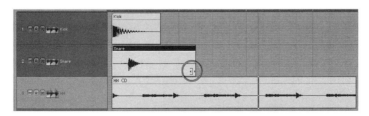

5 Drag left until you've trimmed the silence off the tail of the Snare Region.

In the Audio window, the Region updates to display this edit. This makes sense, because the same Region is displayed in both windows. To reaffirm the point, let's trim the silence off the front of this Region using the Audio window this time.

6 In the Audio window position the Arrow tool over the bottom left corner of the Snare Region.

The pointer turns into a Region-resize pointer.

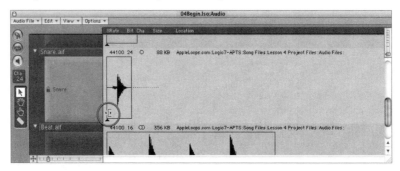

As you complete the next step, watch the Region in both the Audio and Arrange windows.

7 Drag the left edge of the Region toward the waveform, cutting off the silence at the front.

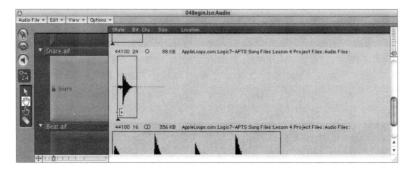

Back in the Arrange window, the silence is not only trimmed from the Region, but the Region pops forward a bit. Why? The answer is, when you trim the front of a Region, you also reset the Region's *Anchor*. You'll learn how to do that in a moment, but first, let's take a second to explore a very cool feature: Logic's ability to automatically search for zero crossings in the waveform.

Searching for the Zero Crossing

Editing in the Audio window is not at all accurate. In fact, all edits in the Audio window are only accurate to within 256 samples. That can cause problems because all edits to Region boundaries should ensure that the boundary intersects the waveform precisely where the waveform crosses zero. If you fail to make an appropriate edit, you will hear unwanted pops and clicks in your song. (It's sort of like trying to shove a doorstop under a door, big end first—there's going to be some noise!) The following figure shows an extreme close-up of an audio file with a Region boundary that does not cross the waveform at zero:

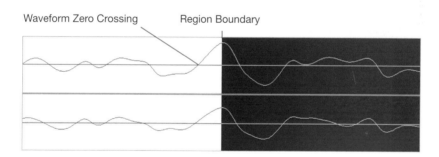

This inappropriate edit will result in a slight clicking or popping sound when the Region begins playing. To avoid this unwanted noise, you must ensure that your Region boundaries cross the waveform at zero, as shown in the next figure.

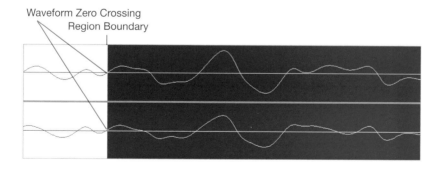

Fortunately, Logic has an option that will automatically find the closest zero crossing to your edit, so you don't need to zoom in on every edit you make. Let's turn this option on to make future edits sound better.

1   From the Audio window's local menu bar, choose Edit > Search Zero Crossings.

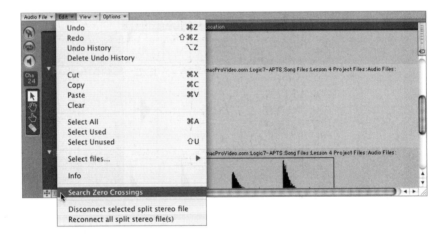

Now whenever you move a Region boundary in the Audio window, Logic automatically moves the edit to the closest zero crossing. If the file is stereo, Logic looks for the nearest point where both the left and right channels cross zero and places the Region boundary there. It's hard to see this in the Audio window, so let's open the Sample Editor and take a close look.

2   In the Audio window, double-click the Snare Region.

The Region opens in the Sample Editor.

3   In the Sample Editor, choose Edit > Search Zero Crossings.

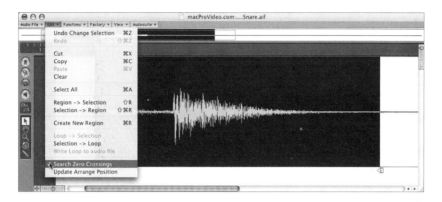

4   Zoom in closely on the Region's start boundary.

5   Grab the S icon, drag the Region's start boundary into the waveform, and try dropping it on a peak in the wave, instead of at the zero crossing.

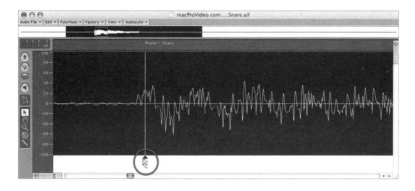

The Region boundary always shifts to the nearest zero crossing. And it does so in a very particular way. In fact, *the boundary shifts to the zero crossing of the nearest ascending wave* (a wave going up from zero, instead of down to zero).

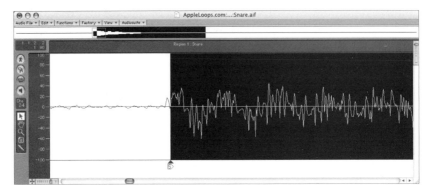

6   Reset the Region's start boundary to the beginning of the waveform's sound.

7   Close the Sample Editor.

Setting a Region's Anchor Point

Every Region has an Anchor that serves as a temporal reference point, or the point Logic uses to snap the Region to the Arrange window's time grid. The resolution of this time grid changes depending on the Arrange window's zoom level, but at all resolutions the time grid's function is the same: It's there to ensure that the Region's Anchor always snaps to a bar or beat position (or division and tick, if you're zoomed in close enough), which in turn lets you confidently move Audio Regions around the Arrange window, safe in the knowledge that no matter where you move a Region, it will always play in rhythm with the other Objects in your song.

In the Audio window, the Anchor is represented by a small triangle under the Region. When a Region is created, an Anchor is automatically placed at its start boundary, but you're free to place the Anchor anywhere you'd like within the Region. For Regions like the HH loop, it's fine to have the Anchor right at the Region's beginning, because the Region starts on the downbeat of a drum loop. But Regions like Snare present a bit more of a challenge. This Region does not begin on a downbeat, but rather begins with a bit of sound that leads into a Snare hit. To ensure this Region lines up correctly with other Arrange window Objects, you should adjust the Anchor so that it falls directly on the peak of the Snare hit.

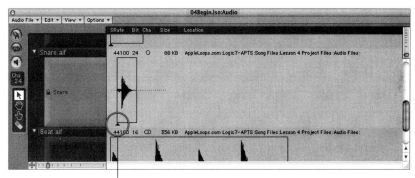

Anchor Point

1   In the Audio window, drag the Snare Region's Anchor point until it falls on the peak of the Snare hit.

Notice that back in the Arrange window, the Snare Region has actually shifted forward a bit, but now the peak of this Region falls directly on beat 1 1 1 1.

2   In the Arrange window, grab the Snare sample and shift it forward to 1 2 1 1.

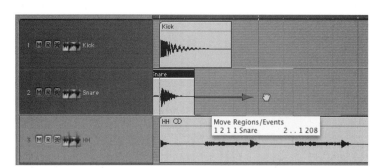

As you drag, the bar, beat, division, and tick numbers you see in Logic's info box reflect the position of the Region's Anchor point and not the left edge (start boundary) of the Region.

Of course, you know from the exercises above that the Audio window allows edits accurate to within 256 samples. That's not terribly accurate, and you probably want your Anchor to be set at exactly the peak of the Snare hit's sound. Let's open the Snare hit in the Sample Editor and refine the Anchor's position.

3   In the Arrange window, double-click the Snare Region.

The Region opens in the Sample Editor.

4   In the Sample Editor, zoom in on the Anchor point (remember, you can press the down arrow key to quickly center the Anchor in the Sample Editor).

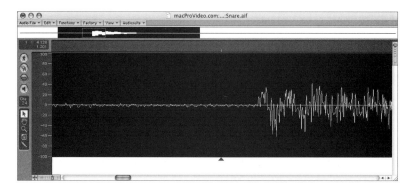

Notice that the Anchor edit you made in the Audio window was very inaccurate! This is audio editing, and audio editing is all about precision. Let's tighten this edit up.

5   Grab the Anchor point and drag it to the beginning of the waveform's peak.

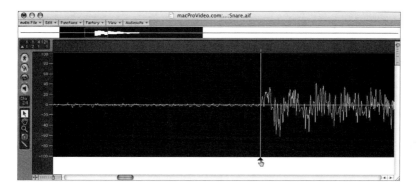

6   Close the Sample Editor.

NOTE ▶ As you move Regions in the Arrange window, the help tags actually show you the position of the Anchor, and not the Region's start boundary.

Repeating Audio Regions

At the moment, the Arrange window has three Regions in it: a kick and a snare hit, and a hi-hat loop. Many songs begin from such humble beginnings—let's take these three Regions and turn them into a beat!

All audio programs have some sort of repeat feature that lets you quickly make multiple copies of MIDI Regions and Audio Regions. However, Logic has a few tricks to add to this process. For example, you can repeat Objects one right after the other, which is great for making multiple copies of a perfectly trimmed audio loop, such as a one-bar beat loop. Regions of a duration that is not exactly a bar (or a beat) benefit from Logic's ability to repeat Regions so that the Anchor point always falls on a bar, a beat, or even the seconds and frames

from the SMPTE time code ruler. As always, practice makes perfect, so let's try
repeating some Objects.

1 In the Arrange window, select the Kick Region.

2 From the Arrange window's local menus, choose Region > Repeat
Regions.

> **TIP** ▶ You will repeat Regions a lot. Consequently, you should assign
> this function to a key command. (See Lesson 3 for more information
> about key commands.) Option-Shift-R is a good choice.

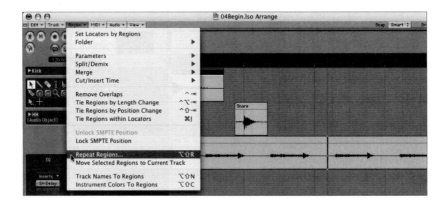

The Repeat Regions/Events dialog opens.

3 In the Number of Copies text box type *3*, choose Auto from the Adjustment menu and make sure the Copies button is selected, then click OK.

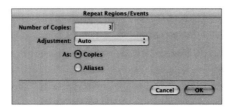

Logic creates three copies of the Kick Region, back to back.

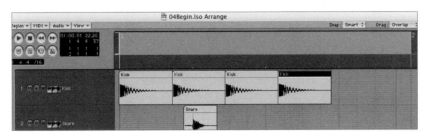

This isn't the most "rhythmic" of repeats. Because the Kick Region is less than a full beat in duration, the repeated Kick Regions fall off beat and the timing of these repeated Objects is strange, to say the least. Let's undo that repeat and try again, using a different setting in the Repeat dialog's Adjustment menu.

4   Press Cmd-Z to undo the last edit.

5   Once again, open the Repeat Regions/Events dialog.

The Repeat Regions/Events dialog opens. The Number of Copies text box should still read 3, so there's no need to change that. Instead, focus on the Adjustment menu—that's where the magic takes place.

6   From the Adjustment menu, choose Beat and click OK.

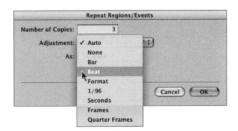

Logic creates three copies of the Kick Region and places each copy on the next beat of the bar.

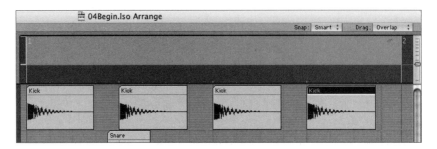

7   Position the Arrow tool over the bottom right corner of any Kick Region and drag left to shorten its duration.

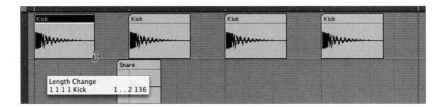

All of the copied Kicks change duration. This demonstrates an important point: When you copy an Audio Region using the Repeat Regions/Events dialog, all copies are treated like aliases that refer back to the original Region. (In fact, the Repeat Regions/Events dialog's Copies and Aliases radio buttons do exactly the same thing when you repeat an Audio Region.) If you look at the Audio window, you'll see there is still just one Kick Region in this song, but that Region has been used multiple times. Thus it makes sense that editing this one Audio Region would cause all instances of the Region to change as well.

Interestingly, the Repeat Regions/Events dialog functions differently depending on the position of the Region's Anchor. Let's repeat the Snare Region once to see how.

8   In the Arrange window, select the Snare Region.

9   From the Arrange window's local menu bar, choose Region > Repeat Regions.

The Repeat Regions/Events dialog opens.

10   In the Number of Copies text box, type *1,* leave the Adjustment menu set to Beat, and click OK.

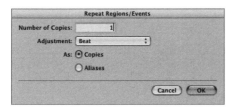

The Snare Region skips a beat.

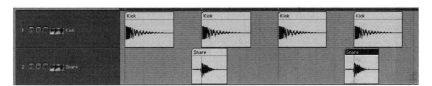

As it turns out, if the Anchor is not at the exact start of the Region, Logic always skips a beat when it repeats! Keep this in mind so that your heart doesn't skip a beat when this happens as you edit your own songs.

Working with Sampling Rates

When audio comes in through your audio interface, analog-to-digital (A/D) converters sample the audio stream a certain number of times per second. That number is the recorded digital audio file's *sampling rate*. CD-Audio uses a sampling rate of 44.1 kHz, which means the audio stream has been sampled 44,100 times per second. This is a lot of little samples, and consequently CD-Audio comes pretty close to representing the original audio waveform.

But the holy grail of digital audio is to copy an analog waveform perfectly. In pursuit of this perfect waveform, audio editors like Logic now enable us to record and edit audio at sampling rates of 48 kHz, 96 kHz, and even 192 kHz (audio hardware permitting). These sample rates provide significantly more samples per second than CD-Audio, which means these higher sampling rates come closer to representing a true analog waveform. Consequently, they sound better!

> **NOTE ▶** Higher sampling rates mean more data to process every second, putting a strain on your computer. If your system's audio interface works with 96 or 192 kHz audio, you may want to edit at this sampling rate to preserve as much of the original analog signal as possible. But unless you're on a cutting-edge Mac, higher sampling rates won't let you use as many audio tracks and DSP effects as you can at lower sampling rates. The most commonly used sampling rate is 48 kHz because it provides good quality without straining your computer to the max.

Working with Sampling Rates

As you saw at the beginning of the lesson, this song uses a sampling rate of 44.1 kHz. All of the song's audio files use this sampling rate too, except for the **HH.aif** file, which has been recorded at 48 kHz. You can still use the **HH.aif** file in the song, but it will not sound correct unless you convert its sampling rate to match the sampling rate of the song. The reason? Logic just plays samples per second. It's much the same as the frames per second (fps) setting in a video editor. If you play a 30 fps NTSC video at 25 fps (PAL), the video plays back much slower than it should because five fewer frames display every second. Similarly, playing a 48 kHz audio file in a 44.1 kHz song still works, but the file sounds like its playing slower than it should because fewer samples per second play than are supposed to.

The following steps demonstrate what happens if you add a 48 kHz file to a 44.1 kHz song.

1   Press the spacebar to start playback.

The Kick and Snare Regions are perfectly in time, but the HH Region is not. In fact, if you look closely at the HH Region in the Arrange window, you can see that although it's supposed to be exactly one bar in length, it's a bit too long.

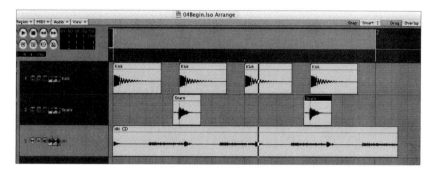

2   Press the spacebar to stop playback.

3   In the Audio window, check the **HH.aif's** sampling rate.

This file uses a sampling rate of 48 kHz. And therein lies the problem. You'll need to change the **HH.aif** file's sampling rate before it will play with proper timing in your song. To do that, you'll use the Sample Editor's Digital Factory.

Using the Digital Factory to Convert Sampling Rates

The Digital Factory™ is a suite of digital signal processors designed to change audio files in several ways. For example, you can use the Factory to time-compress or time-expand an Audio Region, change its pitch, add groove or swing to a machinelike audio loop, or, for the purpose of this exercise, alter its sampling rate.

Under most editing circumstances, Logic is a nondestructive audio editor that does not change your source audio files in the course of editing. But as with most rules, there is a notable exception.

Enter the Digital Factory. Almost all Digital Factory functions are destructive, which means they permanently alter your source audio files. This can cause problems if you ever need to get those source files back or if they are used in another song, so keep this in mind!

1 In the Arrange or Audio window, double-click the HH Region.

The Region opens in the Sample Editor.

2 From the Sample Editor's local menu bar, select Factory > Sample Rate Convert.

The Factory window opens and displays the Sample Rate Convert dialog.

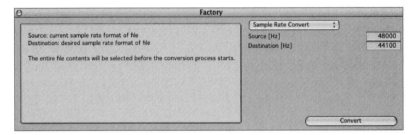

On the right side is a Source [Hz] field displaying the file's current sampling rate (48,000 Hz, or 48 kHz), and a Destination [Hz] field displaying your song's sampling rate (44,100 Hz, or 44.1 kHz). This is all correct, so there's no need to change anything here.

3   Click the Convert button.

If the Region references only a subsection of the audio file, a dialog pops up to inform you that the whole audio file will be converted.

4   Click OK.

If the file is used in any other songs on your computer, Logic pops open a dialog to tell you so.

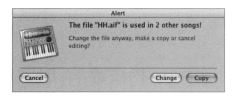

If you see this dialog, it's a very good idea to choose the Copy option. If you don't, the source audio file will be changed, and those changes will ripple into any other song that uses this file. When you choose this option, Logic creates a copy of the source file, and then changes the copy. Your source file is not altered, and it remains available to the other songs that use it (the copied file is placed in the same folder as the original on your hard disk).

5   Close the Factory window.

6 Close the Sample Editor.

Back in the Arrange window, the HH Region is now exactly one bar long because its sample rate has been converted.

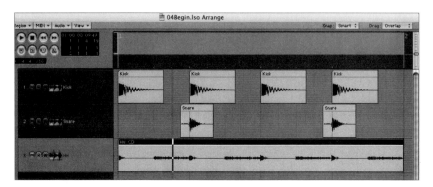

7 Press the spacebar to start playback.

All Audio Regions now play with the correct timing.

8 Press the spacebar again to stop playback.

Working with Tempo and Audio Regions

Earlier in this lesson, you saw that the Anchor point ties an Audio Region to Logic's time grid. This is particularly important for situations where you must change your song's timing, such as when you're changing tempo.

1 Press the spacebar to start playback.

2 Double-click the tempo setting and change the song's tempo to 110 bpm.

Notice that the Kick and Snare hits keep the correct timing, but the HH Region sounds completely off! This is because the Kick and Snare Regions are single hits, and the Anchors in these Regions tie them to the correct place in Logic's time grid, even when you change the tempo.

The HH Region, on the other hand, is an entire loop with just one Anchor point. Unfortunately, as you slow down the playback tempo, this Region begins to play too quickly relative to the other Audio Regions in the song.

But guess what? There's a quick and easy way to fix that.

3 Set the tempo back to 120 bpm.

4 From the toolbox, grab the Scissors tool.

5 Hold down the Option key, and click the Scissors tool at exactly 1 1 3 1 (the beginning of the second eighth note of the bar).

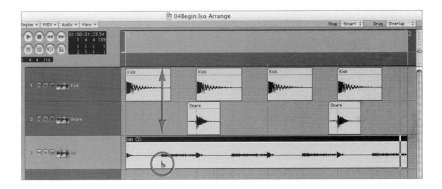

The HH Region is divided into eight equal sections. Pressing the Option key while slicing Objects is a great way to create several equal-size Regions out of one large Region. In this situation it is an ideal edit because there is a single hi-hat hit on each eighth note. Consequently, you have now created eight individual Regions, each with its own Anchor.

6 Next, change the tempo back to 110 bpm.

Because the HH Region has been divided into eight smaller Regions, and each of these smaller Regions has its own Anchor, the HH track now keeps time with the rest of the song. In fact, you can now change the tempo to anything you'd like and the HH will always play in time.

7 Press the spacebar to stop playback.

8 Over in the Audio window, notice that a bunch of new Regions have been created for the **HH.aif** file.

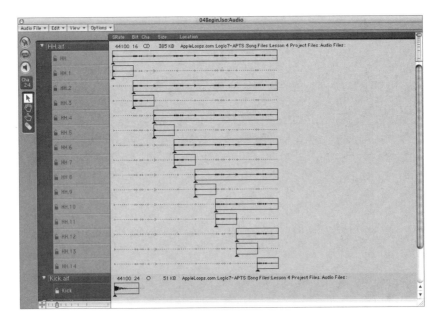

Zoom out of the audio window to see all of the HH Regions, if necessary.

9 Close the Audio window.

Adjusting Tempos to Regions

These days more than ever, music is based on sample loops. Unfortunately, you won't always know the bpm of the loop you're using, and that makes it hard to set your song's tempo or integrate the loop into the song. Thankfully, Logic provides an automatic way to set the bpm based on the length of an Audio Region, and it's called the "Adjust Tempo using Region Length and Locators" function. Let's import the **1-Bar Conga.aif** loop and see how this function works. To import this loop we will use a trick you haven't seen yet, so follow the first few steps closely.

1   From the Arrange window's toolbox, grab the Pencil tool.

2   Press Shift and click the Pencil tool on the Audio 4 track at exactly 1 1 1 1.

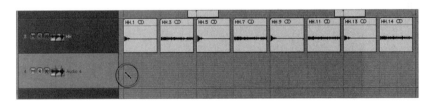

Shift-clicking the Pencil tool in the Arrange area causes the Open file dialog to appear.

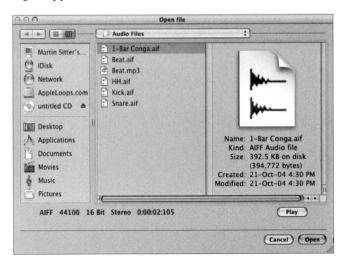

3　Navigate to the Lesson 4 Project Files > Audio Files, then select the **1-Bar Conga.aif** file, and click Open.

The file is added to Track 4 at 1 1 1 1. As you can see, the **1-Bar Conga.aif** file is not quite one bar long at the song's current tempo of 110 bpm. Consequently, you can tell it must use a faster bpm. But how much faster? Let's find out.

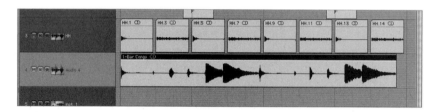

4　Make sure the 1-Bar Conga Region is selected.

5　In the Bar Ruler, make sure that the one-bar Cycle range is enabled.

One-Bar Cycle Range

As you saw in Lesson 3, the Cycle mode always cycles from the left to the right locators. With a one-bar Cycle range enabled, you can be sure the left and right locators are exactly one bar apart. This is important as you do the following step.

6   Choose Options > Tempo > Adjust Tempo using Region Length and Locators (T).

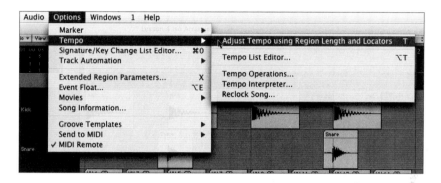

A dialog pops up to ask if you want to change the tempo of the entire song (globally) or if you want to create a tempo change for only the part of the song covered by the 1-Bar Conga Region (in this case, only one bar). If you choose Create, only one bar of your song will have its tempo changed to match the tempo of the 1-Bar Conga Region. All the other parts of the song will stay at their current tempo. If you choose Globally, the tempo changes for the entire song.

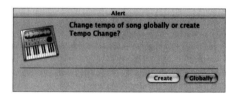

7   Click the Globally button.

The song's tempo changes to 114.0001 bpm. Why? Well, the Region is exactly one bar long, and the song's left and right locators are exactly one bar apart. When you adjust the tempo of the song using the "Adjust Tempo using Region Length and Locators" function, Logic looks at the length of the Region (one bar) and the distance between the left and right locators (also one bar) and makes them exactly the same.

However, 114.0001 bpm is a strange tempo indeed! Perhaps there's a better option for matching the tempo of this Region to the tempo of the song.

8   Press Cmd-Z to undo the tempo change.

The song's tempo reverts to 110 bpm.

Adjusting Regions to Tempos

In the previous exercise you discovered that the 1-Bar Conga Region's tempo was approximately 114 bpm, but your song currently uses a tempo of 110 bpm. To resolve this difference in tempos, you must use a process called *time-stretching* to change the 1-Bar Conga Region to match your song's tempo.

In the old days of audio design, this was a time-consuming task that took a bit of trial and error using the Time and Pitch Machine, located in the Sample Editor's Digital Factory. But with Logic 7, this task is now easily and quickly accomplished right in the Arrange window using the new Adjust Region Length to Locators function.

But first things first: You are about to change the timing of an audio file. Before doing so, you must choose a Time Machine algorithm that suits the aural content of the file.

1   From the Arrange window's local menus, choose Audio > Time Machine Algorithm > Beats Only.

The Conga line is just a rhythmic pattern, with no pitch or melody, so Beats Only is an appropriate Time Machine algorithm choice. However, there are six Time Machine algorithms on offer, each particularly suited to a certain type of audio material. Selecting the correct algorithm will help you avoid introducing unwanted artifacts into your audio file. The available algorithms include:

▶ Version 5—The tried and trusted algorithm used in Logic 5.

▶ Any material—A universal algorithm that produces acceptable results for almost any type of audio material. The best default algorithm choice.

▶ Monophonic—The best one for mono vocal, brass, woodwind, or other mono Audio Regions.

▶ Pads—The setting for Audio Regions with a lot of harmonic content (such as choirs, strings sections, or synth swells).

▶ Rhythmic—The algorithm for steady rhythmic instrumental recordings (including synth stabs, rhythmic pianos, or guitar loops).

▶ Beats Only—One that perfectly maintains the timing of percussive material; should be used with drum loops.

With the correct Time Machine algorithm selected, it's time to adjust the tempo of the 1-Bar Conga Region.

2 From the Arrange window's local menu bar, choose Audio > Adjust Region Length to Locators.

> **TIP** ▶ Adjusting Objects to tempos relies on the Region being a perfect loop. You may need to use the Sample window to trim your Audio Regions to the correct length before performing this function.

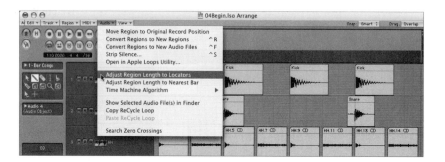

Logic quickly processes the Region, and time-stretches it. However, Logic may not have adjusted the actual Region boundary to match the new length. No problem, just grab the bottom right corner of the Region and stretch it out.

3 Grab the bottom right corner of the 1-Bar Conga Region and drag right until it covers exactly one bar.

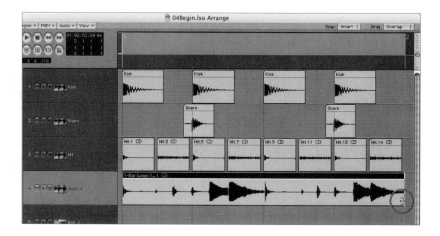

4 Press the spacebar to start playback.

The Conga loop plays in time with your song.

In the next lesson you will discover another great way to work with the tempo of audio files: Apple Loops! In fact, you'll re-insert this Conga loop as an Apple Loop, so let's clear it out of the Arrange window for now.

5 Make sure the 1-Bar Conga Region is selected and press the Delete key to remove it from the song.

Using Folders

Folders let you group many Arrange window Objects into one tight unit that you can edit just like any Audio or MIDI Region. In essence, a folder is a Region that contains other Regions in much the same way a folder in your computer's Finder can contain other folders. Video editors familiar with Apple Final Cut Pro might like to think of a folder as a nested sequence for Audio and MIDI Regions. Basically, a folder is a way to create a song within a song.

Folders provide a great way to group similar Objects together, such as the Audio Regions that make up this song's beat. It's therefore often beneficial to pack all the Objects that make up a chorus into a single folder, and all the Objects that make up a verse into a single folder, and so on. Once the folders are packed, you have only to arrange folders in the Arrange window, and the song is done.

1 Press Cmd-A to select all of the Audio Regions in the Arrange window.

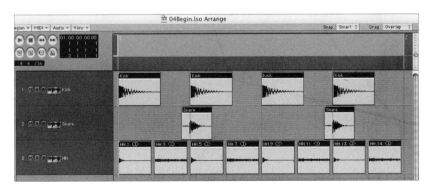

2 Working in the Arrange window's local menu bar, choose Region > Folder > Pack Folder (Cmd-F).

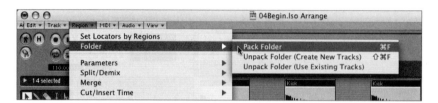

Logic packs all of the selected Audio Regions into a folder one bar long.

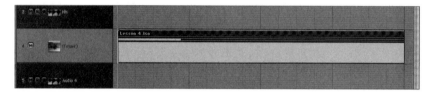

3 Press the spacebar to start playback.

You can hear the beat, so where are the Regions?

4 Grab the Arrow tool and double-click the Folder Object.

Logic opens a lower-level Arrange window to display the Objects in the folder. Notice that this Arrange window has only three tracks—the three tracks you packed into the folder. In essence, this folder now shows a song within a song, and the new song has its own Arrange window one level down from the main Arrange window. You can now edit these tracks and the Objects they contain just as you'd edit tracks in the main Arrange window.

5 To get back to the main Arrange window, do one of the following:

▶ Double-click anywhere on the background of the lower-level Arrange window.

▶ Click the Level-up button in the top left corner of the lower-level Arrange window.

Level-up Button

The main Arrange window comes back and displays the packed folder.

Working with Tracks and Folders

With the folder packed, you have a few empty tracks still populating the main Arrange window—specifically, the Kick, Snare, and HH tracks. These tracks have already been added to the folder and are now just taking up space in the main Arrange window, so let's delete them.

1   In the main Arrange window, select the Kick track.

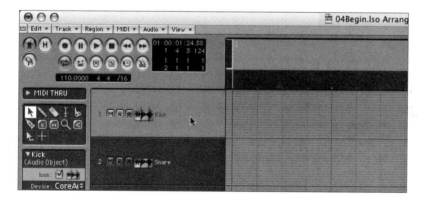

2   Press the Delete key.

The Kick track is deleted.

3   Delete the Snare and HH tracks.

Only the folder is left in the Arrange window.

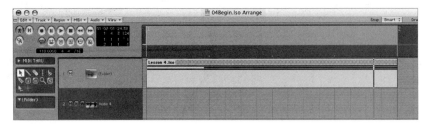

4   Press the spacebar to play the song.

The audio in the folder still plays, even though there are no Audio Regions or tracks displayed in the Arrange window.

5   Press the spacebar to stop playback.

Unpacking Folders

There may come a point in time when you need to unpack the folder to rearrange your song. This process is just as easy as packing the folder in the first place. Let's try it.

1   In the Arrange window, make sure that the folder is selected.

2   From the Arrange window's local menu bar, choose Region > Folder > Unpack Folder (Create New Tracks), or press Shift-Cmd-F.

Logic unpacks each Audio Region to its own track in the Arrange window.

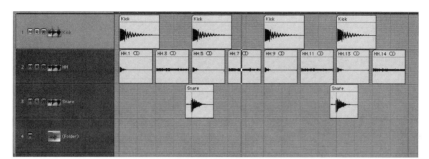

You now know how to unpack folders. However, we want these Audio Regions to be packed in a folder. So let's repack the folder and delete those extra tracks one more time.

3   Press Cmd-A to select all of the Audio Regions in the Arrange window.

4   Choose Region > Folder > Pack Folder (Cmd-F).

5   From the main Arrange window, delete the Kick, HH, and Snare tracks.

Saving the Song as a Project

This is the first time you've saved the project. Keep in mind that the second part of this book is a start-to-finish tutorial that results in a finished song, so each of the next six chapters build upon the previous ones. Consequently, you should save this song using a name you can remember, because you're going to need it for Lesson 5, "Working with Apple Loops".

Just in case something goes awry along the way, you should save the song after (and during!) each exercise, using a different name each time. For example, you could name this saved file *LogicLesson4*, the song for the next chapter *LogicLesson5*, and so on. The name you choose is up to you; just make sure you remember what it is and where you put it.

> **TIP** ▶ You should always save incremental versions of your songs by adding a number to the file each time you save it (MySong1, MySong2, MySong3, etc.). Project files do occasionally become corrupt, and if you haven't saved incremental versions, you have nothing to go back to when something goes wrong. But more practically, say you go off on a musical tangent and then don't like the results. If you save incremental versions of your song, you can return to that great mix from a few hours earlier.

In the following steps you will save the song as a project. This is a great technique to learn, because when you save a song as a project, Logic automatically groups all audio files, plug-in settings, and even EXS instrument samples and Space Designer impulse responses into one folder that you can easily move from computer to computer, back up on a DVD disc, and so on.

1   Choose File > Save as Project.

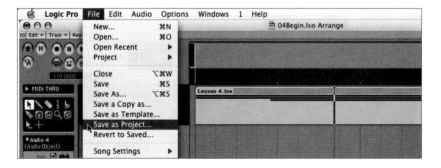

The "Save as project" dialog opens.

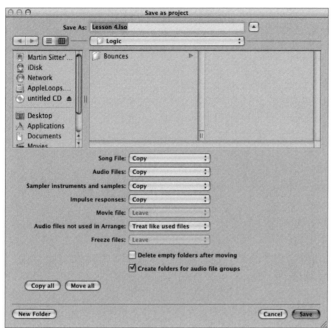

Here you are presented with several choices. You can choose to copy or move your song files, audio files, EXS24 sampler instruments and samples, and Space Designer impulse response files. You can also choose to leave unused audio files behind. All of these options provide a great way to consolidate your song into one tight bundle that has all the parts needed for the arrangement. When it comes time to back up a project, this is the option you should use!

2 Leave the "Save as project" dialog at its default settings.

In most situations, you want to copy files to the newly saved project. In fact, you should only move files if you know exactly what you are doing. For example, if you move the song's audio files to the new folder, they are removed from the old folder and will no longer be available to other songs that reference them. Ditto EXS24 sampler instruments and samples, and Space Designer impulse response files.

3 Navigate to the place on your hard disk where you want to save the song.

TIP ▶ By default, the "Save as project" dialog opens to your User > Music > Logic folder. When in doubt, this is a great place to save the song.

4 Click Save.

Logic consolidates your song and all of its audio files into a single folder on your hard disk.

5 Repeat this process after each of the next six chapters!

What You've Learned

- ▶ The Audio window acts as your song's audio library. All of the audio files you record or import into Logic are listed in this window, along with information about the files' sampling rates, bit depths, channel configurations (stereo/mono), file sizes, and locations.

- ▶ To import audio files directly into the Audio window, choose Audio File > Add Audio File.

- ▶ Logic converts all imported MP3 files to PCM files at the same sampling rate of your song.

- ▶ The Sample Editor is a *sample-accurate* editor. This contrasts with the Audio window, which only allows edits accurate to within 256 samples.

- ▶ The channel setting, located on the left edges of both the Audio window and Sample Editor, is used to set the audio track channel that auditioned audio plays through.

- ▶ The Search Zero Crossings function causes Logic to automatically place edits to Region boundaries and Anchors on the zero crossing of the nearest ascending wave to your edit.

- ▶ Region Anchors determine how the Region is tied to Logic's time grid.

- ▶ The Sample Editor's Digital Factory is used to convert sampling rates for files imported into Logic.

- ▶ Folders provide a convenient way to group several Audio Regions into one Object that can be edited and arranged just like a normal Audio Region in the Arrange window.

- ▶ The Save as Project function allows you to group all necessary audio files into one folder that is easy to back up or move from computer to computer.

5

Lesson Files	APTS_Logic_7 > Song Files > Lesson 5 Project Files > 05Begin.lso
	APTS_Logic_7 > Song Files > Lesson 5 Project Files > 05End.lso
Media	APTS_Logic_7 > Song Files > Lesson 5 Project Files
Time	This lesson takes approximately 1 hour to complete.
Goals	Add Apple Loops to the arrangement to create a finished song
	Add and name tracks
	Audition Apple Loops in the Loop Browser
	Add a collection of Apple Loops to the Loop Browser
	Use the Global Tempo track

Working with Apple Loops

Apple Loops made their first appearance with a helper application called Soundtrack, which comes with Final Cut Pro. (Soundtrack can also be purchased as a stand-alone application.) Though Apple Loops began life as a loop format to make audio editing easy for video editors, Apple Loops have been warmly received by audio editors as well. The reason is simple: Apple Loops contain information used to *automatically* time-stretch *and* transpose the audio file, so it not only plays at the correct tempo but also plays at the correct pitch for the song you are working on. It can otherwise take hours to time-stretch and pitch-convert regular audio files so that they fit into a song. But with Apple Loops all the magic takes place under the hood, leaving you free to concentrate on the important part of audio production—making music!

Apple Loops tend to be complete musical phrases that lend themselves particularly well to looping (hence the name), and they really shine in audio phrases that use recurring rhythmic musical elements or other elements suitable for repetition. Additionally, Apple Loops typically contain tags that enable you to quickly locate files by instrument, genre, or mood. This feature, coupled with the Apple Loop Browser that comes with Logic, means that finding the right loop for your particular purpose is simple and easy.

Taking a First Look at Apple Loops

To get a feel for how Apple Loops work, let's add one to the arrangement.

1   From this book's companion DVD files, open the project file named
    05Begin.lso (in the Lesson 5 Project Files folder), or continue working on
    your song from the previous lesson.

2   Open a Finder window over Logic.

    TIP To open a Finder window over Logic, click the Finder icon in the
    Dock. If any windows are open in the Finder, they will pop to the surface.
    If no windows are open in the Finder, a new one will pop open.

3   From this book's companion files, navigate to the Lesson 5 Project Files >
    Apple Loops folder.

    In that folder is an Apple Loop named **Bongo Groove 05.aif**.

4   Drag the **Bongo Groove 05.aif** Apple Loop from the Finder window, and
    drop it into the track named Audio 4 at 1 1 1 1.

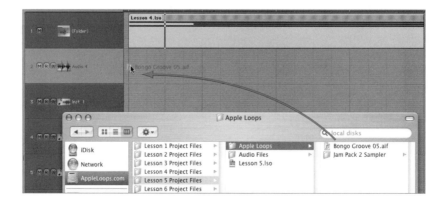

The Apple Loop is added to the song. Notice that the Apple Loop automatically fills one bar of the song at the current tempo. Additionally, check out the Apple Loop icon to the right of the new Audio Region's name—that little loop-the-loop is a good visual indicator to help you spot Apple Loops in your arrangement.

NOTE ▸ Mono Apple Loops have one loop-the-loop, while stereo Apple Loops have two.

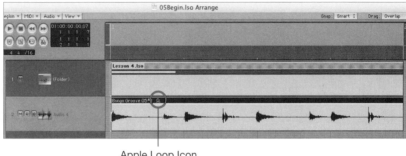

Apple Loop Icon

5   Press the spacebar to start the playback.

6   Change the tempo of the song from 110 to 126.

As you can hear, the Apple Loop adjusts its tempo and plays in time with your song. How cool is that?

7   Stop playback.

Using the Apple Loops Utility

Logic comes with the Apple Loops Utility. With it, you can turn any
AIFF, WAV, or SDII file into ready-to-use Apple Loops. In many cases,
it takes more time to use Logic's internal pitch-converting and time-
stretching functions to fit a loop into your song than it does to open
the Apple Loops Utility and transform the normal audio loop into
an Apple Loop. And once the loop is converted, it will always stay in
time with your song, even if you need to make an unexpected tempo
change later.

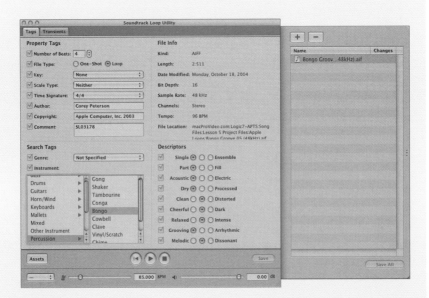

The Apple Loops Utility

Continues on next page

▶ **Using the Apple Loops Utility** *(continued)*

As it turns out, creating Apple Loops is even easier than you might
expect. Just add the audio loop you want to convert to your arrangement
and select it. Then, from the Arrange window's local menus, choose
Audio > Open in Apple Loops Utility, as shown. Converting normal
loops couldn't be any easier.

Working with Tracks

The song you're working on has four empty *Audio Instrument* tracks, but no
remaining *audio* tracks. The Bongo Apple Loop you just added filled the last
audio track with sound, so before you can add any more Apple Loops to the
song, you'll need to create a few more audio tracks. Let's get this housekeeping
out of the way now so we can have fun later.

Adding Tracks

In Logic, all tracks listed in the Arrange window must be assigned to *channels*.
Channels are simply paths that audio and MIDI use to travel into and out of
Logic. For example, MIDI messages travel through MIDI channels as they
leave Logic and travel to your MIDI interface and then to another MIDI device
such as a hardware synthesizer or digital-effects unit. Similarly, audio tracks
are a type of audio channel that can read recorded audio, like a vocal or guitar
part, off the hard drive and send it to your sound card's outputs.

To take this a bit further, Audio Instrument channels use sound generated by one of Logic's internal synthesizers, say an es2, and then send it to a sound card output. You will learn more about MIDI and audio channels in the "Customizing Your Setup" section of this book. For now, just keep this in mind: Each Arrange window track must be assigned to a channel, or you will have no sound because there's no channel for the signal to follow out of Logic.

Creating a new track in Logic is a two-part process: First you create the track, then you assign it to a channel. Let's go through the process now by adding a few tracks to the song.

1 In the Arrange window, select the track named Audio 4.

2 From the Arrange window's local menu bar, choose Track > Create (or press Shift-Return).

TIP You can also double-click an empty track slot at the bottom of the Arrange window to create new tracks.

A new, empty track is created directly under the selected track. By default, a new track is assigned *to the same channel* as the last track selected in the Arrange window, in this case audio track channel 4 (Audio 4). That channel is currently used for the **Bongo Groove 05** Region. Let's assign the new track to its own unique channel.

3   In the Arrange window's Track column, click and hold the name Audio 4 on the newly created track.

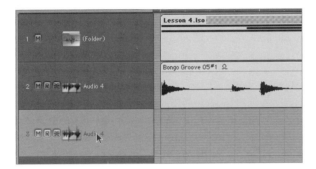

A hierarchical menu appears. This menu lists all of the channels available for use in the song. Notice that in the Audio section of the menu all available MIDI and audio channels are available, including Aux inputs, Busses, Audio Instruments, Outputs, and Audio Tracks. Indeed, you could assign any one of these channels to the track, but for the purpose at hand you must assign an audio track channel, because only audio track channels are designed to play audio loops off your hard drive.

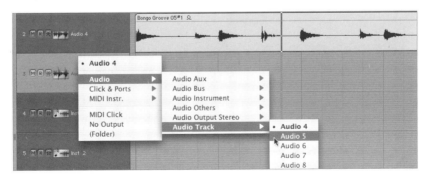

4   From the hierarchical menu, choose Audio > Audio Track > Audio 5.

The track is assigned to play through audio track channel 5. That took a few steps. You can streamline the process using the following trick:

▶   With the track named Audio 5 selected in the Arrange window, choose Track > Create with Next Instrument (Ctrl-Shift-Return).

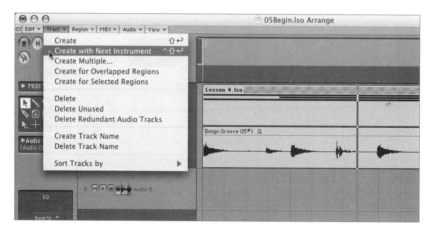

A new track is added to the song, and the new track is automatically assigned to audio track channel 6.

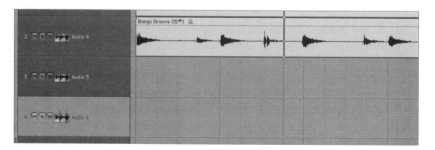

Adding Multiple Tracks

In the steps above you learned how to add tracks one at a time, but Logic contains a great feature for situations where you need to quickly add several tracks to the Arrange window. It's the Create Multiple Tracks function.

1   Scroll to the bottom of the Arrange window and select the last Audio Instrument track (Inst 4).

2   From the Arrange window's local menu bar, choose Track > Create Multiple.

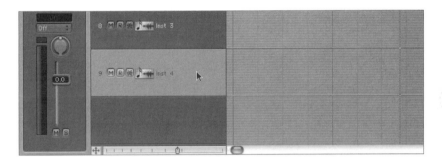

3   The Create Multiple Tracks dialog appears.

4   From the Track Type menu, choose Audio Instrument.

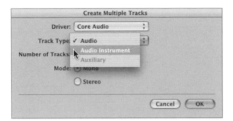

5   In the Number of Tracks text box, type *4*.

6   Click OK.

Logic creates four new Audio Instrument tracks under the last track selected and assigns them to the next Audio Instrument channel.

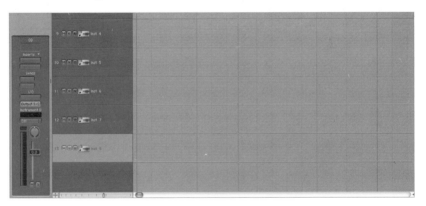

Setting a Track's Stereo/Mono Status

By default, *all newly created audio tracks are mono.* You can change this with the Stereo/Mono button in the Arrange window channel strip. In fact, you can also set a track to play back just the left channel of a stereo file, or just the right channel (this comes in handy with sample loops that contain, for example, a beat in the left channel and a bass line in the right channel).

NOTE ▶ Audio Instrument tracks do not have a Stereo/Mono button. Instead, they assume the stereo/mono status of the instrument assigned to them.

1   Select the Audio 5 track.

The Arrange window channel strip updates to display the channel settings for track Audio 5. At the bottom of the channel strip's level meter there is a Stereo/Mono button. Currently, it shows a single circle, indicating it is set to play back in mono only.

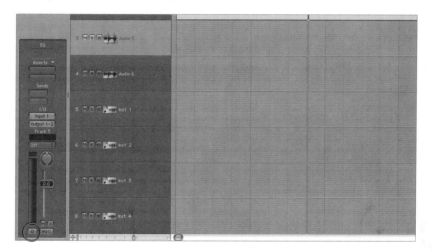

2   Click the Stereo/Mono button.

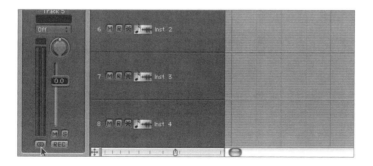

The button updates to show two interlocked circles: Stereo! Additionally, the channel's level meter splits in two, providing a display for both the left and right channels.

The Pan control works differently on mono and stereo tracks. On a mono track, the Pan control moves the mono sound from side to side. On a stereo channel, the Pan control acts like a balance control, adjusting the volume of one channel relative to the other. Consequently, in stereo tracks you cannot move sound from the left side of the stereo spectrum to the right side, or vice versa. Fortunately, there is an easy work-around.

3　Click and hold the Stereo/Mono button.

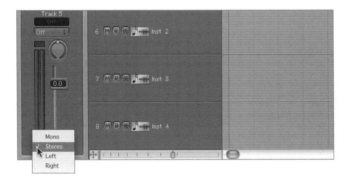

A menu pops up to ask if you'd like this channel to be mono, stereo, or either the left or right channel of a stereo file. Keep this option in mind when you'd like to move the sound from the left side of a stereo file to the right side of the sonic spectrum, or vice versa.

4　Leave the channel set to Stereo.

5　In preparation for adding stereo Apple Loops later in this lesson, set track Audio 6 to stereo playback.

Naming Tracks

It's a good idea to name tracks as you go, not only so you know what's on them, but also so you don't accidentally assign a newly created track to a channel you've already used.

1   In the Arrange window's Track column, press the Option key and double-click the Audio 4 track directly on its name.

A text box opens.

NOTE ▸ If you don't hold Option, double-clicking a track name brings up the Track Mixer, covered in Lesson 9, "Mixing."

2   Type *Bongo* into the text box, and press Return.

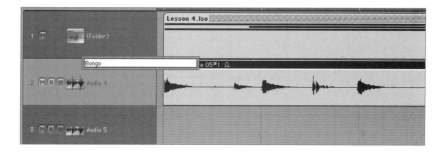

The track adopts the new name. Let's try this one more time to drive the concept home.

3   Option–double-click the Audio 5 track name, type *Bass* into the text box that appears, and press Return.

Audio 5 track is now named Bass. In fact, this name is not only listed in the Track column, but it is also assigned to the channel itself.

4   Click and hold the word *Bass*.

The hierarchical channel menu appears.

5   Navigate to the Audio > Audio Track section.

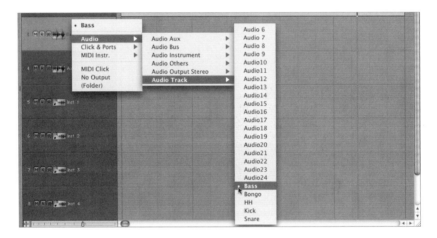

Notice that the named audio tracks appear at the bottom of the channel list. This is a great feature, because otherwise you could easily assign the same channel to two different tracks!

Reordering Tracks

It's common practice to group similar types of tracks in the Arrange window's Track column. For example, you might want to have all your vocal tracks sit one above the other. Depending on the order in which you create the tracks, you may need to move a track up or down the Track column to achieve this.

1   On the left edge of the Track column, position the Arrow tool over the Bass track's *number*.

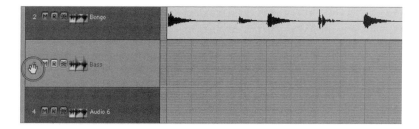

The pointer turns into an open hand.

2   Grab the Bass track, drag it up to the top of the Track column, and release
    it above the (Folder) track.

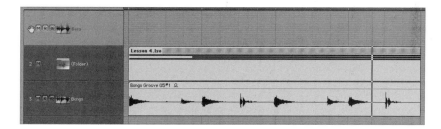

If you need more tracks at any point in this lesson, feel free to create them!

Looping Objects in the Arrange Window

Loops, loops, loops! At the moment, you have two Regions in the Arrange
window. One is in the form of an Apple Loop, while the other is a folder that
contains individual audio samples. Both these Regions are just one bar long,
and one bar does not make much of a song. Loops to the rescue!

Looped Regions are simply aliases that refer back to the original Object. There
are many benefits to using loops. For example, because loops are just aliases
with no extra audio content of their own, loops take up less system memory
than copying the Objects would. But even better (particularly for looped MIDI
Regions), if you change the data in the original Object, that change ripples
through all the loops. Edit once, change all.

NOTE ▶ The Song Information window allows you to inspect the amount of system memory used for the Objects in your song. To open the Song Information window, choose Options > Song information.

Object Type	Objects	Events	Memory
MIDI Regions	7	21	4860
Audio Regions	7		6426
Tempo Alternatives	1	1	202
Internal Objects	1	4	
Signature Objects	1	2	
Environment Objects	135	0	39628
Transform Settings	1		430
Undo Steps	27		110376
Score Styles	31		3972
Score Formats	0		0

The Song Information window shows the amount of system memory used by the Objects in your song.

To create loops, you'll use the *Region Parameter box*. This box sits in the top left corner of the Arrange window, directly above the toolbox, and it always updates to display the unique parameters of any Audio Region or MIDI Region selected in the Arrange window.

1   In the Arrange window, select the Bongo Groove 05 Region.

The Region Parameter box updates to display the Region's name.

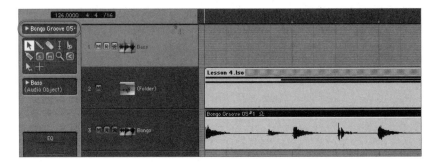

2   In the top left corner of the Arrange window, click the disclosure triangle
    on the left edge of the Region Parameter box.

    The Region Parameter box expands to display the Bongo Groove 05
    Region's properties. Notice the Loop parameter.

Disclosure Triangle

3   Select the Loop parameter's check box.

    The Bongo Groove 05 Region now loops.

4   Press Ctrl–Left Arrow until you can see approximately 25 bars of the song.

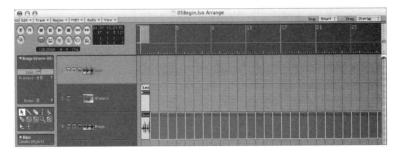

That loop sure goes a long way! It will loop all the way to the end of the song unless another region in the track blocks it. In fact, you can stop a loop at any point by placing an empty region in the way.

5   From the toolbox, grab the Pencil tool.

6   In the Bongo track, click the Pencil tool at exactly 25 1 1 1 (bar 25).

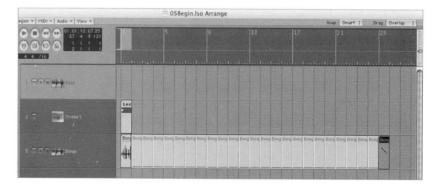

An empty Object is inserted into the track at bar 25, and the loop is stopped dead in its track.

Inserting an empty Object is a great way to stop a loop, but if you know in advance you need your loop to span only a certain number of bars, you can use the following trick:

7   Position the Arrow tool over the top right corner of the Folder Object.

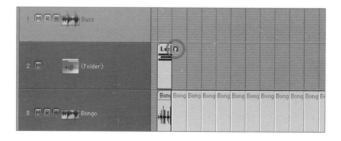

The Pointer turns into a loop icon.

8   Drag the right edge of the Folder Object to bar 25.

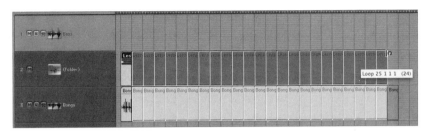

The Folder Object now loops exactly 23 times. Furthermore, this trick works with any Audio Region or MIDI Region in the Arrange window. Remember this when you're laying out Apple Loops later in this lesson.

That's enough groundwork for now. Let's continue on to the fun stuff and explore Apple Loops.

Using the Loop Browser

The Loop Browser is your Apple Loops sound palette. It comes stocked with hundreds of Apple Loops in both Logic Express and Logic Pro, and you can quickly add new Apple Loop collections to the Loop Browser at any time. It's easy to expand your Apple Loops arsenal by, for example, adding Apple's Jam Packs or downloading Apple Loops from Web sites such as appleLoops.com.

1   Choose Audio > Loop Browser.

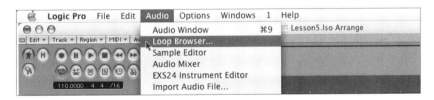

The Loop Browser opens.

Browsing Apple Loops

The Loop Browser is designed to make finding the right loop a simple and intuitive process. In its default view, the Loop Browser uses a matrix to show 54 categories of Apple Loops. You can further refine your search by using the search field in the Loop Browser's top right corner, or by switching to the traditional hierarchical view to locate loops by genre, instrument, or mood.

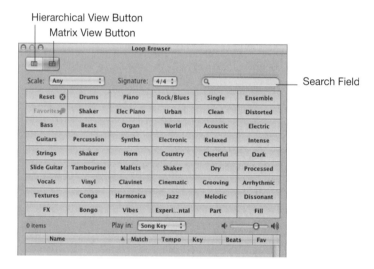

1   In the top left of the Loop Browser, click the Hierarchical View button.

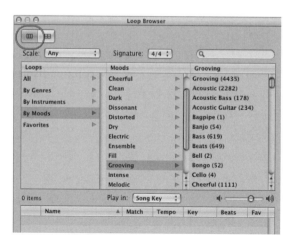

2   Click the Matrix View button to return to the matrix view.

3   Click a category button.

The loops in that category are displayed in the list at the bottom of the Loop Browser.

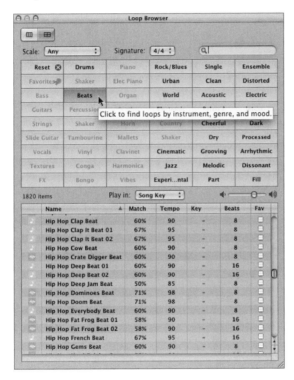

The loop list itself is divided into columns, with each column displaying loop properties, including tempo, key, and beats. You can click the column heads to sort loops according to a column's property.

4   Click the Tempo column head.

The Apple Loops are listed according to tempo.

TIP To customize the matrix view's category buttons, Ctrl-click the category button you wish to change. A hierarchical shortcut menu lets you choose a new category to assign to the button.

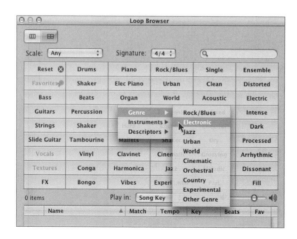

▶ **Using Favorites**

Add GarageBand Jam Packs 1, 2, and 3 to your system and you will have thousands of Apple Loops in your arsenal. With all those loops to juggle, finding the correct loop when you need it becomes a challenge. At times like this, the Loop Browser's Favorites category can really come in handy!

The Loop Browser's list has a Fav (Favorites) column that has a check box for every displayed loop. When you check this box, the loop is automatically added to the Favorites category, located in the top left corner of the Loop Browser's matrix view. As you audition loops, it's a good idea to tag the ones you like so you can quickly find them again later, when needed.

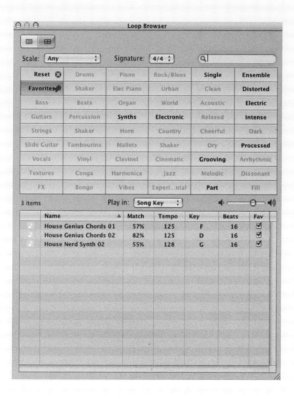

Adding New Apple Loops Collections

With the continuing proliferation of the Apple Loops format into Apple's audio and video editing applications, many third-party loop producers are beginning to create Apple Loops collections (try www.appleLoops.com, or search the Web for *free Apple Loops* and check out any of the dozens of hits that result). Even Apple has entered the fray, offering three Apple Loops Jam Packs. The Jam Packs are designed for GarageBand, but Logic can do everything GarageBand does (and a whole lot more), so the Jam Packs work just as well in Logic. For more information visit the Jam Packs Web page at www.apple.com/ilife/garageband/jampacks/.

Wherever you find your aftermarket Apple Loops, one thing is certain: Logic must first index all new Apple Loops before you can use them, and you must load them into the Loop Browser before they will be available to your Logic songs. The loops themselves can be in any directory on any hard disk connected to your system. However, it's up to you to tell Logic where they are.

A subset of the Apple Loops contained in Jam Pack 2: Remix Tools has been included with this book's DVD. Specifically, the sample Apple Loops include a construction set used to create house music (a form of electronic music using a steady, four-on-the-floor beat in the bpm range of 115 to 130). You can find these Apple Loops in the Lesson 5 Project Files > Apple Loops > Jam Pack 2 Sampler folder. Let's add these Apple Loops to the Loop Browser now.

> **NOTE** ▶ If you are using Soundtrack, you need to add the Soundtrack Apple Loops collection to the Loop Browser to use them in your songs. By default, the Soundtrack Apple Loops collection is located in your startup disk > Documents > Soundtrack Loops folder.

1   Open a Finder window above Logic.

> **TIP** ▶ For best results, open a new Finder window over Logic by clicking the Dock's Finder icon. If you don't, the Loop Browser may disappear.

2   From this book's companion DVD files, navigate to the Song Files > Lesson 5 Project Files > Apple Loops > Jam Pack 2 Sampler folder, and take a quick look inside.

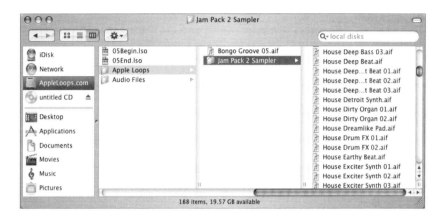

The folder contains Apple Loops that all begin with the word *House.*

3   Drag the Jam Pack 2 Sampler folder out of the Finder window, and drop it on the Loop Browser.

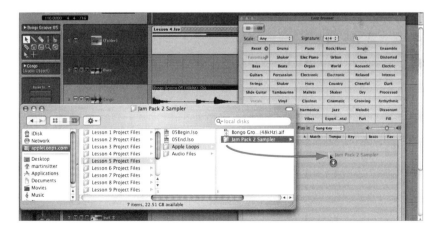

The Loop Browser indexes all of the loops contained in the folder. When Logic finishes, these loops will be available to all of your Logic songs, directly from the Loop Browser.

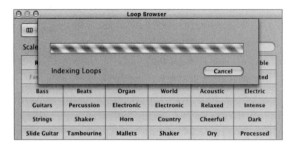

4   In the Finder window, navigate to your Startup Disk > Library > Application Support > GarageBand folder.

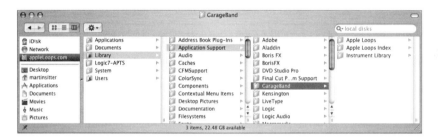

This folder has two important subfolders: Apple Loops, and Apple Loops Index.

5   Select the Apple Loops folder.

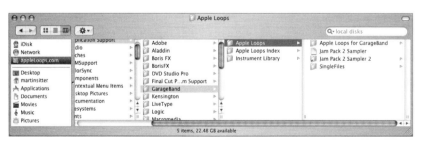

Notice that Logic has added an alias to this folder that refers back to your Apple Loops in their current place on your hard disk(s). This is important to keep in mind, because if you delete this book's companion files after you've finished the lessons, the Jam Pack 2 Sampler loops will also be deleted.

NOTE ▸ The Apple Loops that were installed along with Logic are all contained in the Apple Loops for GarageBand folder.

6   Select the Apple Loops Index folder.

These are Logic's index files. Do not delete these files! If you do, the Loop Browser will not be able to find or display any of your system's Apple Loops (however, you can reindex them following the steps above, so all is not lost).

7   Close the Finder window

8   Switch back to Logic.

9   If the loop Browser has closed, choose Audio > Loop Browser to open the Loop Browser again.

Now that you have some new loops to play with, let's audition some of them to see what they sound like.

Auditioning Apple Loops

The Loop Browser makes choosing loops a very aural process—it plays Apple Loops as you click them!

In the step above you added more than 100 House Apple Loops to the Loop Browser. The song you are working on already has a classic four-on-the-floor house beat (the audio loops in the folder), and the Bongo line is pretty good as a house rhythm. Let's search through these new House Apple Loops and find a few to add to the song.

1   In the Loop Browser's Search field, type *House* and press Return.

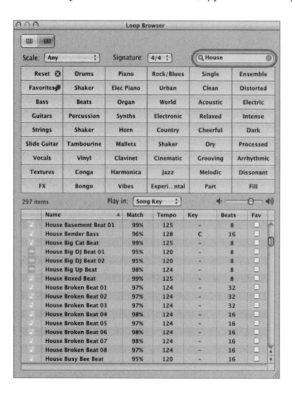

The loop list updates to show all Apple Loops with the word *House* in their name.

TIP ▶ As you audition the House Apple Loops, don't forget to tag the ones you like as Favorites so that you can easily find them when it comes time to add Apple Loops to your arrangement.

2   Click a loop that you wish to audition.

The icon to the left of the loop's name turns into a speaker, and the loop begins to play.

3   Use the up and down arrow keys to move the Selection range up and down the loop list.

As you select new loops, they automatically play. But that's not all; they play at the same tempo and in the same key as your song. In fact, if the song itself is playing, the Apple Loops will play over your arrangement, letting you hear how the loop fits with the song!

4   Press the spacebar to start the song playback.

5   From the Loop Browser's list, select a new Apple Loop.

The selected loop plays at the same tempo as the song. As you can see, the Loop Browser makes finding Apple Loops a cinch.

Directly above the loop list on the right edge of the Loop Browser, there is a volume slider you can use to adjust the Loop Browser's playback volume as you audition Apple Loops.

6   Use the volume slider to adjust the Loop Browser's playback.

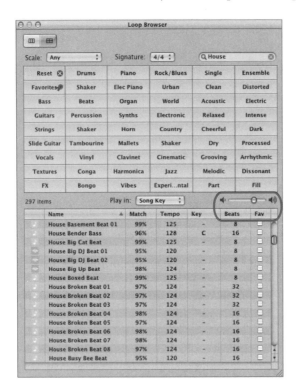

7   Continue auditioning House loops until you find several that sound good with the beat. Tag the loops you like as Favorites.

8   Press the spacebar to stop playback.

> **TIP** ▸ To stop the Loop Browser playback, you can also click the playing Apple Loop a second time.

Adding Apple Loops to Your Song

When you've found the loop you're looking for, it's time to add it to your song. This is a simple process: Just drag the loop from the Loop Browser, and drop it into an Arrange window track.

You already have a Bass track in the Arrange window. Let's drop one of the House Bass Apple Loops into this track now.

> **NOTE ▶** You don't have to use the House Apple Loops. The remaining lessons in this part of the book are designed to work with any Apple Loops you want. If house isn't your genre, feel free to experiment with other Apple Loops until you find a groove you like. We're making music here, and music is a very individual thing! The important thing is to have fun and pump out some great beats.

1   Use the Loop Browser to find a House Bass Apple Loop that sounds good.

2   Drag the Bass Apple Loop from the Loop Browser and drop it into the Bass track at the top of the Arrange window.

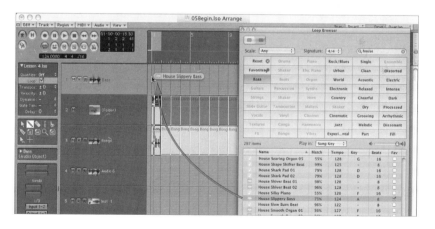

The loop is added as an Audio Region to the Bass track.

3   Loop the new Audio Region to bar 25.

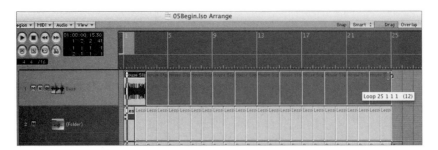

4   Grab the bottom right corner of the Cycle range and drag until the Cycle range spans from bar 1 to bar 25.

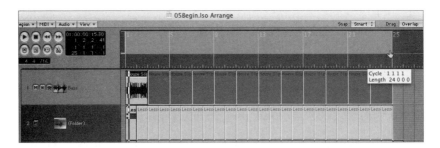

This arrangement is coming along. Before adding any more loops, let's take a look at one of the coolest features of Apple Loops in Logic: green Audio Instrument Apple Loops.

Exploring Green Apple Loops

If you take a close look at the left edge of the Loop Browser's loop list, you'll notice that some Apple Loops have a blue icon, while others have a green icon with a note. While both types of loops can be added to audio tracks in the

Arrange window, Apple Loops with a green icon hide a special trick: When you add an Apple Loop with a green icon to an empty Audio Instrument track, Logic automatically loads a software instrument and all the effects needed to reproduce the loop, and also adds a MIDI Region to the track to play the Audio Instrument. This is an amazing feature with endless possibilities. Let's look at it now.

> **MORE INFO ▶** Green Apple Loops are called *Audio Instrument loops.*
> When you add an Audio Instrument loop to an audio track (instead of an Audio Instrument track), Logic quickly renders a new audio file and creates an Audio Region you can edit.

1   In the Arrange window, select the track named Inst 1.

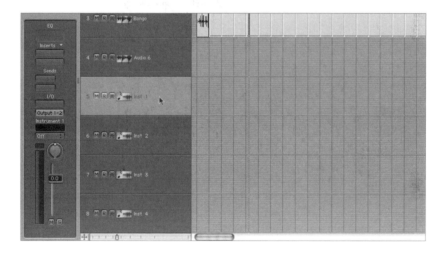

Notice that this is an empty Audio Instrument track. There is no Audio Instrument assigned to the track's inputs. Additionally, no effects have been added to the track's inserts.

2   In the Loop Browser, search through the House Apple Loops until you find a pad loop with *a green icon* that sounds good with the other loops in your arrangement (we choose the House Solitary Pad).

3   Drag the green Apple Loop over the track named Inst 1, and drop it at 1 1 1 1.

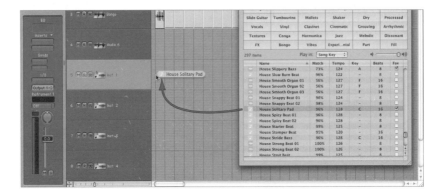

Several things happen. First, Logic loads a software instrument to produce the green Audio Instrument loop's sound. Second, Logic loads several DSP (digital signal processing) effects. And finally, Logic adds a MIDI Region to the track.

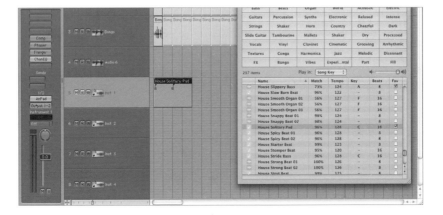

4   Loop the new MIDI Region to bar 25.

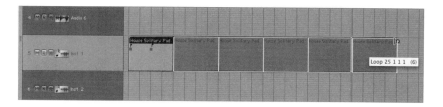

> NOTE ▶ One of the best things about green Audio Instrument loops is that once they are added to an instrument track, you can change the Audio Instrument producing the sound! Not only is this a great way to customize the sound of your song, it's a quick way to instantly build an entire Arrange window full of new instruments. Give it a try.

Using the Global Tempo Track

Global tracks are a new addition to Logic 7. Global tracks provide a way to inspect and change certain song properties, including markers, time and key signatures, chords for MIDI Regions, and most importantly for our purpose here, tempo.

> NOTE ▶ Global tracks are available in the Arrange window, as well as in the Matrix, Score, and Hyper editors.

Exploring Tempo Alternatives

When working with Apple Loops, the Global Tempo track proves invaluable. Using the Tempo track, you can automate tempo changes over time. But even better, from the Tempo track you have direct access to *nine tempo alternatives*. Because Apple Loops automatically adjust the tempo to match the song, these tempo alternatives let you experiment with different tempos, and then quickly apply the one that works best for the song.

1 From the Arrange window's local menu bar, choose View > Global Track Components > Tempo.

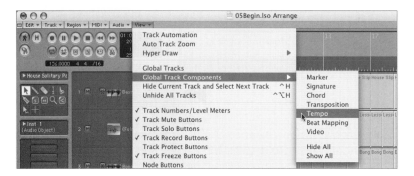

The Global Tempo track appears directly under the Bar Ruler. Currently, there is a horizontal tempo line all the way through it. Directly above the line on the left side is the number 126, the song's current tempo.

You don't want to lose this original tempo, so let's experiment with a tempo alternative.

2   From the Global Tempo track's Tempo Alternative menu, choose 2.

The tempo line changes to 120 bpm.

3   Press the spacebar to start playback.

4   Make sure the Arrow tool is selected.

5   With the Arrow tool, grab the tempo line and drag it up *slowly* to 130 bpm. (Don't drag quickly or you'll make drastic tempo changes.)

When you release the mouse button, the tempo changes to 130 bpm. At any point, you can choose 1 from the Tempo Alternative menu to switch back to 126 bpm. For now, however, stay in tempo alternative 2.

6   Press the spacebar to stop the song playback.

Automating Tempo Changes

Using the Global Tempo track you can actually automate changing tempos over time by clicking new nodes into the tempo line.

1   Using the Arrow tool, double-click just above the tempo line at 9 1 1 1.

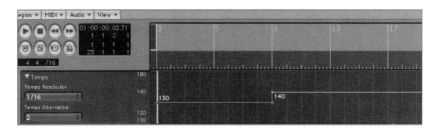

A new node is created, and the tempo increases at bar 9. Clicking in new tempo nodes is not the most exact method of changing tempo. For more precision, use the following trick to open a text box into which you can type the desired tempo.

NOTE ▶ To delete a tempo node, click to select it, and then press the Delete key.

2   At bar 17, press Cmd-Option-Ctrl and double-click.

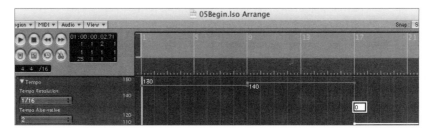

A text box appears.

3   Type *122* into the text box, and press Return.

A new node is inserted and the tempo line changes to 122 bpm.

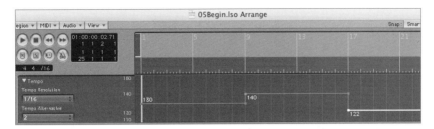

4   Play the song and listen to the tempo changes.

5   When you've heard the changes, stop playback.

Creating Tempo Curves

Currently, the tempo changes are sudden and dramatic. If a more subtle change is what you're after, you can create a continuous transition between tempos (a tempo curve) that slowly changes the tempo over time.

Before you create a tempo curve, you should select a Tempo Resolution setting. It will determine the number of tempo changes performed during the tempo curve: When the tempo resolution is set to 1/16, there will be four tempo changes per quarter note (16 tempo changes per bar); 1/4 will generate one tempo change per beat (four tempo changes per bar).

A different tempo resolution can be defined for each node in the Global Tempo track. With this in mind, select the tempo line you will turn into a curve, and set its tempo resolution before creating the tempo curve.

1   Select the horizontal tempo line between 130 and 140.

The line turns white to indicate it is selected.

2 From the Global Tempo track's Tempo Resolution menu, choose 1/32.

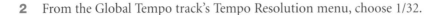

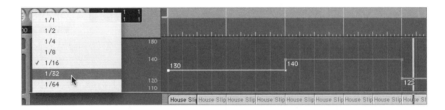

Position the Arrow tool over the node on the right edge of the selected tempo line (directly under 140).

3 Drag the node to the left.

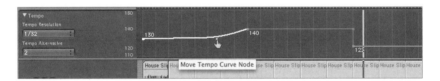

A tempo curve is created.

4 Play the song and listen to the tempo change.

The tempo changes smoothly from 130 bpm to 140 bpm. Cool, but not terribly musical. Let's switch back to tempo alternative 1.

5 From the Tempo Alternative menu, choose 1.

The song reverts to 126 bpm. Currently, the Global Tempo track occupies a lot of space at the top of the Arrange area. Let's hide the Tempo track to get it out of the way.

6 From the Arrange window's local menus, choose View > Global Tracks.

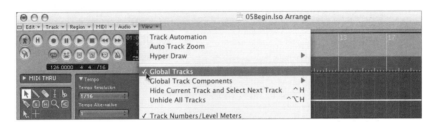

The Global Tempo track is hidden.

Finishing the Arrangement

In the next several lessons you will work with MIDI, record both audio and MIDI into the Arrange window, and use DSP effects and automation to finish your song. Before going any further, take some time to explore the Loop Browser and the Apple Loops on your system. Add loops to your song, use the techniques you learned in the last few lessons to create an arrangement and, in general, have some fun! Make the song as long or as short as you want. When you've created a basic arrangement, continue to the next lesson.

> **TIP** ▶ Many Apple Loops share the same name, but with incrementing numbers at the end. Often, these Apple Loops are intended to work together to create changing musical phrases over time. For example, the House Return Piano 10–13 Apple Loops sound very nice when lined up back to back in the same track. In fact, we used those loops to complete the arrangement.

1   Create a basic arrangement using Apple Loops from the Loop Browser.

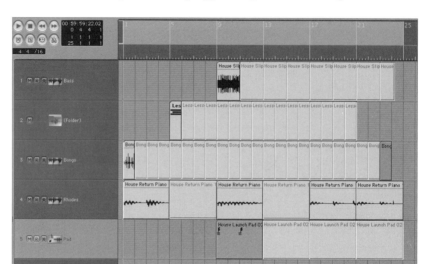

2   Save your song.

What You've Learned

▶   Apple Loops contain information used to automatically time-stretch and transpose the loop so it not only plays at the correct tempo but also plays at the correct pitch for the song you are working on.

▶   All tracks listed in the Arrange window play through *channels*.

▶   To create a new track and automatically assign it to a new channel, choose Track > Create With Next Instrument (Ctrl-Shift-Return).

▶   To loop an Object in the Arrange window, select it and enable the Region Parameter box's Loop check box, or drag the upper right corner of the Object until it has looped as many times as you need.

- ▶ The Loop Browser has categories that allow you to quickly find any indexed Apple Loop.

- ▶ To index a collection of Apple Loops, drag them from the Finder window and drop them onto the Loop Browser.

- ▶ The Loop Browser allows you to audition Apple Loops as your song plays.

- ▶ To add an Apple Loop to your song, drag it from the Loop Browser onto an Arrange window track.

- ▶ Green Apple Loops can be added to empty Audio Instrument tracks. When you add a green Apple Loop to an Audio Instrument track, Logic automatically loads a software instrument and all the effects needed to reproduce the loop, and also adds a MIDI Region to the track to play the Audio Instrument.

6

Lesson Files	APTS_Logic_7 > Song Files > Lesson 6 Project Files > 06Begin.lso
	APTS_Logic_7 > Song Files > Lesson 6 Project Files > 06End.lso
Media	APTS_Logic_7 > Song Files > Lesson 6 Project Files
Time	This lesson takes approximately 1 hour to complete.
Goals	Learn about the Matrix Editor
	Create and modify MIDI events in the Matrix Editor
	Use HyperDraw to automate MIDI control-change data
	Create HyperDraw nodes and curves
	Learn how to quantize notes in the Matrix Editor
	Experiment with note velocity

Editing MIDI in the Matrix Editor

Logic began life as a program called C-Lab Notator (1987) for the Atari ST, and it quickly became the darling of music producers everywhere. One of Notator's key features was the Score Editor, an editing window that used a musical score and actual notes to let traditionally trained musicians "score" music just as they would in the real world, with pen and paper (hence the name Notator). However, most of the people making music then, as now, did not come from a traditional music background. So the creator of Notator, Gerhard Lengeling (the author of this book's foreword), cleverly included what would become the primary MIDI editor in not only Logic, but also every audio production program since the introduction of Notator: the Matrix Editor.

The Matrix Editor has a graphical user interface that provides a keyboard along the left edge. Notes are represented as beams of varying lengths aligned with the keyboard keys. The longer the beam, the longer the duration of the note. You can think of the Matrix Editor as an electronic version of the rolls of paper that scroll through an old-fashioned player piano: The holes in the paper tell the piano which notes to play, and the longer the hole, the longer the note is held. Same concept, different century.

Because the Matrix Editor is graphical and intuitive, it has grown to become the main MIDI editing environment in Logic. This chapter focuses on the Matrix Editor, providing tips and tricks to speed you along your way to making music with MIDI.

Getting Ready to Edit MIDI

In this lesson you will program a MIDI Region to accent the Folder's drum loop. Of course, you'll use the Matrix Editor to do this. However, before you can program a drum MIDI Region, you need a MIDI instrument to create the sound. Happily, Logic provides several drum sets in the GarageBand Drum Kits Audio Instrument. Let's insert this instrument and see how it sounds.

1   From this book's companion DVD files, open **06Begin.lso** (in the Lesson 6 Project Files folder) or continue working on your song from the previous lesson.

2   In the Arrange window, select an empty Audio Instrument track.

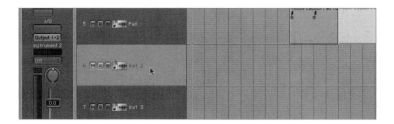

The Arrange channel strip updates to show the channel strip for the selected track.

3 On the Arrange channel strip, click and hold the Input slot.

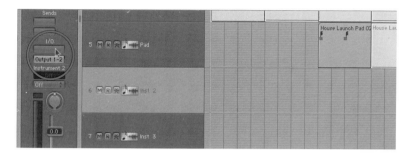

A hierarchical instrument-assignment menu appears.

4 From the instrument-assignment menu, choose Stereo > Logic > GarageBand Instruments > Drum Kits.

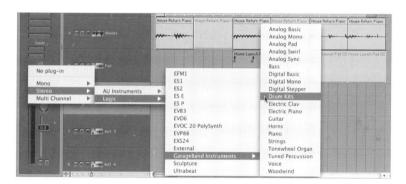

The GarageBand Drum Kits instrument is assigned as the input for the Audio Instrument track.

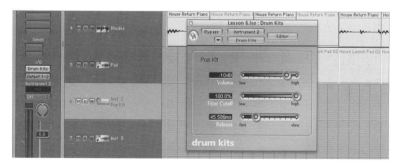

5   Create a one-bar cycle over a part of the arrangement that contains the Folder and Bongo Region.

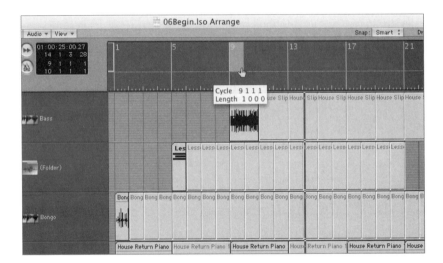

You are going to create a drum loop to accent the existing drum parts, so it's important that your loop play over them.

6   Press the spacebar to start playback.

7   Play your MIDI keyboard and audition the sounds in the Drum Kits drum set.

NOTE ▶ If you don't have a MIDI keyboard, press the Caps Lock key to display Logic's Caps Lock keyboard. For more information, see Lesson 1.

8   Use the Drum Kits Settings menu to find a drum kit you like.

TIP ▶ Don't forget, you can use the Next Plug-In Setting (Cmd-Option-N) and Previous Plug-In Setting (Cmd-Option-B) key commands that you assigned in Lesson 3 to cycle through drum kits without using the Settings menu.

NOTE ▶ The extra drum kits listed in the above figure are installed with Apple's Jam Pack 2.

9   Click the button in the top left corner of the Drum Kits instrument in order to close it.

The instrument will still make sound, but now it's out of sight and doesn't take up valuable screen real estate.

Exploring the Matrix Editor

With a drum kit assigned to the Audio Instrument track, you're ready to program some beats. Let's open the Matrix Editor and take a look at how this interface works. First things first, however. Before you can edit a MIDI Region, you need a MIDI Region to edit.

1   Grab the Pencil tool and click the Audio Instrument track at the same bar as your one-bar cycle.

An empty MIDI Region is created.

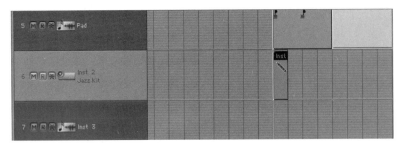

2   Double-click the new MIDI Region.

The Matrix Editor opens.

TIP You can customize the color of the Matrix Editor. From the Matrix Editor's local menus, choose View > Matrix Colors to open Display Preferences. There you can set which colors will be used to represent both black and white keys, and even adjust the color of the grid to make it stand out from the background.

Matrix Editor Keyboard   Bar Ruler

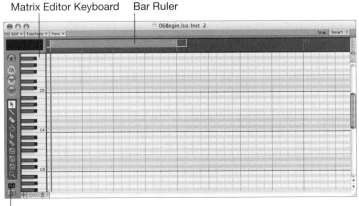

Matrix Editor Toolbox

Along the left edge of the Matrix Editor there is a keyboard, and clicking its keys with the Arrow tool triggers playback of the Drum Kits instrument just as if you were playing a controller keyboard.

3 Along the Matrix Editor's left edge, click the keyboard's keys.

The Drum Kits instrument plays.

TIP ► Logic's Global Preferences pane's Editing tab has a pop-up menu labeled "Double-clicking a MIDI Region opens." You can set this preference so that double-clicking a MIDI region opens any of Logic's MIDI editors. By default, this preference is set to open the Matrix Editor.

Global Preferences pane

Editing tab

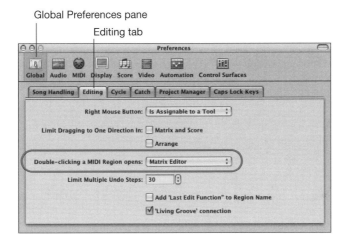

Adding Notes with the Pencil Tool

The Pencil tool provides the primary way to add notes to the Matrix Editor. Using the Pencil tool, you can simply click in the Matrix Editor to add a note.

1 From the Matrix Editor's toolbox, grab the Pencil tool.

2 On the Matrix Editor's keyboard, click keys until you find the note you want to add.

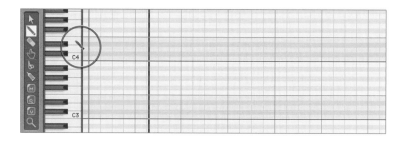

3 Paying particular attention to the time grid, click with the Pencil tool in the Matrix Editor to create a note.

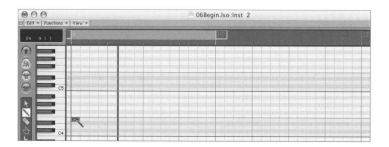

New notes are always created *at the same duration and velocity as the last note selected in the Matrix Editor* (velocity is covered a bit later in this lesson). Consequently, your note may be of a different duration than the one pictured above. However, that is easy to change.

4 Position the Pencil tool over the right edge of the new note and drag until the note is of the correct duration.

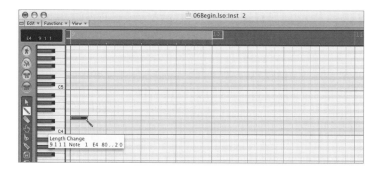

> **TIP** ▶ Logic's Arrow tool can be a bit finicky, so dragging the lower corner of the note sometimes moves it instead of resizing it. If this happens, force Logic to obey your wishes by grabbing the Finger tool. This tool's only function is to resize notes, so the note is sure not to move.

You probably noticed that the note's edge snaps along to certain timing values as you drag to resize it. The values the note snaps to are defined by the Matrix Editor's current zoom value. To temporarily deactivate snapping, begin resizing the note and then press the Ctrl key. To "gear down" while resizing a note, hold down Ctrl-Shift as you drag—the note will resize slowly, letting you set its duration very accurately..

5 Add another note to the Matrix Editor.

The new note is of exactly the same duration as the last one selected.

> **TIP** ▶ If you have several notes of different durations in the Matrix editor, select a note of the duration you want your new note to be *before* creating the new note. The new note will be created using the same duration as the last note selected.

Adding Notes with a MIDI Controller

Adding notes with the Pencil tool works fine, but it is often easier to play notes into the Matrix Editor using a MIDI controller. Here's how it's done.

1 Use your MIDI controller to find the note you want to add.

2 In the top left corner of the Matrix Editor, click the Toggle MIDI In button to turn it on.

As you'll see in a second, when you add notes using a MIDI controller, the new note is always added at the SPL's position. Consequently, you must move the SPL to the place where you want the new note before adding the note.

3 Click the Bar Ruler to position the SPL where you want the new note to be added.

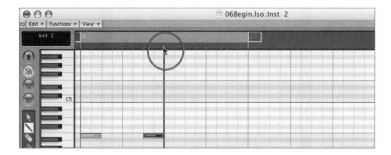

The SPL moves to the clicked position. When you input notes using a MIDI controller, the new notes are added to the Matrix Editor using duration settings from Logic's Step Input Keyboard. Let's open it up and take a look.

4 Choose Windows > Step Input Keyboard. The Step Input Keyboard opens with several note duration values in the top left corner.

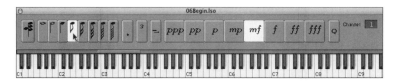

5   On the Step Input Keyboard, choose a note duration.

6   On your MIDI controller, play the key for the note you wish to add.

The note is added to the Matrix Editor, and the SPL jumps to the end of the new note.

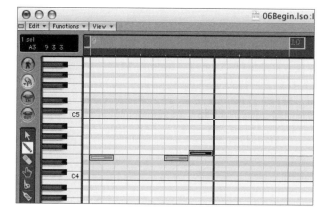

7   Click the Toggle MIDI In button to turn it off so that you don't accidentally add any new notes by pressing keys on your MIDI controller.

8   Close the Step Input Keyboard.

Repositioning Notes

From time to time you might drop a note on the wrong key—it happens! Fortunately, it's easy to reposition notes in the Matrix Editor. In fact, you can do so using either the Arrow tool or a MIDI controller. The following steps show you both methods.

1   From the Matrix Editor's toolbox, grab the Arrow tool.

2   Grab a note and drag it to a new position in the Matrix Editor.

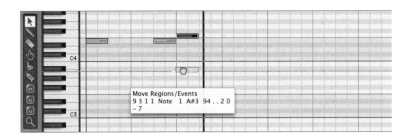

Notice that Logic triggers the sound of the keys you drag the note over. This lets you audition keys to ensure that you drop the note on the correct one. However, you can disable this feature.

3   In the top left corner of the Matrix Editor, click the Toggle MIDI Out button to turn it off.

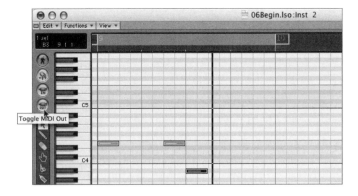

4   Once again, grab the note and drag it to a new position.

You no longer hear the keys as you drag the note past them.

5   Click the Toggle MIDI Out button to turn it on again.

In general, it's best to have this button on as you edit.

So, dragging notes is a good way to reposition them, but you can do the same thing a bit quicker using a MIDI controller.

6   In the top left corner of the Matrix Editor, double-click the Toggle MIDI In button.

Take a close look at the Toggle MIDI In button. Notice that double-clicking the button causes a Lock icon to appear on the left side of it.

7   In the Matrix Editor, select the note you wish to reposition.

8   Press a key on your MIDI controller.

The note jumps to the played key.

TIP ▸ If you have multiple notes selected in the Matrix Editor, this trick moves them *all* to the pressed key.

9   Click the Toggle MIDI In button to turn it off so that you don't accidentally reposition other selected notes.

Setting Note Velocity

The notes in the Matrix Editor can be several different colors, with the colors representing their velocity values. Each note also has a horizontal line that stretches backward from its front edge, and the length of this line in relation to the length of the note is also an indicator of its velocity.

Note Color vs. Velocity Value

Color	Velocity Value
Purple	01–15
Dark blue	16–31
Light blue	32–47

Note Color vs. Velocity Value

Color	Velocity Value
Light green	48–63
Green	64–79
Yellow	80–95
Orange	96–111
Red	112–127

1　Grab the bottom right corner of any note in the Matrix Editor and drag right to increase the note's duration.

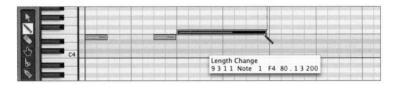

When experimenting with velocity, it helps to use a note with a long duration so that you can see how velocity affects the thin horizontal line stretching back from the front of the note.

2　From the Matrix Editor's toolbox, grab the Velocity tool.

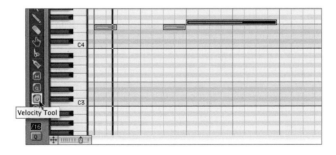

The Velocity tool has a *V* on it, and as you may have guessed, it's used to change a note's velocity.

3   With the Velocity tool, click and hold the long note, then drag up and down.

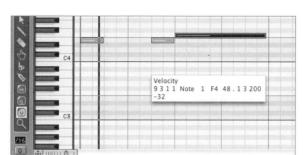

The note's color changes and the thin line grows longer or shorter to indicate the changing velocity. As you drag, the note plays at each new velocity so that you can hear the results of your edit.

You can also adjust the velocity of multiple notes at one time:

4   With the Velocity tool, rubber-band select several notes.

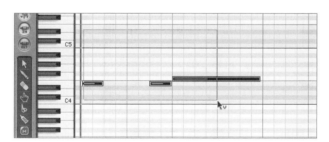

5   With the Velocity tool, click and hold any selected note, then drag up and down.

All the selected notes change velocity together, but in a very smart way—each note keeps its velocity relative to the others. Consequently, notes with higher velocities will retain their higher velocities.

NOTE ▶ When you're adjusting the velocities of multiple selected notes, once any note reaches a velocity of either 0 or 127, it is no longer possible to edit any of the selected notes further.

Quantizing Notes

Quantization corrects the rhythm of notes so that they conform to a specific time grid. Logic actually records two positions for each note in a sequence. The first is the note's original position, and the second is its playback, or *quantized*, position (for sequences that are not quantized, both positions are exactly the same). This fact means that quantization settings are nondestructive—only the playback position (not the original note position) is changed. If you quantize a sequence but later decide you want to revert to the nonquantized version, just turn quantization off and your notes will revert to their original positions inside the sequence.

While quantization is typically used to "clean up" the recording of a loose performance, it is equally effective at "humanizing" the timing of a sequence programmed using the Matrix Editor. For example, the notes you've entered are strictly quantized to Logic's time grid. This is great if you're producing techno or machine music à la Kraftwerk, but often such a rigid timing structure does not produce natural-sounding music. Logic has several *swing quantization* settings that can reverse the effect of rigidly quantized notes to make them sound as if a person—not a computer—is playing them.

Swing-quantizing works exactly the same way as other methods of quantizing, so let's experiment a bit with swing-quantizing the notes in your sequence.

1   From the Matrix Editor's toolbox, grab the Quantize tool (the one with the *Q* on top).

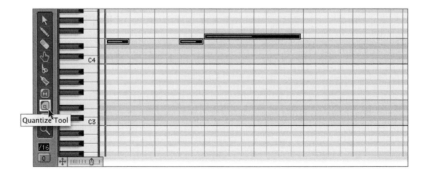

2   With the Quantize tool, rubber-band select the notes in the Matrix Editor.

3   Click and hold any of the selected notes.

A menu of quantization values appears.

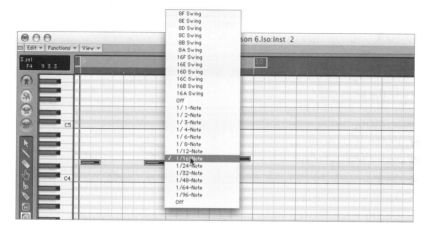

To help you put a bit more of an organic gloss on your MIDI Regions, the top of the quantization menu holds several swing settings. Let's choose one now.

NOTE ▶ In the middle of the quantization menu there's an Off setting that turns quantization off and returns the notes to their nonquantized position in the sequence.

4   From the quantization menu, select a swing quantization option.

Some notes shift off the standard time grid. Not all the notes shift—only enough shift to give the sequence more of a human feel.

NOTE ▶ Swing quantization is more noticeable if you have many notes in the Matrix Editor. In the next figure there are only three notes, but even still you can see how the second and third notes have shifted off the time grid. For this example, an eighth-note swing quantization was used.

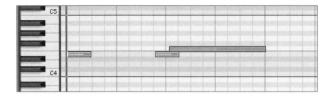

5   Press the spacebar to play the song.

6   Choose a quantization setting you like.

7   Press the spacebar to stop playback.

Using HyperDraw

HyperDraw is a system for automating MIDI-controller values, such as volume, pitch, modulation, or any of the 127 controller values that are part of the MIDI specification. The thing that makes HyperDraw appealing is that controllers are drawn in as lines between nodes. You can freely edit nodes, and even draw curves between them to make swooping changes in automation. With a bit of practice, HyperDraw allows you to make incredibly detailed evolving ambiences in your songs.

HyperDraw is located in the Matrix Editor, Score Editor, and Arrange window. It works exactly the same way in each editor, so for the purpose of experimenting, we'll explore HyperDraw in the Matrix Editor. But before we do so, a quick word of advice: As you experiment with editing HyperDraw information, remember Cmd-Z (undo)! It's easy to make mistakes when editing HyperDraw information, so Cmd-Z can be a real lifesaver.

1   From the Matrix Editor's local menus, choose View > Hyper Draw, and take a look at the choices presented in the HyperDraw menu.

The HyperDraw menu lists all of the standard control-change or MIDI-controller types you will commonly use while editing your sequences, including Volume, Pan, and Modulation.

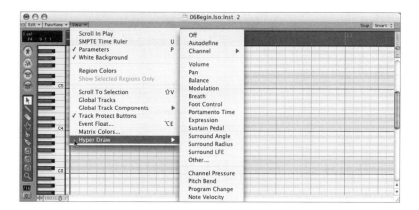

NOTE ▸ If you need a MIDI controller that's not displayed in the HyperDraw menu's main list, choose the Other option, and a dialog will open to let you enter any controller you need.

2 From the HyperDraw menu, choose Pan.

The blue HyperDraw area appears at the bottom of the Matrix Editor and displays the sequence's pan data (or lack of pan data—you'll add some in a minute).

HyperDraw Area

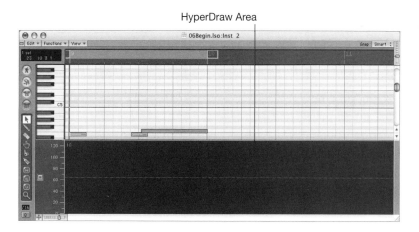

Creating Nodes with the Pencil Tool

HyperDraw, as its name suggests, is an area used to *draw* MIDI-controller values. While recorded MIDI-controller values also show up here, the chief benefit of HyperDraw is that you can quickly and conveniently draw in controller curves. In the following exercises you'll use a couple of different techniques to draw in HyperDraw information. First, let's look at using the Pencil tool.

1   From the Matrix toolbox, grab the Pencil tool.

2   Draw a curve through the first bar of the Matrix's HyperDraw area.

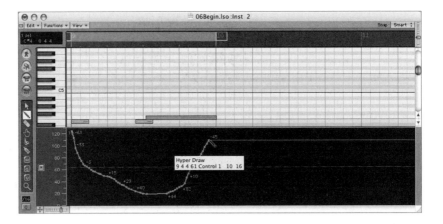

Notice that Logic draws a series of nodes, and the nodes are all connected by a line. You should still have a one-bar cycle enabled (if you don't, enable one now), so let's see how this HyperDraw data affects panning.

3   Press the spacebar to start playback.

4   In the Arrange window, make sure that the Audio Instrument track that plays the Drum Kits instrument is selected.

5   Watch the Pan control in the Arrange channel strip.

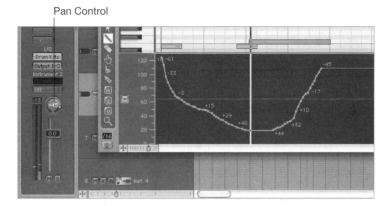

Pan Control

As the cycle plays, the Pan control moves to follow the HyperDraw data.

NOTE ▶ Logic displays values next to some nodes.

Selecting and Moving Nodes

Logic is very intelligent in the way it deals with nodes, and in most cases you'll find node editing to be an intuitive process. For example, to move a node, just grab it and drag it around the HyperDraw area. However, there are still a few tricks to keep in mind, so let's practice moving a few nodes.

1   From the Matrix Editor's toolbox, grab the Arrow tool.

2   Click and hold the last node in the HyperDraw area.

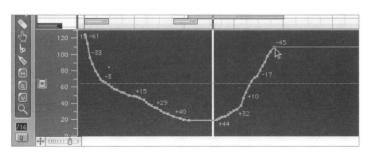

Let's move the selected node around the HyperDraw area.

TIP ▶ If you quickly click a node, it is deleted! To select a node without deleting it, either click and hold the node, or slowly click the node with a long press of the mouse button.

3   Drag the node up or down.

TIP ▶ To restrict node movement either horizontally or vertically, hold down Shift as you drag the node. The node's movement will be restricted to whichever axis you first begin dragging along.

The node follows the pointer movements. You can also move multiple nodes together.

4   Hold down Shift and click several alternating nodes in the line.

This is a good exercise, because by selecting alternating nodes, you can see how intuitively HyperDraw works.

5   Grab any of the selected nodes and drag up.

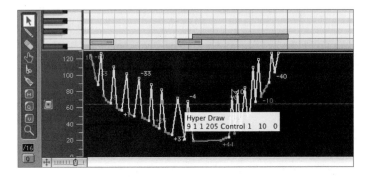

As you might expect, the selected nodes rise, while the other ones remain right where they were.

6   Hold Shift and then click the HyperDraw area's background to deselect all nodes.

7   Grab any line between two nodes, and drag it up or down (make sure you grab directly on the line).

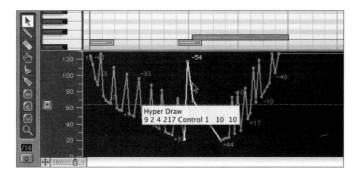

The line turns white, and the nodes at either end move in unison.

Deleting Nodes

Logic provides three different ways to delete nodes, so let's try out each one and learn how it works. The first method is one you may have learned earlier—the hard way—if you clicked a node too quickly during a previous exercise.

1   Quickly click a few nodes.

They are instantly deleted.

2   Select the node at the far right side of the HyperDraw area, and drag it to the left (don't release the Arrow tool).

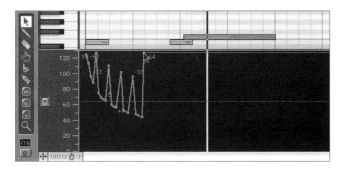

As you drag the node, each time you pass another node, the passed node disappears. However, these nodes are not gone for good, and as long as you continue to hold down the mouse button, you can backtrack this edit.

3   Drag the selected node back toward the right.

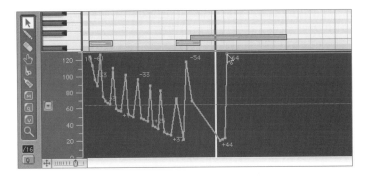

The erased nodes reappear!

4   Hold down Shift and rubber-band select all nodes in the HyperDraw area.

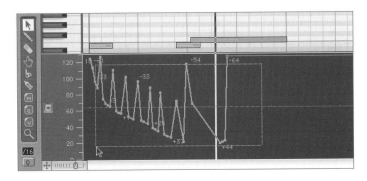

NOTE ► To rubber-band select nodes, you *must* hold down the Shift key. If you don't, trying to rubber-band select nodes instead creates new nodes, as you'll learn in the following exercise.

5   Press Delete.

All nodes are erased from the HyperDraw area.

Creating and Copying Nodes with the Arrow Tool

A bit earlier in the lesson you used the Pencil tool to draw in a line of nodes. You can create single nodes without using the Pencil tool, by simply clicking the Arrow tool in the HyperDraw area. Logic automatically interpolates a line between the new node and the nodes immediately to its left and right.

1   With the Arrow tool, click in the HyperDraw area to create three nodes over the first two beats of the bar, as pictured in the following figure:

   TIP ▸ If an extra node is created right at the beginning of the HyperDraw area, just give it a quick click to delete it.

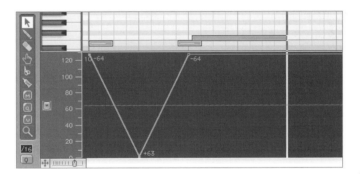

With a little practice, creating nodes becomes a quick and intuitive process. Copying nodes is easy as well. The following steps show you how to copy several nodes at the same time, though you can also use these techniques to copy single nodes.

2   Hold down Shift and rubber-band select all three nodes.

3   Hold down Option, click and hold any selected node (or any line between the selected nodes), and then drag to the right until your HyperDraw area looks like that shown in the following figure. (Be sure to keep the Option key held down until *after* you release the mouse button.)

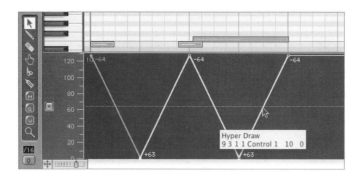

Holding down Option is a great way to copy nodes, and indeed it's a method you'll often use because it's convenient. However, you can also copy and paste nodes in the HyperDraw area.

4   Press Cmd-Z to undo the last edit.

The copied nodes disappear, and the first three nodes are reselected (if they are not, press Shift and rubber-band select them now).

5   Press Cmd-C to copy the selected nodes.

The selected nodes are copied to the Clipboard. You'll paste these nodes back into the HyperDraw area in a second, but first you have to move the SPL to the place where you want the first node to be pasted, because Logic always pastes copied nodes beginning at the SPL's position in the song.

6   In the Bar Ruler at the top of the Matrix Editor, click the beginning of the third beat in the bar to move the SPL.

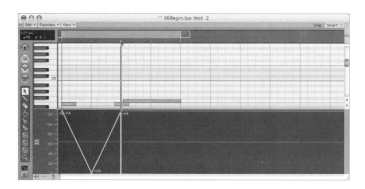

7   Press Cmd-V to paste the copied nodes back into the HyperDraw area.

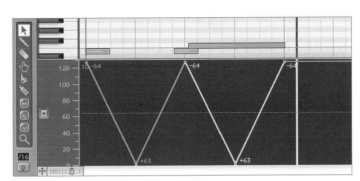

Creating Curves

NOTE ▶ The following feature works only in Logic Pro.

Curves are arguably the coolest feature of Logic's HyperDraw area, because they let you quickly create complex automation sweeps such as customized volume fades or, for the purpose of this example, smooth pan sweeps from one side of the stereo spectrum to the other.

1   Hold down Ctrl-Option and drag down the line between the first two nodes.

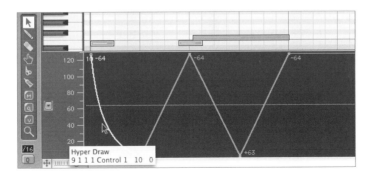

A sweeping automation curve is created.

There are four different types of automation curves, each of which you create by holding down Ctrl-Option and dragging a line in one of the following four directions: down (to create a concave curve), up (convex curve), right (horizontal S-curve), or left (vertical S-curve). Let's try creating one of each.

2   Hold down Ctrl-Option, and then drag the first of the remaining three lines up, the second right, and the last one left.

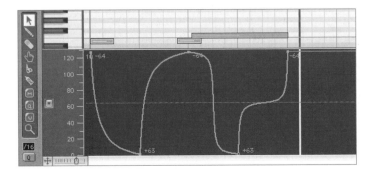

If you decide that a curve isn't exactly what you want, you can revert to the straight line by using the following trick.

3   Hold down Ctrl-Option and quickly click one of the curves.

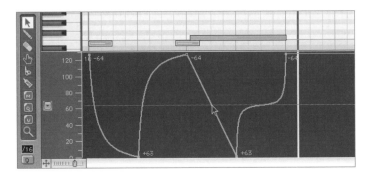

The curve reverts to a straight line.

Using the HyperDraw Menu

On the left edge of the HyperDraw area sits a small downward-pointing arrow button that serves as a shortcut to the HyperDraw menu.

HyperDraw Menu Shortcut Button

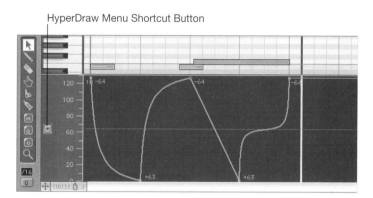

1 Click and hold the HyperDraw menu button to open the menu, and take a look at the options.

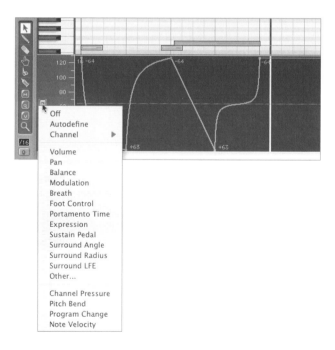

This menu lists all the same options as the HyperDraw menu that's accessible from the Matrix Editor's View menu.

2 At the top of the menu, choose Off.

The HyperDraw area is hidden.

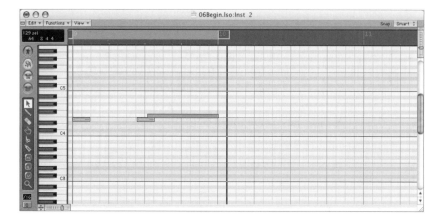

3 Close the Matrix Editor.

Using HyperDraw in the Arrange Window

HyperDraw is also available in the Arrange window, and HyperDraw works exactly the same way here as it does in the Matrix Editor—with an extra benefit: Opening HyperDraw in the Arrange window saves you from opening the Matrix Editor, which conserves screen real estate. As an added bonus, you can open HyperDraw for several different sequences and then compare their settings.

Let's see how to access HyperDraw in the Arrange window.

1 Select the MIDI Region in the Drum Kits Audio Instrument track.

2   Zoom horizontally so that you can clearly see the MIDI Region.

Notice that the pan controller information is already visible as vertical bars in the sequence.

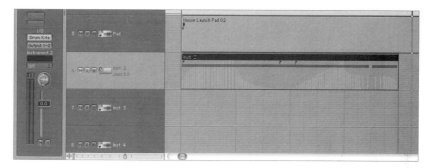

3   From the Arrange window's local menu, choose View > HyperDraw > Pan.

The selected MIDI Region turns blue, and the pan data entered in the Matrix Editor's HyperDraw area is displayed. The following figure shows a close-up of the sequence in the Arrange window:

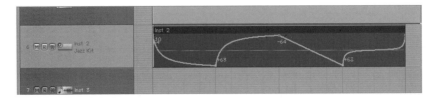

4   To edit this HyperDraw data, use the techniques you learned in the earlier sections of this lesson. That's all there is to it!

What You've Learned

▶   The Matrix Editor displays MIDI data graphically, showing individual notes as boxes whose size represents duration and whose position relative to a keyboard represents pitch.

▶   New notes created with the Pencil tool in the Matrix Editor are always of the same duration and velocity as the last note selected.

▶   To change the duration of a note in the Matrix Editor, position the Pencil tool or Arrow tool over the right edge of the note and drag until the note is of the correct duration.

▶   When turned on, the Toggle MIDI In button lets you enter notes into the Matrix Editor using an external MIDI controller.

▶   If you double-click the Toggle MIDI In button, a lock appears on the left of the button, and pressing an external MIDI controller key moves the note selected in the Matrix Editor to the same note as the pressed key.

▶   To ensure that the MIDI instrument is not triggered as you move notes around the Matrix Editor, turn off the Toggle MIDI Out button.

- ▶ The notes in the Matrix Editor can be several different colors, and these colors represent their velocity values.

- ▶ To create a node, click inside the HyperDraw area.

- ▶ To move a node, grab it and drag it to a new position.

- ▶ To delete a node, click it quickly.

- ▶ To create a HyperDraw curve, hold down Ctrl-Option and then drag the line between two nodes. The type of automation curve you create depends on whether you drag the line up, down, right, or left.

7

Lesson File   APTS_Logic_7 > Song Files > Lesson 7 Project Files > 07Begin.lso

                   APTS_Logic_7 > Song Files > Lesson 7 Project Files > 07End.lso

Media   APTS_Logic_7 > Song Files > Lesson 7 Project Files

Time   This lesson takes approximately 40 minutes to complete.

Goals   Create a custom hyper set for a drum fill using the Hyper Editor

                   Add new MIDI event definitions to a custom hyper set

                   Set the Hyper Editor's time grid resolution

                   Edit the drum fill in the Event List

                   Filter MIDI events in the Event List

Lesson **7**

Editing MIDI in the Hyper Editor and Event List

The Hyper Editor and Event List are MIDI editors designed to let you analyze individual MIDI events—including note-on, note-off, and continuous controller messages—in your song's sequences. During the first half of this lesson, you will use the Hyper Editor to reprogram the MIDI Region in the Drum Kits Audio Instrument track. Along the way you will see how the Hyper Editor's grid view is suited to programming rhythmic MIDI Regions such as drum parts. Later in the lesson, you'll open the Event List and dive deep down into the individual MIDI events that make up the Drum Kits sequence.

Exploring the Hyper Editor

The Hyper Editor is arguably one of Logic's least used MIDI editors, and that's a shame, because the Hyper Editor excels at two particular tasks:

▶   Adding or editing control-change data in individual MIDI Regions, such as pan settings, velocities, or even program-change messages that tell your synthesizer which sounds to play.

▶   Creating drum sequences.

The secret to the Hyper Editor is its ability to organize MIDI events along a user-defined time grid, which in turn enables you to quickly program rhythmic MIDI Regions. Let's open the Hyper Editor and take a first look.

1   From this book's companion DVD files, open **07Begin.lso** (in the Lesson 7 Project Files folder), or continue working on your song from the previous lesson.

2   In the Arrange window, click the top of the MIDI Region in the Drum Kits Audio Instrument track to ensure it is selected.

Because HyperDraw is enabled for this sequence, you must click the thin beam above the blue HyperDraw area to select it. If you click the blue HyperDraw area, you'll accidentally add HyperDraw nodes!

3   Choose Windows > Hyper Edit (Cmd-5).

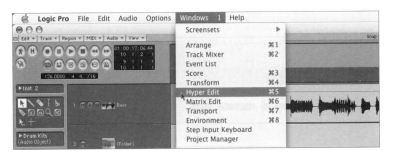

The Hyper Editor opens.

4   Make the Hyper Editor wide, and use the horizontal and vertical zoom
     controls to zoom in until you can clearly see the pan events.

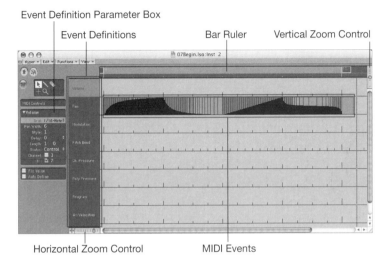

Erasing Events in the Hyper Editor

Take a close look at the Hyper Editor and note the curves in the pan events.
These are the curves you entered using HyperDraw in the previous lesson.
Right now there are a lot of individual MIDI events—in fact, there are so
many it's hard to tell where one pan event ends and the next begins. Let's use
the Hyper Editor to erase the current pan events in preparation for adding a
new, cleaner pan curve with fewer MIDI events.

1   From the Hyper Editor's toolbox, select the Eraser tool.

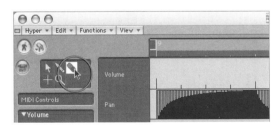

2   Drag across the pan events to erase them all.

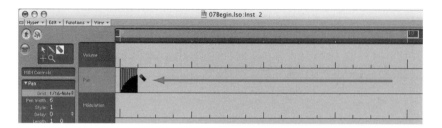

TIP ▶ You can also erase events by selecting them and then pressing the Delete key.

Modifying an Event Line's Time Grid

Now that the old pan events are gone, let's modify the time grid. By default, the pan event grid is set to 1/16-Note—that's 16 events per bar. In the following steps we'll increase this resolution to make the pan events sound smoother.

1   Make sure that the Pan line is selected in the Hyper Editor.

2   On the left edge of the Hyper Editor, from the Event Definition Parameter box's Grid menu, choose 1/32-Note.

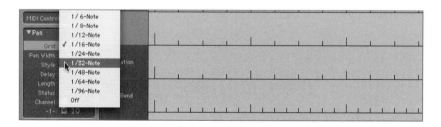

The Pan line changes to display a 1/32-Note grid.

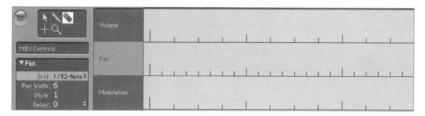

Using the Crosshair Tool to Add MIDI Events

The Crosshair tool is used to create straight lines of MIDI events. It works in a very particular way: You must first click to create the beginning of the line, then release the mouse button and drag out the event line, and finally click to create the end of the event line. Let's try it out now.

1   From the Hyper Editor's toolbox, select the Crosshair tool.

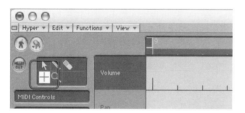

2   Click and press the Crosshair tool at the top of the Pan line's first 1/32-Note.

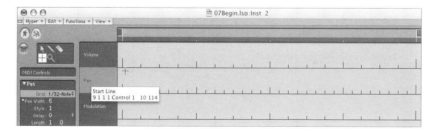

Notice the help tag that appears under the pointer. This help tag tells you the pan value at the point you've clicked.

3   While still pressing the mouse button, refine the value at the beginning of the Pan line by dragging up or down until the event value displayed in the help tag is close to 120.

4   Release the mouse button and move the pointer to the last 1/32-Note in the bar.

A line extends behind the Crosshair pointer. Once again, watch the help tag to see the exact pan value under the pointer.

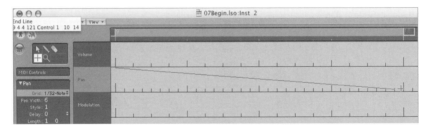

5   When the Crosshair pointer is where you want the last event to be, Ctrl-click the pointer.

TIP > Don't just click the Crosshair pointer. To lock in the changed events, you must Ctrl-click.

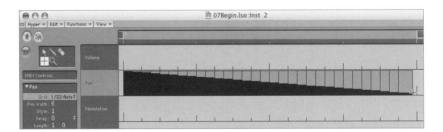

A line of events is drawn.

6   Click the Arrange window to make it the active window.

Notice the line of pan events in the MIDI Region's HyperDraw area. It is a straight line with one node every 1/32-Note.

TIP ▶ If you can't see the line of events in the HyperDraw area, select the actual sequence in the Arrange window by clicking just above the blue HyperDraw area.

7   Make the Hyper Editor the active window once again.

Using Hyper Sets

The Hyper Editor is a deeper window than a first glance might suggest. In fact, the Hyper Editor is divided into layers, called *hyper sets*. A hyper set is a user-defined collection of MIDI events. The events displayed in the Hyper Editor are part of the default MIDI Controls hyper set. But there's also another default hyper set that's very useful: The GM Drum Kit hyper set. To switch to the GM Drum Kit hyper set, use the Hyper Set menu.

1   Click and hold the Hyper Set menu.

Hyper Set Menu

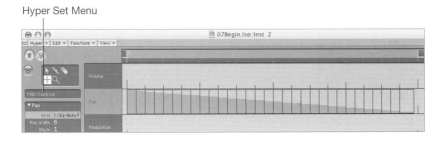

A menu of hyper sets appears.

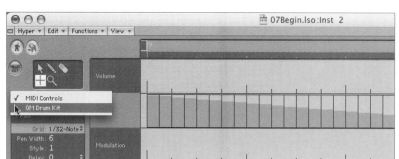

2   Choose the GM Drum Kit hyper set.

The Hyper Editor updates to display a hyper set that lists MIDI note events using GM drum kit names. This is a great bonus when programming drum sequences using Logic's Drum Kits Audio Instrument, because the Drum Kits instrument uses the GM drum kit standard to organize sounds.

NOTE ▶ *GM* stands for General MIDI, a MIDI standard invented by Roland that was intended to synchronize sound sets between different MIDI instruments. Any synthesizer that supports this standardized sound set can play MIDI Regions designed for GM. GM is commonly used in video games and the polyphonic ring tones found in the current generation of cell phones.

3   Scroll down the Hyper Editor until you see the notes you added to the Matrix Editor in the last lesson.

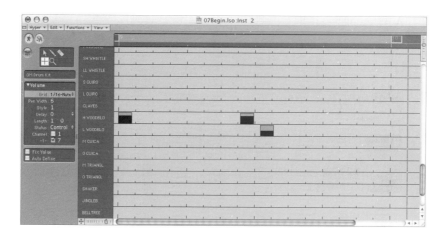

The event lines for the notes are properly labeled for the sound that the note produces. Now isn't this an easy way to find the right drum sound? Undeniably, this is better than clicking notes along the Matrix Editor's keyboard until you find the correct sound.

4   Select the Pencil tool and click a new note into the Hyper Editor.

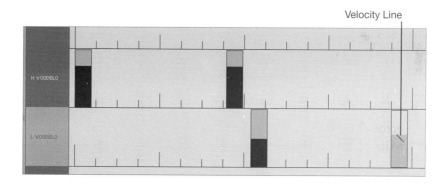

Notice that the new note has a head and a body. The line between head and body represents the note's velocity.

You should still have a one-bar cycle set up in the Bar Ruler (if not, create one now). Let's play the song and reprogram the drum sequence.

5   Click the Play button to start playback.

6   Use the Pencil and Eraser tools to create a drum sequence that augments the song.

Use any sounds you want—it's your song, after all!

7   When you're finished programming the drum sequence, stop playback.

Creating Custom Hyper Sets

The GM Drum Kit hyper set has a lot of event definitions. Most of the sounds on offer are not useful for your drum sequence, and scrolling past all of those events to find the ones you want can distract you from the serious business of programming beats. Thankfully, you can create your own custom hyper sets consisting of only the event definitions you want to use.

1   From the Hyper Editor's local menu bar, choose Hyper > Create Hyper Set.

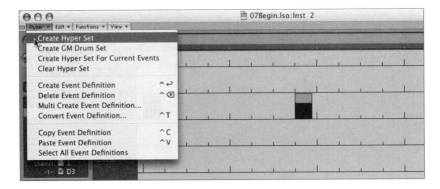

A new hyper set is created. By default, the new hyper set is provided with a default Volume event line.

2   Click and hold the Hyper Set menu.

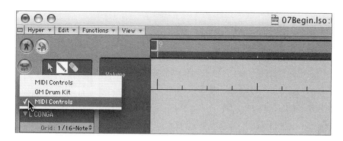

Notice the new hyper set is listed under the GM Drum Kit hyper set and is provided with the default name MIDI Controls. Let's change that name to something more descriptive.

3   Double-click the hyper set's name in the Hyper Set menu.

A text box appears.

4   Type *My Beats,* and press Return.

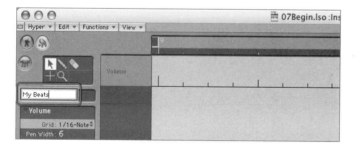

Adding Event Definitions to the Hyper Set

With a new hyper set created, you must now add new MIDI event lines (called event definitions) until the hyper set lists all the MIDI events you require. To do so, you can either copy event definitions from the GM Drum Kit hyper set and paste them into the My Beats hyper set, or use the Auto Define feature. We'll explore both methods in the following steps.

1 Use the Hyper Set menu to switch back to the GM Drum Kit hyper set.

2 To select an event definition you wish to copy into the My Beats hyper set, click its name in the Event definition list.

3 Choose Hyper > Copy Event Definition.

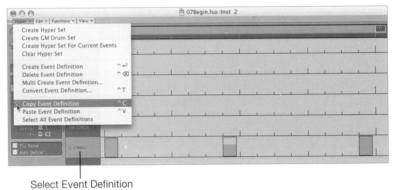

Select Event Definition

4 Switch back to the My Beats hyper set.

5 Choose Hyper > Paste Event Definition.

The event definition is pasted into the My Beats hyper set. That worked pretty well, but there's an even slicker way to add event definitions to the hyper set: *Auto Define*. When enabled, Auto Define allows you to click MIDI events in other Logic MIDI editors, and the clicked events are automatically defined and added to the hyper set as event definitions.

6   On the left edge of the Hyper Editor, click the Auto Define check box.

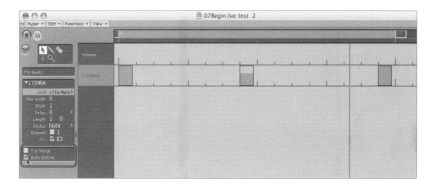

7   Make sure the MIDI Region in the Drum Kits Audio Instrument track is still selected, and choose Windows > Matrix Edit (Cmd-6).

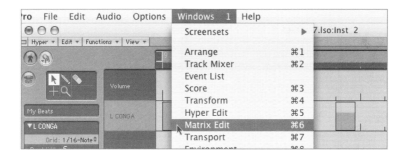

The Matrix Editor opens.

8   Position the Hyper and Matrix editors so you can clearly see both at the same time.

9   In the Matrix Editor, use the keyboard along the left edge to select keys corresponding to the notes you wish to add as event definitions in the new hyper set.

NOTE ▶ Only notes that currently have MIDI events will be added to the hyper set.

TIP ▶ With Auto Define enabled in the Hyper Editor, you can also select individual note events in the Matrix Editor to automatically add them to the new hyper set.

The notes are automatically added to the hyper set. However, the new event definitions are named for the clicked notes and lack the proper drum names. Let's fix that now.

Event Definition Added to Hyper Set

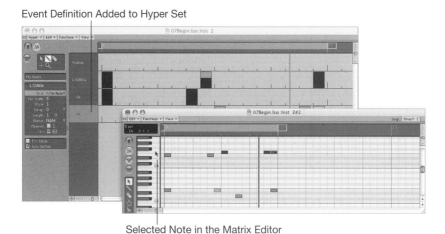

Selected Note in the Matrix Editor

10 In the Hyper Editor, select the event definition lane you wish to rename.

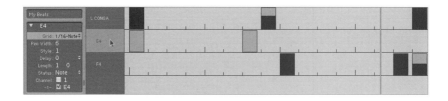

The Event Definition Parameter box is updated to show the event's parameters. At the top of this box the event definition's name is displayed.

11 In the Event Definition Parameter box click the name.

A text box opens.

12 Type a new name for the event definition.

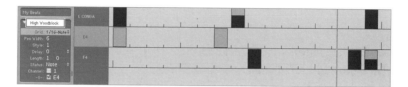

13 Name the other event definitions you added to the hyper set.

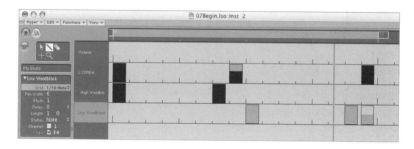

Perfect! This custom hyper set is now available anytime you open this sequence in the Hyper Editor. Let's close the Hyper Editor and move on to examine the Event List editor.

14 Close the Hyper Editor.

Exploring the Event List Editor

The Event List can be daunting at first glance, because it shows a long list of words and numbers that are a bit harder to read than the graphic displays found in the other MIDI editors. Nonetheless, the Event List makes it easy to filter MIDI events to find just the type of event you want. This is a priceless tool when you need to quickly find certain types of data and make precise edits that are difficult to do using the other editors. An example might be finding a single program-change message in a complex MIDI Region.

Opening the Event List

Let's open the Event List now and take a look around.

1 In the Arrange window, make sure that the MIDI Region in the Drum Kits Audio Instrument track is selected, and choose Windows > Event List.

The Event List opens.

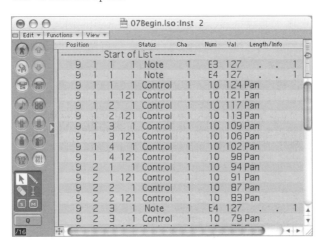

Your Event List might look a bit different from the one in the figure above, but that doesn't really matter. It still shows basically the same thing—a chart displaying MIDI events. Across the top of the Event List several headings are displayed: Position, Status, Cha, Num, Val, and Length/Info.

Position Displays the event's bar, beat, division, and tick.

Status Displays the event type (for example, a note or control-change event).

Cha Displays the MIDI channel used to record events (this is not the channel used to play back the event!).

Num For note events, Num displays the note's keyboard position; for control-change events, it displays the controller number.

Val For note events, Val displays the note's velocity; for control-change events, Val displays the control-change value.

Length/Info For note events, this column shows the note's length; for control-change events, it shows the controller name.

Editing Event Settings

Now that you have an overall picture of what the Event List controls, let's use it to change some event settings.

1 If it is not already open, open the Matrix Editor.

As you experiment with the Event List, it helps to have the Matrix Editor open to provide a visual display of the changes you make in the Event List.

2 Position the Event List beside the Matrix Editor so you can see both clearly.

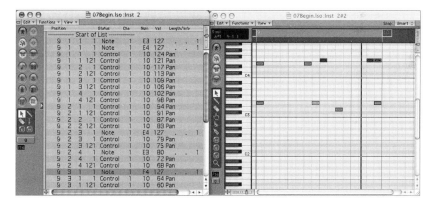

3 In the Matrix Editor, select a note.

The note is highlighted in the Event List.

Selected Note

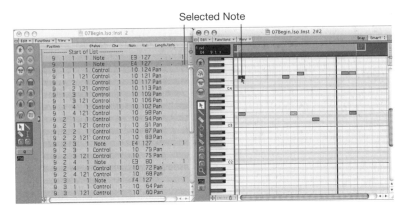

4 In the Event List, double-click the selected note's Num setting, enter *C4*, and press Return.

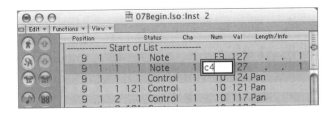

In the Matrix Editor, the selected note jumps to C4.

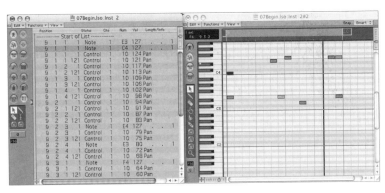

5   In the Matrix Editor, select the Arrow tool and then move the note back to
its original position.

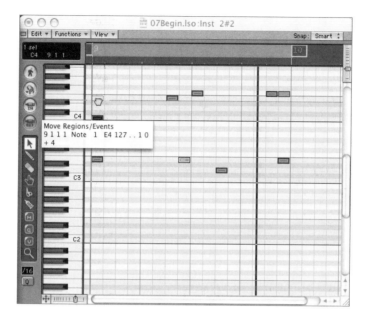

The Event List's Num setting reverts.

Filtering Events

The Event List is currently a mess of data, and with all these entries it's difficult to find exactly the event you're looking for. Event type buttons to the rescue! The event type buttons filter the Event List so it shows only a specific type
of event, making it easier to find the event(s) you need to change.

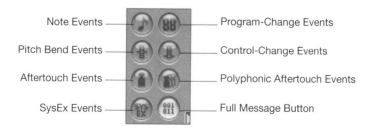

1   Click the Note Events button to disable it.

All note events are removed from the Event List display, and it now displays only pan control-change events.

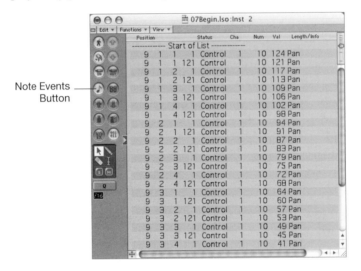

Note Events
Button

2   Click the Control-Change Events button.

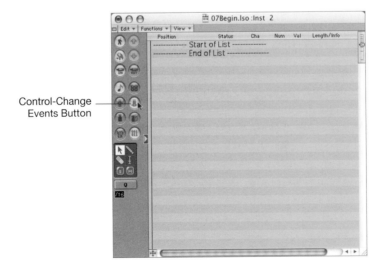

Control-Change
Events Button

The MIDI Region contains only note and pan events. All note events are already filtered out of the Event List. Because pan events are control-change events, clicking the Control-Change button filters all remaining events out of the Event List, which clears the list completely!

3   Click the Note and Control-Change Events buttons again to activate them.

What You've Learned

- ▶ The Hyper Editor is used for programming rhythmic control-change data and MIDI drum Regions.

- ▶ In the Hyper Editor, MIDI events appear as vertical beams along a grid.

- ▶ The Hyper Editor's Crosshair tool lets you create smooth lines of MIDI events.

- ▶ The Hyper Editor is organized into layers called hyper sets. A hyper set is a collection of MIDI event definitions.

- ▶ You can create custom hyper sets that contain only the event definitions you need.

- ▶ Using the Hyper Editor's Auto Define button, you can click MIDI events in the Matrix Editor, and those events appear as event definitions in the Hyper Editor's currently selected hyper set.

- ▶ The Event List charts MIDI events line by line as a sequence progresses.

- ▶ On the left edge of the Event List, the filter buttons let you filter MIDI events to find the exact type of event you are looking for.

8

Lesson Files APTS_Logic_7 > Song Files > Lesson 8 Project Files >
08Begin.lso

APTS_Logic_7 > Song Files > Lesson 8 Project Files >
08End.lso

Media APTS_Logic_7 > Song Files > Lesson 8 Project Files

Time This lesson takes approximately 90 minutes to complete.

Goals Record both MIDI and audio to further augment the song

Set up Logic's metronome and count-in

Filter MIDI input for recording

Experiment with the Cycle Record and Capture Last Take
features

Choose sampling rate, bit-depth, and stereo/mono settings

Learn to punch in and out on a recording

Recording

To this point you've arranged a song with the Matrix, Hyper, and Event List editors, inputting sampled audio and MIDI by hand. These techniques can take you a long way, but to really make a song your own you need to start recording.

Recording is a simple process in Logic, but it's also one you should practice, because recordings must be done correctly. There's an old saying in the digital world: Garbage in, garbage out. In other words, it's important to start with the best possible recordings, because if the original recording is bad, there's very little you can do to fix it inside Logic. The following lesson will walk through several techniques used to record both MIDI and audio. With a little practice, you'll nail your recordings almost every time. In turn, that will speed up your workflow, helping you to create great-sounding audio.

Setting Up the Metronome

Piano players practice playing to the click of a metronome, because the metronome helps them keep a steady rhythm. Similarly, as you record MIDI data into Logic it is beneficial to have a steady click play to help you keep your timing correct. For this purpose, Logic provides an internal metronome (sometimes called a *click track*).

> **NOTE** ▶ The Metronome's click sound is created by Logic's Klopfgeist Audio Instrument (*Klopfgeist* is German for knocking ghost). By default, the Klopfgeist is inserted on Audio Instrument 128.

The metronome's sole purpose is to provide a steady beat for you to play along to. You can enable or disable it at any time as you program, play, or record your arrangements. Of course, the metronome really shines when it's time to record because its steady click ensures you play in time with the song. To prepare for recording MIDI later in the chapter, let's set up the metronome.

1   Open the file named **08Begin.lso**, or continue working on your song from the previous lesson.

2   In the Transport panel, click and hold the Metronome button (the one with a picture of an old-fashioned metronome).

Metronome Button

A pop-up menu appears.

3   From the pop-up menu select Metronome.

The Song Settings window opens to display the Metronome pane.

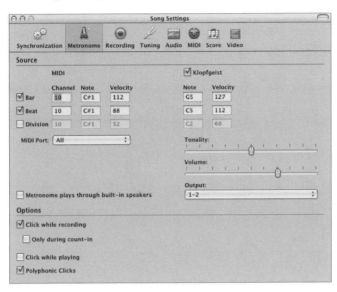

4   In the Options area at the bottom of the Metronome pane, ensure that
     "Click while recording" is checked.

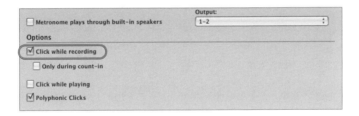

"Click while recording" enables the metronome to automatically be heard
each time you enter Record mode.

TIP If you check the "Only during count-in" box, the metronome clicks just until you begin recording. (Count-ins are discussed in the next section.) This option is very handy for vocals, because you get a good timing reference while you're setting up to record, but the metronome turns off once the vocal starts, so you're not distracted by the clicking metronome during recording.

5   Leave the Song Settings window open.

Setting a Count-in

A count-in gives you a bit of a head start before recording by engaging the SPL one or more bars early.

1   In the Song Settings window, select the Recording pane.

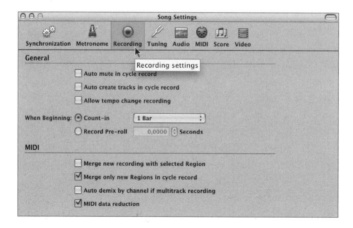

2   Make sure the Count-in setting (Logic Pro only) is checked.

3   From the Count-in menu, choose 1 Bar.

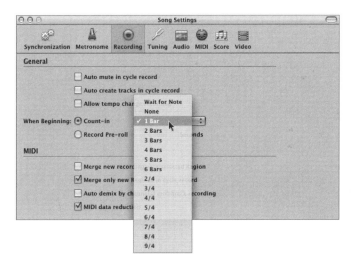

NOTE ▶ The Count-in menu will let you set up to six bars as a count-in.

4   Close the Song Settings window.

5   In the Arrange window make sure that an Audio Instrument track is selected.

At this point, you're just going to test the count-in. MIDI-based tracks do not record anything unless you generate MIDI data. You don't need to record anything just yet, so for the purpose at hand, an Audio Instrument track makes a good test subject.

6   Position the SPL at bar 5.

7   Make sure Cycle mode is turned on.

If Cycle mode is on, Logic begins recording at the beginning of the cycle mode instead of at the SPL's position.

8   Click the Record button (press * on the numeric keypad).

Record Button

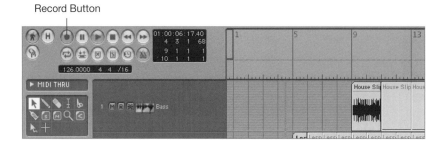

The Bar Ruler turns red (for *record*), the SPL jumps back to bar 4, and it then starts playing. This one-bar jump-back represents the 1 Bar count-in you selected in step 3. During this one-bar count-in, nothing will be recorded, but the metronome clicks along to get you into the tempo and prepare you to record.

9   Press the spacebar to stop recording.

Recording MIDI

In the last lesson you added a drum loop using the Hyper Editor's GM Drum Kit hyper set. That's a great way to program beats, but there's nothing quite as intuitive as playing a beat out and recording it. In the following steps you will redo the beat by playing your MIDI keyboard and recording the MIDI events created by pressing keys.

In the exercise above, you got a quick introduction to the Record button. Just as on an analogue tape deck, the Record button is the Transport button with a circle on it. Press the button, and you're recording! When it comes to recording MIDI, Logic always records to the track currently selected in the Arrange window. In fact, as you select MIDI or Audio Instrument tracks in the Arrange window, they automatically become record-enabled and ready to accept MIDI input (you've already used this feature several times while playing Logic's internal Audio Instruments). All that's left is to actually record. Let's give it a shot now.

Currently, you have a MIDI Region in the Audio Instrument track that plays the Drum Kits instrument. Let's get rid of that sequence and clear the way to record a new one.

1   In the Arrange window, select the MIDI Region in the Drum Kits Audio Instrument track, and press the Delete key.

The sequence is deleted.

2   Create a four-bar Cycle range at a point in your song where all of the drum Regions are playing.

> **TIP** You may have to zoom out before creating the Cycle range.

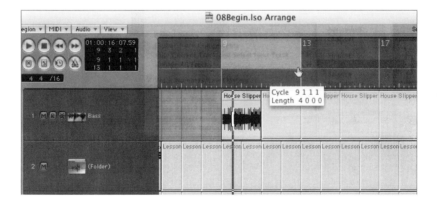

Because you are going to record a drum part, it's important that you can hear all of the other drum sounds in the song, so make sure you select an appropriate part of the arrangement.

3   Make sure the Drum Kits Audio Instrument track is selected.

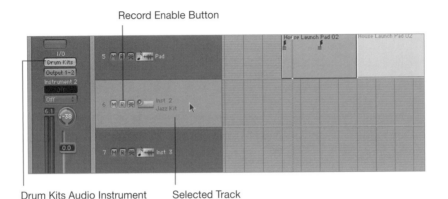

Record Enable Button

Drum Kits Audio Instrument   Selected Track

When you select a MIDI or Audio Instrument track in the Arrange window, the Record Enable button turns red. This means the track is now able to accept MIDI input and is also armed for recording. If you play your keyboard, the track's instrument will make sound.

NOTE ▶ If you click the Record Enable button to turn it off, you cannot play the instrument assigned to the track, and Logic will not record MIDI data to the track.

4   Play your MIDI controller keyboard.

NOTE ▶ If you don't have a MIDI keyboard, press the Caps Lock key to open Logic's Caps Lock Keyboard.

The Drum Kits Audio Instrument plays.

5   Press the spacebar to start playback.

6   As the cycle plays, practice a rhythm part until you find a good groove you're ready to track out.

7 When you're ready to record, press the spacebar to stop playback.

8 Move the SPL to the start of the Cycle range.

9 Press the Transport's Record button, or press the asterisk (*) key on your keyboard's number pad.

The Bar Ruler turns red to indicate you are recording, and the SPL jumps back to one bar before the Cycle range begins (the one-bar count-in set in the previous section) and then plays.

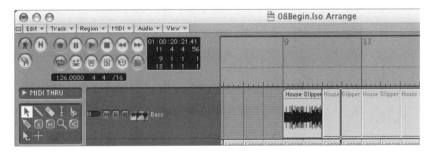

10 Play your MIDI controller and lay down some beats.

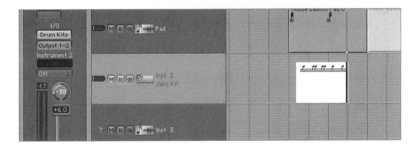

Logic records the MIDI events as you play them.

11 Press the spacebar to stop recording.

Using Cycle Record

In the previous section, you attempted to record a drum sequence using a four-bar Cycle range. As the cycle continued to play and you continued to enter MIDI events on your controller keyboard, the new events were added to the first recorded MIDI Region. That can be a fine way to record if you need to keep adding new MIDI events to a sequence, but for most situations, there's a better way to record short loops like this one: *Auto create new tracks in cycle record.*

With the "Auto create new tracks in cycle record" song setting, each time you finish a cycle while recording, Logic automatically creates a new Arrange window track using the same output channel as the track you are recording on, and then automatically records to the new track. It works like a charm, so let's try it out.

> **NOTE** ▶ Cycle record also works when recording audio.

1   Delete the newly recorded Region.

2   In the Transport, click and hold the Metronome button, then choose Recording from the menu that appears.

The Song Settings window opens to display the Recording pane.

3   In the General section of the Recording pane, select "Auto create tracks in cycle record."

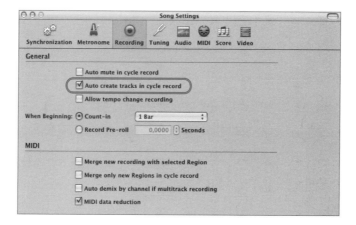

You can mute the passes you've already laid down. It helps to avoid a confusing clash of sounds as you attempt to play in your new passes of the MIDI Region. You can do this in the Song Settings window's Recording pane, too.

4   In the General section of the Recording pane, select "Auto mute in cycle record."

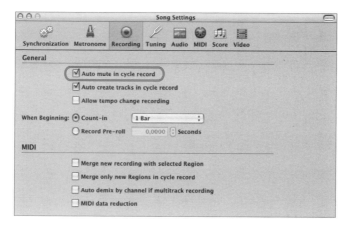

5 Close the Song Settings window.

6 Press the Transport's Record button, and lay down some beats.

7 Continue recording through several passes of the cycle.

> **NOTE ▶** You must let two cycles pass before Logic creates the first new track. With "Auto create tracks in cycle record" enabled, you must record a full cycle before Logic will save the MIDI Region and create the new track.

Logic creates a new track at the end of each cycle and moves the last recorded MIDI Region down to the new track. Additionally, Logic mutes all the previous recording passes so you don't hear their sound over the sound you are playing.

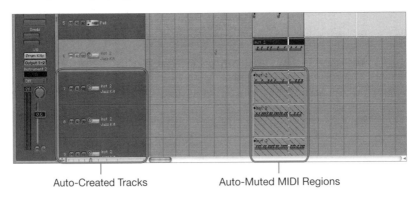

Auto-Created Tracks   Auto-Muted MIDI Regions

8 Continue recording new tracks until you've got the groove you're after.

9 Press the spacebar to stop playback.

You now have a lot of tracks in the Arrange window—more than you need. In fact, you should only select the best pass from the many you've recorded. Let's clean up the Arrange window by deleting the tracks you don't need.

First, you'll have to audition the recorded passes to find the one that sounds best.

10 From the toolbox, select the Mute tool.

> **NOTE ▶** To toggle the mute status of any Region that is *currently selected* in the Arrange window, press the M key.

11 Press the spacebar to play the cycle.

12 As the cycle plays, click the muted MIDI Regions to toggle their muted status, and audition the sequences until you find the one you like best.

> **TIP ▶** Muted regions have a dot before their name and are a lighter color than similar unmuted regions. To make muted regions visible, Logic Pro users can check the "Muted regions are textured" check box, located on the Arrange tab of the Display Preferences window.

13 Delete the tracks that contain recording passes you don't like.

14 Make sure your remaining MIDI Region is not muted.

You are left with one perfect recording!

15 Stop playback.

16 From the toolbox, select the Arrow tool.

Filtering MIDI Input

Logic provides two ways to filter MIDI input. Using the Song Settings window's MIDI pane, you can filter out incoming MIDI events such as note events, program changes, pitch bend data, and aftertouch information. Additionally, you can also adjust quantization as you record MIDI events into Logic using the MIDI Thru feature. The following section details both techniques.

Using Input Filtering

MIDI controllers can generate a variety of MIDI commands. In addition to note-on and note-off information, they also send information like continuous control numbers and aftertouch (pressure) commands. In some cases, you may not want to record every type of information that your controller is generating. For example, you may not want to record aftertouch information if you have a sound that reacts strangely to aftertouch and you sometimes inadvertently press too hard on the keys. You can use input filtering to prevent this information from getting to the track.

1   Choose File > Song Settings > MIDI.

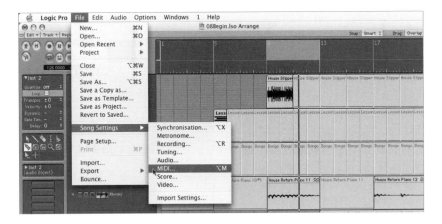

The Song Settings window opens to display the MIDI pane. By default, the General tab is displayed.

2   From the Song Settings window's MIDI pane, select the Input Filter tab.

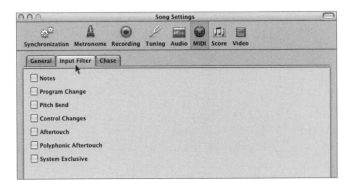

3 Select the Notes check box, and play the keyboard.

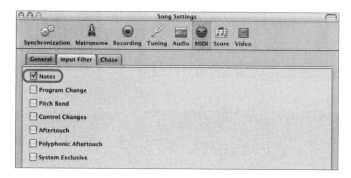

You don't hear anything, because you've filtered all incoming note messages so that they never make it into Logic's sequencer.

4 Make sure you have the Drum Kits track selected in the Arrange window.

5 Click the Notes check box to deselect it; then play your MIDI controller
keyboard.

There is sound again. Take note of the other input filter options—they are
here when you need them.

6 Close the Song Settings window.

Using MIDI Thru Filtering

MIDI Thru filtering adjusts quantization as MIDI events are recorded into
Logic. This ensures that notes conform to perfect rhythmic positions on Logic's
time grid and can really help to clean up loose playing as you record. Let's
try it out.

1 Click the background of the Arrange window to ensure no MIDI Regions
or Audio Regions are selected.

With nothing selected in the Arrange window, the Region Parameter box
updates to say MIDI Thru, and you are now in MIDI Thru mode.

2 From the Region Parameter box's Quantize menu, choose 1/2-Note.

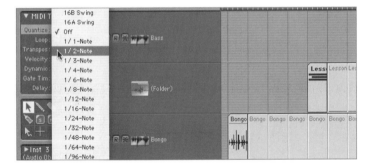

The 1/2-Note setting will hard-quantize all input events to half notes—
that's two notes per bar. This is a very obvious quantization, so it works
well for the next experiment.

3   Select an empty MIDI track (we selected the Audio Instrument track named Inst 3).

This next step is just for experimenting with MIDI Thru, so it's fine to record to an empty track. You will delete the newly recorded sequence in a few steps, so don't worry about adding sounds to the song.

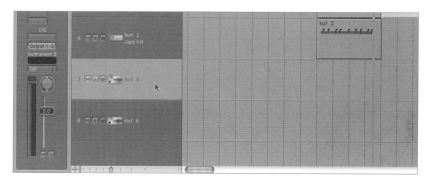

4   Press the Record button (or press * on your keyboard's number pad) and begin recording.

5   Play MIDI events very rapidly on your controller keyboard so that you create a lot of MIDI notes.

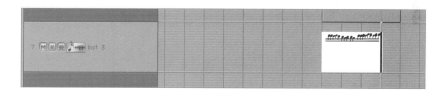

6   Stop recording.

7   Double-click the newly recorded sequence to open it in the Matrix Editor.

All of the input notes have been quantized to 1/2-Note.

8   Close the Matrix Editor.

9   Delete the newly recorded MIDI Region.

10   Set the MIDI Thru quantization to Off.

Using Capture Last Take (Logic Pro Only)

Capture Last Take as Recording is one of those little features that endear Logic to its users. Ever had a moment when you're jamming along to a track, and you realize you just played a perfect take but weren't in record? Then, after pulling the SPL back, pressing Record, and playing the take again, you don't quite do as well the second time. Or the third. Or the fourth. At those times, Capture Last Take as Recording can be a song saver!

Capture Last Take as Recording automatically prints the MIDI notes you've just been playing into the selected MIDI track. Logic maintains a log of all incoming MIDI events anytime its sequencer is playing. Because Logic keeps track of your performance, it's a simple matter to turn that performance into a MIDI Region—Logic just retrieves it from memory and prints it into the Arrange window.

TIP ▶ The Transport window's memory display shows you how much memory is available. If you jam along on your MIDI keyboard as Logic plays, you'll notice this number decreases with every key pressed, because each incoming MIDI event is stored in memory in case you need to recall it using Capture Last Take as Recording.

Memory Display

Capture Last Take as Recording is only available to Logic Pro users, and you must set up a key command to use it. Let's do that now, and then experiment.

1   Press Option-K.

The Key Commands window opens.

2   In the top right corner of the Key Commands window, type *Capture* into the search field.

Capture Last Take as Recording   Type "Capture" into Search Field

Capture Last Take as Recording is listed under Global Commands.

3   Select the Capture Last Take as Recording key command.

4   Click the Learn by Key Label button.

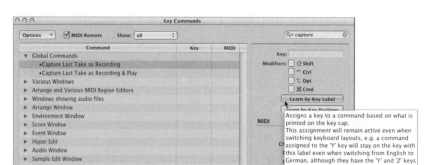

5   Press Cmd-K (think of it as "Command-<u>K</u>eep").

Cmd-K is assigned as the key command for Capture Last Take as Recording.

6   Close the Key Commands window.

7   Make sure that an empty track is selected in the Arrange window.

Once again, we are only experimenting with this feature, so—without recording—let's just play a MIDI Region in an empty track for the moment. You'll delete it in a few steps.

8   Press the spacebar to start Logic's sequencer.

9   Play your MIDI keyboard for a few bars.

10   Stop playback.

There is currently no MIDI data in the empty track. Not for long.

11 Press Cmd-K.

The played MIDI notes are printed as a MIDI Region. How cool is that?

12 Delete the new MIDI Region.

> **NOTE** ▸ Capture Last Take as Recording works only for incoming MIDI events. It does not work for incoming audio.

Setting Audio Options

Before you record audio into Logic, we need to address some basic functions and features. Think of Logic as being like a high-end professional camera. It offers a lot more features and flexibility than that cheap throwaway. You have many more options that give you control over the final image. Before you snap the picture, however, you need to make sure that all the settings are just right so that they'll create the best possible image. In Logic, some options are set just once, before you start to record, while others may need changing during the process of creating your song. You'll choose some settings based purely on personal preference. Nevertheless, it's best to think through all your choices before beginning your work.

Choosing a Sampling Rate

We first addressed sampling rate in Lesson 4, "Editing Audio Regions," when you used the Sample Editor to convert the **HH.aif** file from 48 kHz to 44.1 kHz to match the sampling rate of the song. It is extremely important that you are aware of your song's sampling rate setting, because it greatly affects your computer's performance. Logic can support sampling rates of up to 192,000 samples per second, but a rate that high takes well over four times the disk space and four times the digital signal processing power as the 44,100 samples per second

used for this song. You must also make sure that the sampling rate you've
selected in Logic is compatible with the audio interface you are using. Most
audio interfaces support 44,100 samples per second (44.1 kHz), so you should
be fine using the 44,100 setting when recording audio in this lesson.

1   Choose Audio > Sample Rate.

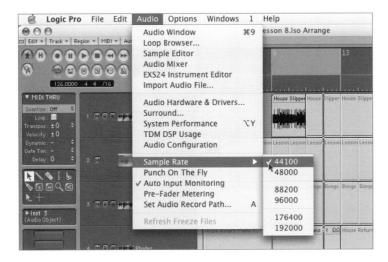

This song is already set to 44100 (44.1 kHz). There's no need to change
anything. However, keep sampling rates in mind when you do your own
recordings, because the song's sampling rate is used as the sampling rate
for your recorded files.

2   Leave the Sample Rate set to 44100.

Setting the Bit Resolution

Logic can record using 16- or 24-bit resolution. The higher the bit resolution,
the more accurately Logic can represent the audio waveform. Using 24-
instead of 16-bit resolution will require more processing power from your
computer's CPU and take slightly more disk space when you start to record
audio. However, with the current generation of technology, 24-bit recording
has become quite standard.

1   Choose Audio > Audio Hardware & Drivers.

The Preferences window opens to display the Audio pane, with the Drivers tab selected.

NOTE ▶ If you're using Logic Express, your Drivers tab will look different than the figure below, which was taken in Logic Pro. However, all of the preferences covered in this section are available in Logic Express, so you can still work through the following steps.

2   Select the 24 Bit Recording check box.

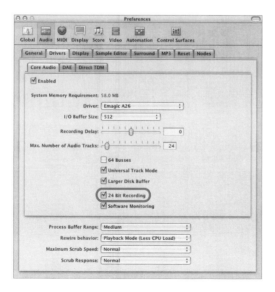

You need to make a few more settings in this window before recording, so let's leave the Preferences window open for the time being.

Setting the I/O Buffer Size

Logic's buffer setting controls how big a bite the computer tries to chew at one time when working with audio. This setting, which is measured in samples, can dramatically change the way in which your system performs, especially when recording. Typically, the bigger the buffer size, the more recorded channels of audio can be played at the same time, and this reduces the processing power required by your computer's CPU.

However, bigger buffers make the system react more slowly when recording. For example, with a large buffer setting you may notice an audible delay between playing a note on your MIDI controller and hearing one of Logic's Audio Instruments react to that note. This delay is called *latency*, and it can also seriously affect your audio recordings. For example, you may sing a note into a microphone and then experience a delay before hearing it through the speakers. Should this happen, you'll need to use a smaller buffer setting. But it's a trade-off, because a smaller buffer setting forces your computer's CPU to work harder, which means that fewer total audio tracks, plug-ins, and Audio Instruments can play simultaneously.

With these considerations in mind, start with a buffer setting of 64. If you later find you need more tracks, plug-ins, or Audio Instruments, you can increase the buffer size.

1   In Logic's Preferences window, make sure the Audio pane's Driver tab is selected.

    Near the top of the Core Audio tab is an I/O Buffer Size menu.

2   From the I/O Buffer Size pop-up menu, select 64.

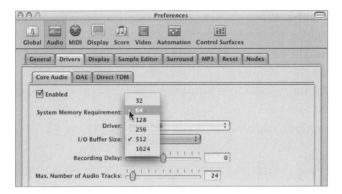

An Alert dialog pops up and asks you to reboot Logic. However, you don't have to actually restart the program.

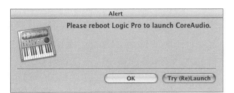

3   On the Alert dialog, click the Try (Re)Launch button.

Logic automatically reinitializes the Core Audio, and your driver settings are enabled.

Leave the Preferences window open for the next exercise.

Enabling Software Monitoring

When you're recording an audio track, software monitoring allows you to hear the signal in your speakers after it has passed through all the Audio Input, Track, and Output Objects you have created in Logic's environment. This enables you to hear how settings such as level, panning, and plug-ins affect the audio as you are recording it. The potential drawback is that since you are recording the audio live, the computer can't look ahead at what's coming. If you have a slower computer or are using large buffer settings, you may notice a delay between when the audio is created and when you hear it.

1   In Logic's Preferences window, make sure the Audio pane's Drivers tab is selected.

    Near the bottom of the Core Audio tab is a Software Monitoring check box.

2   If the Software Monitoring check box is not already selected, select it now.

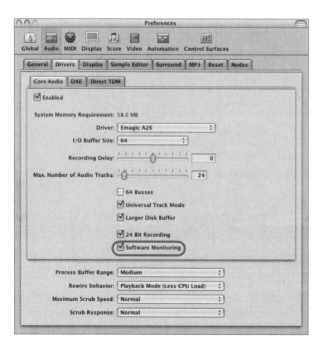

Leave the Preferences window open for the next exercise.

Selecting a File Type

When Logic records audio, the audio is stored as PCM (pulse-code modulated) audio files on your computer's hard drive. These are simply uncompressed audio files, and Logic can create your choice of WAV, AIFF, or SDII PCM audio. AIFF files are the most common type of uncompressed audio files on the Macintosh, so let's choose AIFF as the file type for recording.

1   In the Preferences window's Audio pane, select the General tab.

2   Make sure the Recording File Type menu is set to AIFF.

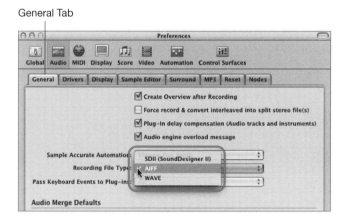

3   Close the Preferences window.

Specifying a Record Path and Name

Unlike MIDI data, which is stored directly within the Logic song file, audio files are stored separately on your computer's hard drive. Audio files can be kept anywhere on your hard drive, though typically you should record to an Audio Files folder located in the same directory as your Logic project file. This type of file management makes it easy to find the files recorded for your song, and it also simplifies the process of backing up songs once you're done, because all the audio files are right there beside the project file. However, Logic provides you with full control over where audio files are recorded by allowing you to set your audio record path.

Each audio file you record needs a unique filename. Instead of manually naming each one, you can have Logic automatically use the name of the track as the filename. Logic will automatically add numbered extensions to the filename to prevent duplicates when you record on the same track multiple times.

Let's specify an appropriate record path and file-naming convention for your audio files.

1   Choose Audio > Set Audio Record Path (Logic Pro users can press the A key).

The Set Audio Record Path dialog opens.

2   At the top of the Set Audio Record Path dialog, select the Use Audio Object
Name for File Name check box.

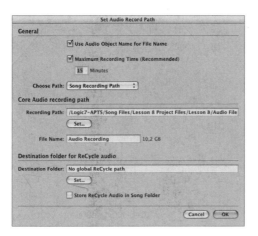

NOTE ▶ Having Logic use the Audio Object name as a basis for filenames
is especially useful when you're recording multiple tracks at the same time.

3   In the "Core Audio recording path" area, click the Set button.

A dialog drops down from the Set Audio Record Path dialog's title bar.

4   Navigate to the Lesson 8 Project Files > Audio Files folder.

5   In the Save As text field, type an initial name for your audio recording.

6   Click the Set button.

The Audio Record Path is set and all new files will be recorded into the Lesson 8 Project Files > Audio Files folder.

TIP ▶ If you do not choose a record path ahead of time, you will be prompted to choose a record path the first time you record-enable an audio track.

7   Click OK to confirm your settings and to close the Set Audio Record Path dialog.

Selecting Auto Input Monitoring (Logic Pro Only)

An audio track either can output the Audio Regions it finds as the SPL moves across them, or it can output the signal it receives from its input. Typically you want to hear the Audio Regions during playback and hear the input in the following two situations: when the track is record-enabled but the Transport is still (so you can set levels), and when the Transport is moving and in Record mode (which is the actual act of recording). Enabling Auto Input Monitoring automatically switches between the signals that are to be monitored, depending on the conditions just described.

Since this automatic switching is very helpful, let's go ahead and select Auto Input Monitoring.

1   Make sure that the Audio > Auto Input Monitoring option is selected.

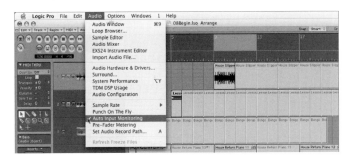

▶ Choosing a Maximum Recording Time

When you record audio in Logic, a Progress dialog pops open to tell you how long you can record. By default, you are able to record for only 15 minutes. This is a small safeguard that keeps you from filling up your hard disk with accidental recordings, but you can change this maximum recording time if necessary. To do so, visit the Set Audio Record Path dialog and deselect the Maximum Recording Time check box, or enter a new maximum recording time in the text box immediately underneath this setting.

Additionally, even with this setting off you may not have enough time to record, for example, a full 80 minutes' worth of audio, and this can make it difficult to master a CD-Audio disc in Logic. For example, if you are recording at 120 bpm, Logic will allow you to record only 71:16 minutes of audio. Happily, there's an easy answer. Due to the way Logic's sequencer works, each song can be a maximum of 2,158 bars in duration. Consequently to gain more recording time, just halve the bpm of your song! The available recording time will double.

Enabling the Replace Mode

In most cases when you are recording, you'll want to use something called the Replace mode. This simply means that when Logic is recording onto a track, any information on that part of the track is overwritten with a new Object. In other words, Logic behaves like a regular audiocassette recorder. However, Logic does not rewrite or delete the previously recorded audio on the hard drive—it's still part of the audio file and you can get it back at any time. This gives a huge advantage over the cassette recorder: You can always undo your recording and go back to where you were before!

> **NOTE** ▶ Recording without the Replace mode can get very confusing. Without Replace engaged, Logic will present multiple recorded Objects on the same track. In an audio track, only one of these Objects can be heard at a time. But in a MIDI track, multiple Objects can be heard from the same track. Sometimes the Objects overlap to the point where you may be hearing things that you can't see in the Arrange window.

1 Click the Replace button in the Transport panel. (The Tool Tip for this button says Toggle Erase Mode, but don't get confused–it is the Replace Mode).

Replace Mode Button

Getting Ready to Record

For the next set of exercises, you'll need a microphone with a preamplifier plugged in to one of your audio interface inputs. Many audio interfaces have mic preamps built into them. If yours doesn't, you can connect an external preamp to one of your interface's line inputs.

> **NOTE ▶** It is possible to do this exercise with any device that sends out a line-level signal. Instead of singing along (as indicated in the exercise), just play a note for each word.

In the last section you had to deal with a lot of general settings. Fortunately, those are primarily set-and-forget kinds of options that you will not need to change during the course of your song. The following settings, however, may need to be changed each time you record a track.

Creating a Track for Recording

Audio track channels are used for recording audio. Consequently, you need to ensure there is an audio track available. Let's create one now.

1   In the Arrange window, position the Arrow tool over the name of any empty track (Inst 3 in the figure).

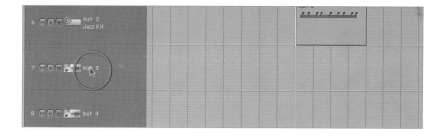

2   Click and hold the track name.

A hierarchical channel selection menu appears.

3   Choose an unused audio track channel.

The track is assigned to the channel.

4   Hold down the Option key and double-click the track's name.

A text box appears.

5   Name the Track *MyAwesomeRecording*.

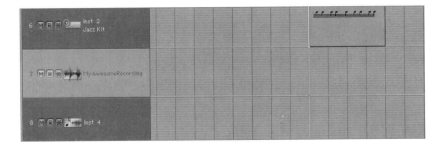

The new track is ready and available for recording.

Choosing Mono or Stereo

As you know by now, Logic can work with either mono or stereo audio tracks. Before recording, select whichever option is appropriate for what you are trying to record. Because you are about to record your very own golden voice, you only need a mono track, so let's ensure that the new track's Stereo/Mono status is properly configured.

1   Make sure the MyAwesomeRecording track is selected in the Arrange window.

    The Arrange Window channel strip updates to show the settings for the MyAwesomeRecording channel.

2   Make sure the Arrange Window channel strip's Mono/Stereo button is set to Mono (single circle).

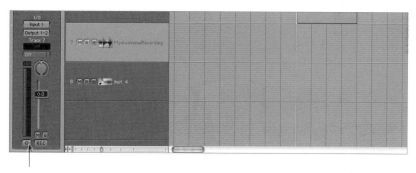

Stereo/Mono Button

Setting an Input

Now you will need to assign the audio track's input. The Input setting is located just below the Sends area, and it should correspond to the physical input that you have your microphone hooked up to. Many audio interfaces (including the stock audio inputs of your computer) only have stereo inputs labeled L (left) and R (right). In this case Input 1 in Logic represents the left input of your audio interface, and Input 2 represents the right input.

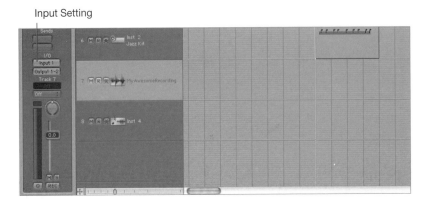

From the Input setting, select the input appropriate for your studio.

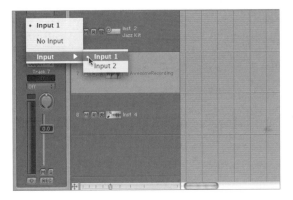

In this case, Input 1 is being selected.

Preparing a Track for Recording

Audio tracks need to be record-enabled before you can record onto them. Once a track is record-enabled, you can see and hear the signal going through the track without actually recording.

For this exercise you will be recording only one track at a time, but it is possible to record to more than one track at a time by simply clicking the Record Enable buttons on the tracks. You might do this to record a drum kit for which you need to record kick, snare, overhead, and tom tracks simultaneously.

> **TIP** To avoid feedback, make sure your speakers aren't turned up loud and your microphone isn't pointed directly at them—or use headphones instead of speakers. If you are using a PowerBook or iBook, the internal mic is very close to the speaker. Be sure to disable software monitoring, or else you will experience a feedback loop that can be very loud.

1   In the Arrange window's channel strip, click the Record Enable button.

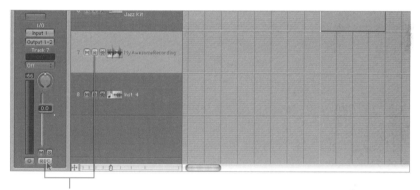

Record Enable Button

2   Make sure that the input levels are strong but not clipping the track by peaking above 0 dB on the level meter. Speak into the microphone, and adjust the level on your preamp until you get a strong level without clipping.

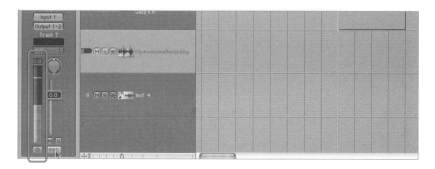

TIP ▶ Many people feel more comfortable singing in the shower than singing in the streets. Besides the obvious privacy aspect, an enclosed shower has a natural reverb that makes you sound great. Get the same effect by inserting a reverb directly on the record track before you record. The effect will not be recorded onto the audio file that's created.

Recording

Here it is—the big moment! You are about to make your first live recording. Feel free to sing along to your song, or else just count out loud as the beats go by. Whatever you choose to do, the important thing is that you actually record some audio. This is just for practice, and you can always delete your recording when we're done with the lesson.

Recording is an action-packed process. It may help to read through this recording exercise first to get the big picture of what is about to happen. Once you feel comfortable, proceed with the following steps.

1 If it's currently on, turn off the Cycle mode.

2 Make sure the SPL is at bar 1.

3 Click the Record button or press the asterisk (*) key.

A one-bar count-in occurs (four clicks).

4 Count the bars and beats out loud as the SPL reaches them.

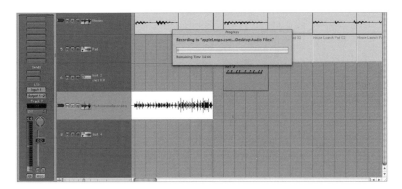

Keep counting all the way to bar 8. While recording, notice the remaining-time indicator that appears.

5   On the Transport, click the Stop button, or press 0 on the numeric keypad after bar 8.

Logic quickly creates a waveform overview, and the audio is now recorded.

NOTE ▶ If you've clipped your recording, Logic will notify you just as a precaution. Simply click Continue.

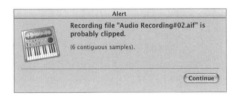

6   Move the SPL back to bar 1 and press Play to listen to what you've recorded.

That's you! Don't worry, most people don't like the sound of their own voice on a recording. The next exercise addresses what to do.

Deleting and Redoing Your First Take

If your first performance wasn't what you had hoped for, you can easily delete
it and try again.

1 Press the Delete key.

The Region you just recorded will already be selected, so pressing the
Delete key is all you need to do.

A dialog pops up to ask if you want to delete the selected audio file.

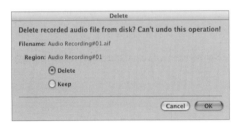

Selecting Delete removes the file from your hard disk. Selecting Keep
removes the file from the Arrange window but keeps the file on your hard
disk and in your Audio window. Keeping old files that you are not going
to use will fill and clutter your hard drive, so it's typically best to just
delete unwanted audio recordings.

2 Click the Delete radio button, and click OK.

The file is removed from your song and deleted from your hard disk.

3 Record yourself speaking the numbers again in the exact same way to prepare for the next exercise.

Recording over Existing Audio

You may find that you want to record over only a certain section of your previous recording. Here's what you can do.

1 Move the SPL to bar 5.

2   Click Record. You will still get the one-bar count in. Recount bars 5 and 6, but stop before you get to bar 7.

Notice that even though Logic was recording during the counting, the Region starts exactly at bar 5. Sometimes this can cut off part of the audio that you want to hear.

3   If necessary, grab the lower left corner of the new Region and drag from bar 5 to just before bar 5 so that you can hear the entire number.

Punch-Recording

Punching in and out on a recording is a concept that goes back to traditional analogue multitrack recorders. This is not something that your typical consumer tape deck can do. The basic idea is that you may want to play the track you've just recorded up to a certain point, then start recording, and then revert back to playback, in one continuous process. This is handy for replacing certain parts of a track that don't sound right. Trying to record right at the offending part (as in the past exercise) makes it difficult to hear and feel the context of the part you are trying to replace.

> **NOTE ▶** Only the tracks that are record-enabled will be affected by punching.

There are two ways to punch: by predefining punch-in and punch-out points with Logic's Autodrop feature, or by using key taps to punch in and out as you record (that is, punching *on the fly*).

Using Autodrop

Autodrop is Logic's way to predefine the area you want to punch. Autodrop uses a process similar to creating a cycle Region to set punch-in and punch-out points. Once you define this area, the recording happens only between these two points, in your *autodrop zone*—even if you start to record or play back from before the area you want to punch. In this exercise you're going to rerecord yourself speaking over bar 4, using the Autodrop feature.

1 In the Transport panel, click the Autodrop button (the Tool Tip says Toggle Drop).

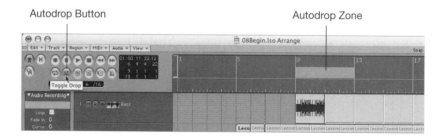

In the top portion of the Bar Ruler an autodrop zone appears. The autodrop zone looks very similar to a Cycle range, except it's half as tall. You can move and resize the autodrop zone exactly the same way as you'd move or resize a Cycle range: Grab it in the middle and drag to move it, or grab the lower corners and drag to resize it.

2 Adjust the autodrop zone so it starts at 4 1 1 1 and ends at 5 1 1 1.

NOTE ▶ You can also drag an autodrop zone into the Bar Ruler by Option-dragging from left to right.

Locators

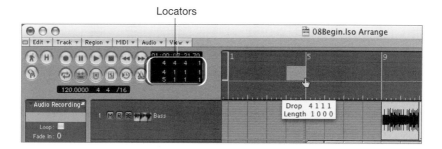

As you adjust the autodrop zone, the Transport panel's locators update to display the autodrop zone's left and right boundaries. Use the locators to confirm your position.

3   Place the SPL at bar 1 and click Record. When the SPL gets to bar 4, start counting.

TIP ▶ You can start counting sooner, but anything you say before the SPL reaches bar 4 will not be recorded.

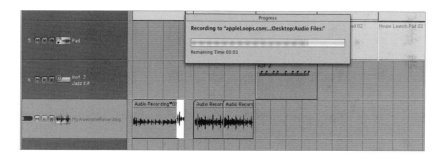

Notice that Logic automatically punched you in and out where you told it to. You should now have a new Object in the area that you autodropped in on. If you make a mistake, simply undo it (Cmd-Z) and try it again.

4   Turn the Autodrop mode off.

> **NOTE ▶** Undoing a record operation does not erase the file from the drive. The file will still remain in the Audio window. You'll learn how to clean up unused files in just a few exercises.

Punching on the Fly (Logic Pro Only)

Instead of predefining the area you want to record, you can tap keys to punch in and punch out whenever and wherever you want. For this to work, Logic needs to be in the Punch on the Fly mode. This lets it know to be ready for a recording at any time.

When you're punching on the fly, it's important to initiate each punch-in and punch-out by using a command called Record Toggle. (Logic tends to behave sluggishly when you punch in by simply hitting the Record button while in playback.) Record Toggle is only accessible through a key command that is not assigned in the default Logic key command set. This key command toggles between the Playback and Record mode. During playback you use this key command to punch in, and then again to punch out. You can even punch in and punch out multiple times throughout the same track.

Let's set up the Record Toggle key command and try punch-on-the-fly recording.

1   Press Option-K.

The Key Commands window opens.

2   In the Key Commands window's search field, type *Record Toggle*.

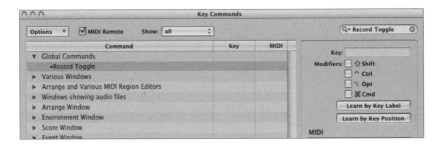

The Record Toggle key command is displayed in the Key Commands window.

3   Click the Learn by Key Label button.

4   Press Shift-*.

Shift-* is added as the Record Toggle key Command.

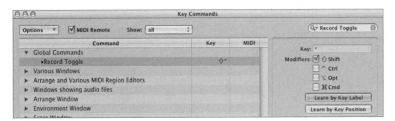

TIP ▶ You may want to assign the Record Toggle function to a single-stroke key command that doesn't require a modifier key like Shift.

5   Close the Key Commands window.

The key command is set, so let's enable punch-on-the-fly recording and try it out.

6   From Logic's main menu bar, make sure that the Audio > Punch On The Fly option is enabled.

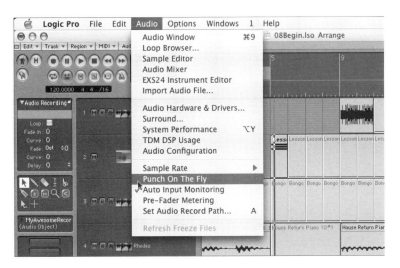

7   Position the SPL at bar 1.

8   Click the Play button.

9   Just before bar 3, press Shift-* and say *three* at bar 3. Just after you say it, press Shift-* again to punch out.

You end up with a new Object around bar 3 for the area you recorded.

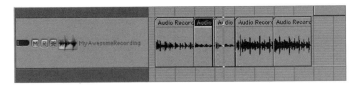

10   Stop playback.

This may take some practice. Remember, if you mess up, just undo it and try again.

Merging Recordings

Once you've punched in and out a few times, you'll notice that the track has been divided into several Objects. This is not a problem until you want to move the entire passage. Having to select multiple Objects can get confusing, and mistakes can easily be made. In this case, once you're sure that everything sounds correct, you can simply glue all the Objects back together again. This will not change the sound of the track at all.

1   Select all Audio Regions in the track you've been recording to.

2   From the toolbox, select the Glue tool.

3   Click any of the Objects with the Glue tool.

> **NOTE ▶** By default, pressing the J key merges all selected Regions in the Arrange window.

An Alert dialog pops open. In essence this dialog says you have Audio Regions from several different files selected. Consequently, to create a single Audio Region out of multiple audio files, Logic needs to combine the selected Regions into a single, new audio file.

4   In the Alert dialog, click Create.

Logic mixes down the selected Regions to create a new Region, and a Progress dialog pops open so you can keep track of how long the mixdown will take.

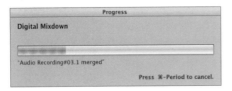

When the mixdown is completed, you are left with a single continuous Region in the Arrange window. This new Region will sound identical to what you had before you merged the Objects.

Cleaning Up After Recording

After a session of tracking audio, you will most likely have a lot of audio that was recorded but is no longer used. Remember when you punched in over your track? The audio you recorded over is still on your hard disk, eating up precious space. There are certain advantages to keeping this audio around. For example, if you need to, you can always go back to a previous recording by finding the file in the Audio window and adding it to your arrangement. However, when the recording is done and you're happy with the result, it's a good idea to clean the unused (and unwanted) recordings off your system to free up disk space for . . . well, more recordings! The steps in this exercise show you how to do this cleanup easily, without accidentally throwing out something you need.

1   Open the Audio window (Cmd-9).

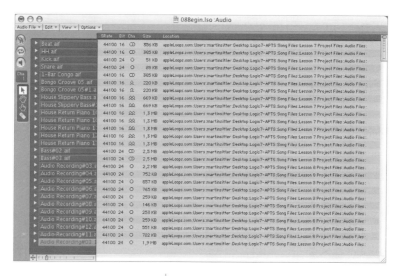

You have many audio files and Regions in your list. Several of those files are not used in the song.

2   From the Audio window's local menu bar, choose Edit > Select Unused.

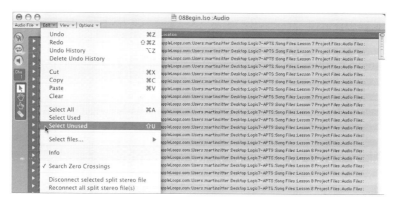

All of the audio files *not* used in the song are selected.

3   From the Audio window's local menu bar, choose Audio File > Delete File(s).

An Alert dialog pops open to tell you how many files will be deleted. Notice that the dialog warns that you can't undo this operation! The files will be removed from your song and also deleted from your hard disk. Pay attention, because after the next step, these files are gone—forever!

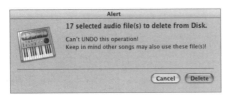

4   Click the Alert dialog's Delete button.

The unused audio files are removed from the song and deleted from your hard disk. Now things should be nice and tidy, with only the audio files that are used in the song appearing in the Audio window.

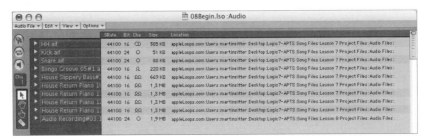

5   Close the Audio window.

At this point you have a decision to make: Do you like the sounds you've recorded? If so, use the skills you've learned so far to arrange the recorded MIDI and Audio Regions so they fit into the song, or alternatively, delete them!

What You've Learned

- ▶ You can configure the metronome as an audible-click track guide.

- ▶ MIDI performances can be recorded even if the Record mode wasn't engaged, by using the "Capture last take as recording" command.

- ▶ You can apply input filters to prevent certain types of MIDI information from being recorded into a track.

- ▶ Buffer settings allow you to control the track count and audio latency.

- ▶ You can use input monitoring to hear what you're recording in real time.

- ▶ Audio files are recorded independently of the Logic song file to a directory you define on the hard disk.

- ▶ You can use the Audio window to view, manage, and delete audio files within your song.

- ▶ Autodrop and Punch on the Fly help you rerecord only certain areas of a track.

- ▶ The Glue tool lets you merge Objects after punching to create one seamless Object.

9

Lesson Files
APTS_Logic_7 > Song Files > Lesson 9 Project Files > 09Begin.lso

APTS_Logic_7 > Song Files > Lesson 9 Project Files > 09End.lso

Media
APTS_Logic_7 > Song Files > Lesson 9 Project Files

Time
This lesson takes approximately 1 hour to complete.

Goals
Create a unique mix

Set levels and control clipping in the channel strip

Experiment with the Track Mixer

Add cross fades to Audio Regions

Use Sends to send a signal to a system bus

Use the CPU window to monitor system performance

Freeze a track in the Arrange window

Mixing

Mixing is the art of adjusting the volume and pan positions of your song's tracks until each sound is sitting in its own space in the sonic spectrum. And it *is* an art, because mixing takes practice. While there's no substitute for a trained ear, Logic tries hard to make mixing a painless process. For example, the Arrange window's channel strip has a fader, a level meter, and a pan pot that help you visualize (as well as hear) how your song's tracks fit into the mix. There's even a dedicated window, called the Track Mixer, that's designed to mimic the layout of a hardware mixing console. With a little practice, you'll soon be using both the Arrange window channel strip and the Track Mixer to create mixes that sparkle!

The last half of this lesson covers some other important mix techniques, such as creating fades, using a bus channel, and freezing tracks to free up system resources for other important things (like adding more plug-ins!).

Setting Volume Levels

All of Logic's audio channel strips have a level meter that displays the channel's volume in decibels (dB). The bottom of this meter represents a dB value of $-\infty$ (that is, silence), while the top of the meter represents 0 dB, which is the maximum allowable volume level before the signal clips the channel. As the level meter pulses up and down, the peak level is held for a few seconds, so you have time to see its value. The numerical value of the peak level is also displayed in the clip detector at the top of the level meter. With this in mind, let's take a moment to explore what *clipping* really means.

Controlling Clipping

Clipping occurs when too much signal is fed through a channel. Clipped audio sounds fuzzy and distorted—you certainly don't want clipped audio in your song. Fortunately, you don't have to rely on your ears alone. All audio channels have a *clip detector* that shows you when the channel is in danger of clipping.

The clip detector is above an audio channel's level meter. When too much signal is fed into the channel, this detector turns red to tell you that it's time to turn down the volume. Furthermore, once a channel clips, the clip detector stays on until you turn it off by clicking anywhere on the channel's level meter.

Because Logic uses 32-bit floating-point processing for all internal calculations, you *can* actually clip Logic's internal audio channels *a little bit* without creating distortion in your final mix. However, as soon as the audio leaves Logic through an output channel, you must be sure it peaks no higher than 0 dB. This is a very important concept, so let's create an output track in the Arrange window and use that channel to explore clipping.

1   Open the file named **09Begin.lso**, or continue working on your song from the previous lesson.

2   If you do not have an empty track at the bottom of the Arrange window, create one now.

3 Click and hold the empty track's name.

A hierarchical channel-selection menu appears.

4 Choose Audio > Audio Output Stereo > Out 1-2.

The track updates to say Out 1-2, and the Arrange channel strip now displays the channel strip for Stereo Output 1-2 (the first Stereo Output on your sound card). Now the channel's level meter displays the level of the signal as it leaves Logic.

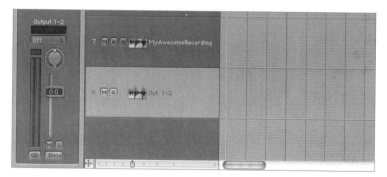

All of Logic's audio is currently being sent to Stereo Output 1-2, so in essence this channel acts as a master fader for your song. It is very important that you don't clip this output; should this happen, your song will sound bad. Period. But don't trust me—trust your ears.

5   Decrease your computer's volume.

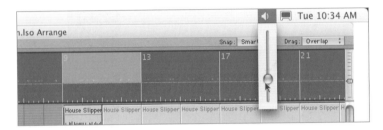

You are about to massively increase the volume coming out of Logic. Protect yourself and your equipment by turning down the volume on your computer!

6   To get a good, strong signal to work with, create a four-bar Cycle range that spans all the sounds in your song.

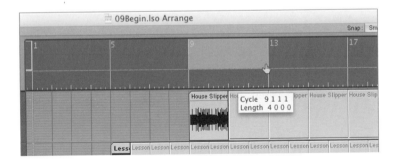

7   Press the spacebar to play the cycle.

8   With the Out 1-2 track still selected in the Arrange window, drag the channel strip's volume slider to the top (+6.0).

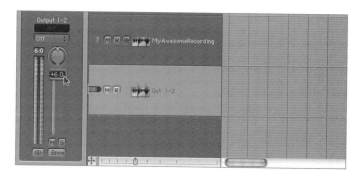

As the song plays, watch the Output 1-2 level meter and notice how it peaks past the top of the scale. If you listen closely, you'll hear distortion in your audio each time the level meter spikes past its top. (If you don't hear distortion now, trust me, you will in the final bounced file). This is clipping.

9   Stop playback.

10   Click the clip detector.

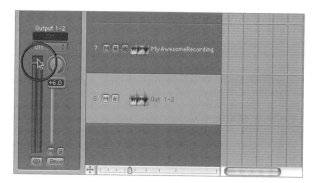

The clip detector turns off, and the red light disappears.

NOTE ▶ If an audio channel clips, the clip detector remains on until you manually turn it off.

Reverting a Slider to Its Default Setting

The Out 1-2 channel strip's volume level is set to +6. Let's revert it to 0 using a handy trick: In Logic, Option-clicking a slider or a knob always returns it to its default setting. This works not only for the channel strip, but also for all Audio Instrument and effects plug-ins.

1　Option-click the Out 1-2 channel's volume slider.

The slider returns to 0, the default setting.

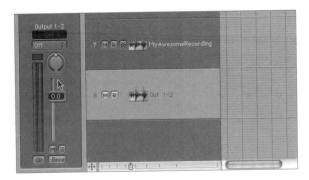

Adjusting Volume Levels

Under normal conditions the clip detector is off, and the numerical value it displays shows you the amount of headroom left above the channel's most recent volume peak. *Headroom* means the number of dB left before the channel clips. For example, if the clip detector is off (the background is brown), and the number it displays is 4.9, the channel can be raised a maximum of 4.9 dB before the audio clips. As you saw in the last exercise, when the clip detector turns red, the channel's audio has clipped, exceeding 0 dB. In this situation, the number printed in the clip detector shows you the number of dB over 0 at which the channel has peaked, which in turn is exactly the number of dB by which the track needs to be attenuated, or reduced, in order to avoid clipping.

Let's use the Out 1-2 channel's level meter to adjust the volume of the Output 1-2 Object so that it comes as close as possible to 0 dB without clipping the channel.

1   Play the cycle and watch the clip detector to determine its maximum value.

In the figure above, the channel clips by 3.6 dB. Consequently, the channel's volume must be lowered 3.6 dB to avoid clipping.

> **NOTE ▶** The fader values given in this exercise are all approximations and may vary from the values you need to use to achieve the intended result, given the Apple Loops you added to your song in Lesson 5, "Working with Apple Loops."

2   Click the clip indicator to turn it off.

3   Decrease the Output 1-2 Object's fader by the amount of dB needed to avoid clipping (for the song pictured, that is 3.6 dB).

4   Press the spacebar to start playback.

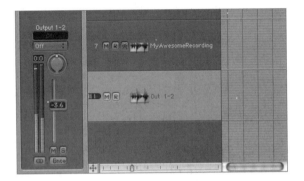

In the figure above, a volume slider setting of –3.6 causes the song to peak at 0 dB. That's as loud as the song can get without clipping the channel.

TIP ▶ By default, level meters show a channel's volume as adjusted by the fader. If you'd like to see the volume of a channel's source signal, choose Audio > Pre-Fader Metering (Logic Pro only).

5   Press the spacebar to stop playback.

Using the Track Mixer

In the previous exercises you used the Out 1-2 channel strip to make some simple changes to the audio level of your entire song. The Arrange channel strip is a very handy tool when you need to adjust the volume of individual tracks, but when it's time to do some serious mixing, Logic's Track Mixer is really the place to be. The main advantage of the Track Mixer is that it displays all the tracks in your song—both audio and MIDI tracks—in a classic mixing console view.

Opening the Track Mixer

Let's open up the Track Mixer and position it under the Arrange window so that both are clearly visible.

1   Choose Windows > Track Mixer (Cmd-2), or double-click any track name in the Arrange window.

The Track Mixer opens.

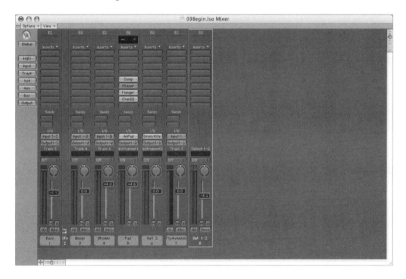

Let's organize the screen so that both the Track Mixer and the Arrange window are clearly visible.

2   Select the Arrange window.

The Arrange window becomes the active window.

3   Choose Windows > Tile Windows horizontally.

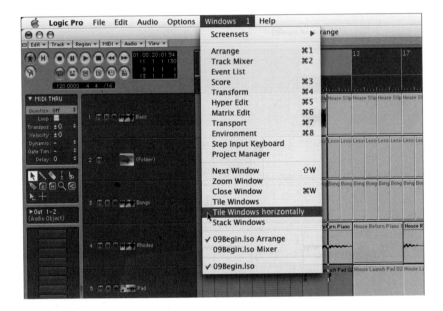

The Arrange window is horizontally aligned above the Track Mixer. You can now clearly see both.

NOTE ▸ The tile-horizontally command places the top left corner of the active window in the top left corner of the screen.

Working with Tracks in the Track Mixer

Logic's Track Mixer adapts to your track order in the Arrange window. When you open the Track Mixer, Logic automatically organizes tracks based on the order of tracks currently available in the Arrange window. The order of the Arrange window's tracks from top to bottom determines the order of the Track Mixer's tracks from left to right. If you reorder tracks in the Arrange window, the Track Mixer updates to reflect the changes.

NOTE ▶ In the Track Mixer, the Folder track is very thin and does not have a channel strip. However, if you double-click it, the Folder opens to let you adjust its tracks, just like double-clicking the Folder in the Arrange window to display its internal tracks.

1   In the Arrange window, select a track.

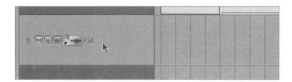

Notice that the selected track is also selected in the Track Mixer. Similarly, if you select a track in the Track Mixer, it is selected in the Arrange window.

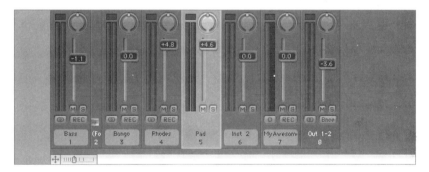

2   In the Arrange window, reorder a few tracks.

As you reorder the tracks, the Track Mixer reflects the changes.

NOTE ▶ You cannot reorder tracks in the Track Mixer.

Filtering Tracks

The *filter buttons* along the Track Mixer's left edge are used to display only the tracks you're interested in. If you have dozens of tracks in your project, these buttons make it easier to find the exact track you're after.

Let's experiment with filtering the Track Mixer display so that it shows only certain tracks.

1   On the left edge of the Track Mixer, click the Track button.

All tracks disappear except for the song's audio tracks.

2   On the left edge of the Track Mixer, click the Inst button.

The Track Mixer now displays only Audio Instrument tracks.

3   Click the Inst button once again to revert the Track Mixer back to its normal display mode.

4   On the left edge of the Track Mixer, click the Global button.

The Global button displays all Audio and MIDI Instrument channels that exist in this song. (You'll learn more about these channels in the part titled, "Customizing Your Setup.")

NOTE ▶ Clicking the Global button causes the track order to change. First, the MIDI instruments are displayed, followed by Input, Audio Track, Instrument, Auxiliary, Bus, and then Output channels.

5   With the Global button still selected in the Track Mixer, double-click any track that is not already part of your arrangement.

The track is added to the bottom of the Arrange window. This is a great way to add new tracks to your arrangement.

6   Click the Global button once again to revert the Track Mixer back to its normal display mode.

7   Delete the new track from the Arrange window.

Exploring the Fader Area

The bottom half of each channel displays the Fader area. You've already explored some of this area's functions, such as the fader, level meter, Pan control and Record Enable button. Let's take a moment to look at a few of the others, including muting, soloing, and setting up mix groups.

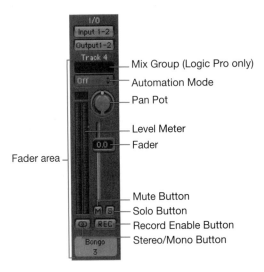

Muting and Soloing Tracks

At the bottom of the Fader area is the Mute button, and next to that is the Solo button. You click the Mute button to turn off a track's sound and click the Solo button to turn off the sound of all tracks except the one being soloed.

1   Press the spacebar to start playback.

2   Experiment with the Track Mixer's Mute and Solo buttons, and listen to how they affect playback.

    You can also mute and solo tracks in the Arrange window. Interestingly, muting and soloing in the Arrange window works a bit differently from muting and soloing in the Track Mixer. Let's experiment to see how.

3   From the Arrange window's local menus, ensure that the View > Track Mute Buttons and View > Track Solo Buttons options are checked.

Take a close look at the tracks in the Arrange window. They all have their own Mute and Solo buttons.

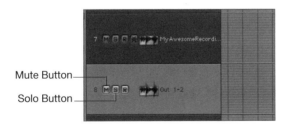

4   In the Arrange window, experiment with the Mute and Solo buttons to see how they affect the sound.

NOTE ▶ When you solo a track in the Arrange window, the Bar Ruler turns yellow to visually indicate that Solo mode is engaged. As a quick time saver, you can even click one Solo or Mute button and then drag down across other tracks to mute/solo them!

As you click the Arrange window track Mute and Solo buttons, notice that the tracks in the Track Mixer *are not* muted or soloed! In fact, both sets of buttons function independently of the other, and the reason is ingenious. Logic allows you to assign several different Arrange window tracks to a single channel. Because you can mute and solo these tracks independently of the channel itself, you can ensure that only one track plays through the channel at any one time—very handy when it comes time to audition, for example, multiple vocal takes through the same series of effects.

5   Make sure that no tracks are muted or soloed in either the Arrange window or the Track Mixer.

Using Groups to Link Channels Together (Logic Pro Only)

Groups let you link multiple channels together so that you can control them all at once. For example, if multiple channels are assigned to a group, you can increase the volume of one channel, and all the other channels in the same group will also increase in volume.

This is a great technique to use when you need to preserve relationships between tracks. For example, you've probably assigned the Bass and Bongo tracks different volume levels. If you later decide that the combined sound of these tracks is too loud or too quiet, you currently have to change each track's volume individually. This makes it very easy to lose the relative relationships between these tracks' volume levels. By assigning the tracks to a group, you can change the volume of one, and the other automatically follows.

1   On the Bass track, click and hold the Group display.

The Group pop-up menu appears.

2   From the Group pop-up menu, select Group 1.

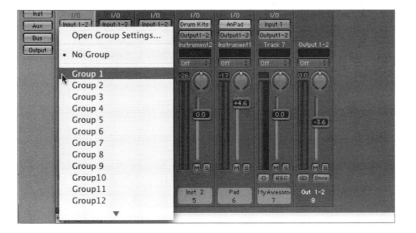

This initializes the group, and the Group Settings dialog opens.

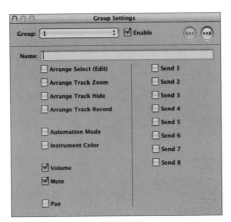

The settings in this dialog dictate which edit operations affect grouped tracks. By default, Volume and Mute are selected.

NOTE ▶ The Group Settings dialog automatically opens when you first initialize a group. (If you assign a track to a group but the Group Settings dialog doesn't open, it means that the group has already been initialized.) After that, you can open the Group Settings dialog at any time by selecting Open Group Settings from the Group pop-up menu.

3   Check the Pan box.

4   On the Bongo track, click and hold the Group setting, and choose Group 1 from the pop-up menu.

The Bass and Bongo tracks are now both assigned to Group 1.

5   Adjust the Bass track's fader and Pan control.

The Bongo track's fader and Pan control also adjust relative to the Bass track.

6   In the Group Settings dialog, uncheck the Enable box.

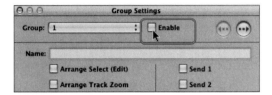

The Group setting in the channel strip turns from yellow to blue, indicating the group is disabled.

7   Once again, adjust the Bass track's fader and Pan control.

The Bongo track does not follow the Bass track, since you have temporarily disabled the group.

8   Close the Group Settings dialog.

> **NOTE ▶** The Toggle Group Clutch key command is very handy for temporarily disabling a group. Press the Toggle Group Clutch key once to have Logic disable all of your song's groups, allowing you to adjust individual faders and pan pots. Press it a second time to re-enable all groups. To set up the Toggle Group Clutch key command (it's a good idea to assign the G key), visit Logic's Key Commands window (Option-K).

9   Close the Track Mixer.

Creating Fades

The Arrange window has a dedicated tool for making fades, and as you may have guessed, it's called the Fade tool. Fades created with the Fade tool are nondestructive, which means your audio files are not permanently altered in any way. Instead, when the song begins playing, a fade audio file is created on your hard disk, with one Region for each fade, and Logic refers to this fade file as it plays the fades.

Let's experiment with fades by creating a fade-in and a cross fade.

1   From the Arrange window's toolbox, grab the Magnifying Glass and
    drag around the Bongo Audio Region to zoom in.

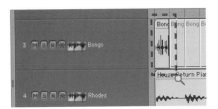

Fades are hard to see unless you zoom in very close. With the Bongo
Audio Region filling the Arrange area, it's easy to see the fades you'll
make in the following steps.

2   From the toolbox, grab the Fade tool (the one with the sideways
    V on it; the Tool Tip says Auto Crossfade Tool).

3   Drag the Fade tool over the beginning of the first half of the Bongo
    Region.

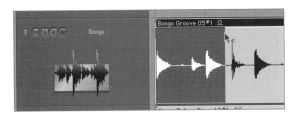

A fade-in is created.

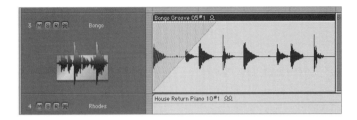

4   With the Fade tool still selected, hold down Control and click and drag up or down on the fade.

The pointer turns into a magnifying glass and the fade curves!

NOTE ▶ Fade curves are not available to Logic Express users.

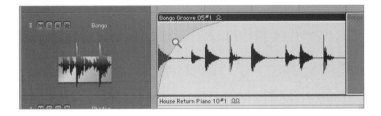

A cross fade is created in exactly the same way as a fade-in, except instead of dragging the Fade tool over the beginning of a Region, you drag across the boundary between two adjacent Regions.

5   Locate two adjacent Audio Regions in the Arrange window, and drag the Fade tool across the boundary between them.

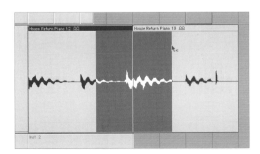

A cross fade is created between the Regions.

6   Hold down Control, and drag up or down on the cross fade.

The cross fade's center point moves left and right as you drag.

NOTE ▶ Logic Express users are not able to adjust the cross fade's center point.

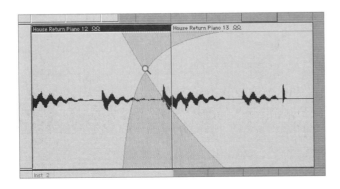

7   Hold down Option and click the cross fade.

The cross fade is deleted.

8   For practice, go ahead and create a few fades. When you're done, click Play to hear what they sound like.

Before Logic plays your song, it creates a fade file that contains the added fades.

NOTE ▶ If your computer is quick or if the fades are small, the Progress dialog might not appear.

The fade file itself is stored in a folder called Fade Files, located in the same directory as the song's project file. The fade file is named after the song, with the extension *-f16m* for 16-bit recordings, or *-f24m* for 24-bit recordings. If this fade file is moved out of the folder or goes missing, it's not a big deal. Logic will simply create a new fade file the next time you play the song.

TIP ▶ If your Finder window is in column view (as shown in the figure above), you can play the fade file to hear what it sounds like. To enter column view in a Finder window, press Cmd-3 or click the Column View button in the top left corner.

Using Sends

When you insert a DSP plug-in into a channel's Insert slot, 100 percent of the channel's sound passes through the plug-in, so all of the channel's signal is processed by the effect. For equalizing or dynamic range compression, this is perfect because you want to equalize or compress the entire signal. But for other effects, such as reverbs and delays, you will normally want only a portion of the signal to be processed so that you can control how wet the signal is (how much reverb there is compared with the amount of the source signal). While a Mix slider is used with these types of effects to adjust, for example, the amount of reverb compared with the amount of source signal, in many situations using a Send provides a far better method for working with these types of effects.

Sends split a portion of a channel's sound out and *send* it to a system bus. The signal that travels out through a Send is exactly the same as the signal passing through the channel itself, so it makes a good source signal for DSP effects. Furthermore, you can send the signal from several different tracks to the same bus. This allows you to process the sound from several different tracks using the same set of DSP plug-ins!

Setting Up a Bus Channel

Before using a Send, you must have a destination ready to receive the Send's signal. Sends always transfer a signal to a system bus. To see how this works, let's set up a bus channel now and then send some signal to it.

1   Double-click the empty track slot at the bottom of the Arrange window's Track List.

A new track is created.

2   Click and hold the new track's name, and choose Audio > Audio Bus > Bus 1 from the pop-up menu that appears.

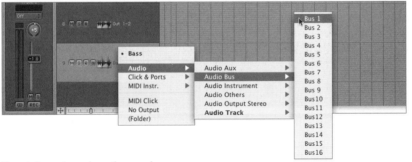

Bus 1 is assigned to the track.

3 Make sure that Bus 1 is a stereo channel.

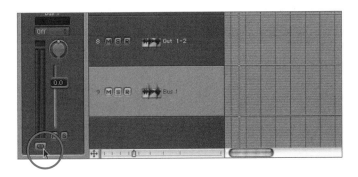

4 On the Arrange window's channel strip, click and hold Bus 1's first Insert slot, and then in the pop-up menu choose Stereo > Logic > Reverb > SilverVerb.

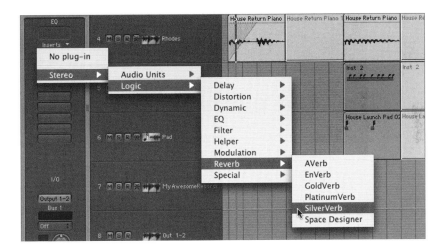

The SilverVerb appears in a plug-in window.

5   At the top of the SilverVerb window, click and hold the Settings menu and choose the Ambience preset. (You can change the preset later, if you like.)

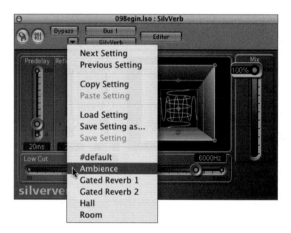

6   Make sure that the SilverVerb's Mix slider is set to 100%.

Why 100%? The Mix slider adjusts the ratio of processed signal to source signal. In this case, the Bus channel is there to provide only processed sound, and you don't want any of the original signal sneaking through. So, setting the Mix slider to 100% means that the Bus channel's output contains only reverb.

7   Close the SilverVerb plug-in window.

Initializing Sends

With the Bus 1 channel set up with a reverb, it's time to send some signal to it.

1   Press the spacebar to start playback.

2   Create a Cycle range that spans four bars of the Bongo track that contain an Audio Region.

3 In the Arrange window's Track List, select the Bongo track.

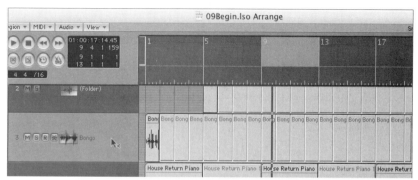

The Arrange channel strip updates to show the Bongo track's channel strip.

4 On the Arrange channel strip, click and hold the first Send slot.

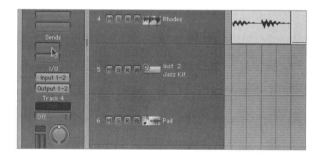

A hierarchical menu appears.

5 Choose Bus > Bus 1.

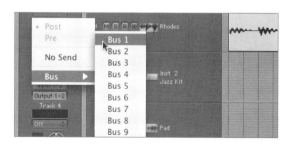

The Send is assigned to Bus 1, and a Send Level control appears to the right of the Send slot. The Send Level control is currently set to the off position, $-\infty$.

6 Drag the Send Level control up to set it to 0.

Send Level Control

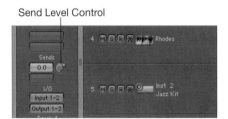

As you drag, the Send slot temporarily changes to show you the value of the Send Level control. The sound of the Bongo track is now being processed by the SilverVerb inserted in the Bus channel. Can you hear the reverb?

TIP ▶ Setting the Send level to 0 is called *normalizing the Send level*. To do this quickly, hold down Option and click the Send Level control.

7 Experiment by sending the audio from other tracks to Bus 1.

8 Press the spacebar to stop playback.

Exploring Pre and Post Sends

Channel Sends can be set to pre or post fader. *Pre fader* ensures that the Send signal remains constant regardless of the channel's main Volume Fader setting, while *post fader* means that the level passing through the Send changes as the channel's main fader is raised or lowered. Sends default to post fader, and in most situations this is exactly what you want. For example, with the Sends set to post fader, lowering the Bongo track's level transmits less signal to the Bus 1 channel, which means that lowering the volume of the Bongo track also causes the volume of the reverb to lower. If you were to set the Sends to pre fader, raising or lowering the Bongo track's volume fader would have no effect on the volume of the reverb.

Once you start playing around with pre- and post-fader Send settings, it's much easier to see how they work. Let's experiment with the Bongo track now.

1   Press the spacebar to begin playback.

2   In the Arrange window's Track List, select the Bongo track.

3   In the Arrange channel strip, click and hold the first Send slot, and choose Pre from the pop-up menu.

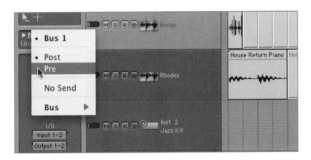

4   Lower the Bongo track's fader to the bottom.

The Bongo track no longer transmits signal, but you can still hear the reverb coming out of Bus 1. This is because the signal traveling from the Send to Bus 1 is pre fader, and thus the Send pays no attention to the Bongo track's volume fader.

5   Click and hold the Bongo track's first Send slot, and choose Post from the pop-up menu.

The Sends are reset to post fader, and Bus 1 stops producing sound! Why? Because the signal traveling from the Send to Bus 1 is now post fader. But the fader is at $-\infty$, so no sound is traveling to Bus 1.

6   Raise the Bongo track's volume fader.

The SilverVerb raises along with the Bongo track.

7   Press the spacebar to stop playback.

Monitoring System Performance

Digital audio editing is a system-intensive process. With multiple audio files zipping around your computer and DSP effects chewing up your CPU power, your computer is working hard! As you apply more and more DSP plug-ins to your song's tracks, you'll notice your system beginning to slow down. In a few minutes you'll learn how to use Logic's Freeze function to combat this problem, but in the meantime, your single biggest asset in monitoring your computer's performance is Logic's CPU window.

The CPU window shows you how much of your system's resources are being devoured by your song. Let's open the CPU window and watch it work.

1   Press the spacebar to start playback.

2   Choose Audio > System Performance (Option-Y).

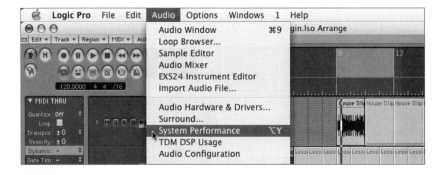

The CPU window opens.

The Audio meter on the left of this window monitors your CPU's performance. As you apply more and more DSP effects, this meter will pulse higher. At the very top there's a bright yellow warning band. When the Audio meter level nears this band, it's time to free up system resources, because your system will start to bog down and become slow. (If this occurs, you'll need to freeze some tracks, but more on that in a moment.)

The Disk I/O meter on the right keeps track of the strain on your hard disks as audio is pulled off them. This meter follows a very simple rule: The more audio tracks used in your song, the more strain is put on your hard disks. A slow hard disk, such as the 4200 rpm disks that come with PowerBooks, will not let you use as many tracks as a faster disk, like the 7200 rpm discs in Power Macs.

3   Place the CPU window in the bottom right corner of your screen, and refer to it often!

Using the Freeze Function

Freezing tracks is a feature that greatly increases Logic's power to process audio. If your system-resources monitor (the CPU window) begins peaking too close to the top of its meter, you can click the Freeze button and then keep working.

Freeze performs an offline bounce for each frozen track. In other words, it renders the track and its plug-ins into a freeze file, and then automatically plays back this freeze file instead of the original one. After freezing, the track's plug-ins are temporarily deactivated, and they will place virtually no strain on your system until you unfreeze the track.

The Freeze button appears on every audio track and Audio Instrument track in the Arrange window, and it looks like a little snowflake. In a few moments you'll click this button to freeze a few tracks. But before doing so, there's something you need to know...

Setting the Song Start and End Markers

Freeze files are always rendered between the song start and song end markers. This has significant implications for short songs, like the one you're working on, because if you click the Freeze button now, you'll have to sit and wait as Logic freezes a lot of empty space at the end of the song. Fortunately, this is a waste of only time, not disk space. Logic automatically trims all silence from the end of a freeze file. Still, time is money, so let's take a moment to snug up the song start and end markers to the active part of the song.

> **NOTE ▶** The song start and end markers also form the default bounce Region.

1   Grab the song start marker and drag it to bar 0. (The song start marker looks like a white-outlined rectangle at the beginning of the Bar Ruler.)

Adding a bar of silence to the start of the song gives you four beats to add MIDI control-change and automation data to configure your MIDI instruments before the song starts playing.

> **NOTE ▶** Clicking the song start marker has a side effect: All Objects in the Arrange area are automatically selected.

Like the song start marker, the song end marker is a white rectangle in the top portion of the Bar Ruler. However, the song end marker is currently way down the Bar Ruler. You can scroll down until you find it and then drag it forward to the end of your song, but a far easier method involves using the Transport window's song end setting.

2   Choose Windows > Transport (Cmd-7).

The Transport window opens. In the bottom right corner of the Transport window is the Song End box, which displays the number of the bar where the song currently ends.

NOTE ▸ The song end setting is available only in the Transport window—the Arrange window's Transport panel does not give you access to it.

3   Double-click the song end setting.

A text box appears.

4   Type *27* into the text box that appears, and press Return.

Why 27? A quick glance at the Arrange area shows that our song finishes at bar 25. Adding two additional bars gives a little extra room to catch reverb and delay tails, or long release settings from Audio Instruments.

NOTE ▸ Depending on your arrangement, your song might end at a different bar than the one pictured. If so, set the song end setting to two bars after the last Region finishes playing.

After you press Return, the song end marker jumps to bar 27.

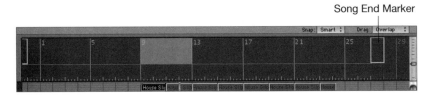

Song End Marker

5   Close the Transport window to get it out of the way.

Freezing Tracks

Freeze files are created using 32-bit floating-point processing to preserve the full signal quality of Logic's DSP effects and Audio Instrument plug-ins. In other words, frozen tracks sound exactly the same as unfrozen ones, so you don't have to worry about changing your sound when you freeze.

NOTE ▸ The word *freeze* is a pun. *Freezing* tracks *frees* your processor for other calculations. Get it?

With the song start and end markers appropriately set, it's time to freeze a track. Let's practice with the Bongo track to see how the process works. But first, you'll need to insert a few effects plug-ins so that you have something to freeze. To do so quickly, let's use a channel strip configuration.

1   In the Arrange window, select the Bongo track.

The Arrange channel strip updates to display the channel strip for the Bongo track.

2   In the Arrange channel strip, click and hold the Inserts label.

A pop-up menu appears.

3   Choose 02 Drums > Percussion > Bongos.

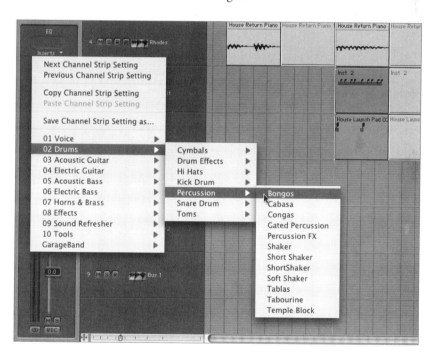

A set of effects suited for bongo sounds is inserted into the channel strip.

The Bongo Channel Strip Configuration includes an instantiation of the Fat EQ, which is not available to Logic Express users. Just to put everyone on the same page, let's change the Fat EQ to a Channel EQ.

4   Click and hold the Fat EQ insert slot, and Choose Mono > Logic > EQ > Channel EQ.

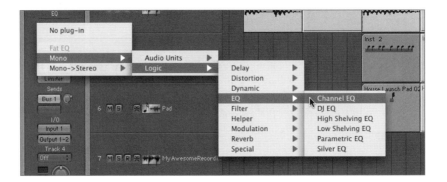

The Channel EQ opens.

5   Close the Channel EQ.

You'll use this EQ throughout Lesson 10, "Automating the Mix," but for now, close the Channel EQ to get it out of the way.

6   Play the song and listen to the inserted channel strip effects.

As the song plays, pay particular attention to the CPU window's Audio meter.

7   Stop playback.

8   In the Track column, click the Bongo track's Freeze button.

Freeze Button

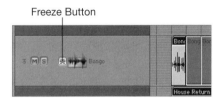

NOTE ▶ When you click the Freeze button, the track's Record Enable button disappears, because it's not possible to record onto a frozen track.

Nothing happens right away. Logic waits until the next Play command to freeze the track, which provides you the opportunity to freeze more than one track at the same time.

9   Press the spacebar to initiate a Play command and, by association, the freeze process.

The SPL races through your song, following the process of the Freeze function, and the Freezing Progress dialog appears.

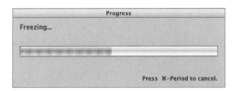

Logic renders out the track, along with all associated plug-ins assigned to its Insert slots. Until you unfreeze the Bongo track by clicking the Freeze button again, Logic will play the Bongo freeze file instead of the original audio track.

The freeze file itself is stored in a new Freeze Files folder that Logic auto-matically creates in the same folder as the song's project file. This freeze file remains only as long as the track is frozen. The instant you unfreeze this track, Logic deletes the new freeze file, so you don't need to worry about filling up your hard disk with unneeded frozen tracks.

10 Press the spacebar to play the song.

The Bongo track sounds just as it did before, and you can still hear the effect of the inserted DSP plug-ins, but a quick glance at the CPU window shows that the strain on your CPU is lower.

What You've Learned

▸ The clip detector at the top of each level meter turns red if a channel's volume is too high.

▸ If the clip detector is black, the number in it shows how many dB below 0 the channel peaks at, and thus how much higher the volume can go before clipping occurs. If the clip detector is red, it shows how many dB *over* 0 the channel peaks at, and thus the number of dB by which you need to reduce the volume to bring the channel's level back under 0 dB.

▸ Level meters hold the channels' peak levels for a few seconds, making it easy for you to see volume peaks.

▸ The Track Mixer displays the same channels as the Arrange window, in the same order.

▶   The Track Mixer's filter buttons are used to hide or display specific track types.

▶   Fades created in the Arrange window are nondestructive and do not change the original audio files.

▶   To create a curved fade, hold down Control and drag up or down on a fade.

▶   A Send (located below a channel's Insert slots) splits a portion of a channel's sound out and *sends* it through a system bus to another Audio Object.

▶   The CPU window is used to monitor your computer's performance.

▶   The Freeze button, which looks like a little snowflake, appears on every audio track and Audio Instrument track in the Arrange window.

▶   When you freeze a track, Logic renders the track and all its plug-ins into a high-quality audio file that it plays instead of the original track. All plug-ins are temporarily deactivated, and they will place no further strain on your system until you unfreeze the track.

10

Lesson Files APTS_Logic_7 > Song Files > Lesson 10 Project Files > 10Begin.lso

APTS_Logic_7 > Song Files > Lesson 10 Project Files > 10End.lso

Media APTS_Logic_7 > Song Files > Lesson 10 Project Files

Time This lesson takes approximately 30 minutes to complete.

Goals Learn about Track Automation

Enter automation nodes by hand

Experiment with automation modes to record automation in real time

Use Automation Quick Access

Assign multiple MIDI controllers to automate more than one plug-in parameter at a time

Automating the Mix

Some high-end hardware mixing consoles can record fader movements, and if you've ever watched one of those mixing consoles in action, you can almost see ghostly hands moving the faders up and down to make volume adjustments. This feature is called *automation*, and as you may have guessed from this lesson's title, Logic can automate fader movement, too. But Logic does not stop there: It can automate all MIDI controller data, and even the sliders and knobs on every DSP plug-in, including software instruments and effects such as Delay and EQ. Automation really is the icing on the sonic cake, because it takes an otherwise straight-ahead mix and breathes life into it by changing its sound over time to create a constantly evolving ambience. If you want to make your mixes truly shine, automation is the answer.

Using Track Automation

Track Automation is quite similar to HyperDraw. But while HyperDraw works with individual Regions, Track Automation, as its name suggests, is tied to specific tracks in the Arrange window. Right now, if you don't have Track Automation enabled, all the Objects in the Arrange area look normal. With Track Automation enabled, a gray automation track appears, as you'll see in the next exercise.

Exploring Track Automation

Let's enable Track Automation and automate volume changes in the Bongo track.

1   Open the file named **10Begin.lso** in the APTS_Logic_7 > Song Files > Lesson 10 Project Files folder or continue working on your song from the previous lesson.

2   From the Arrange window's local menu bar, choose View > Track Automation.

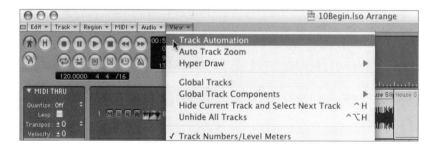

If this is the first time you've enabled Track Automation for your song, the following dialog appears (if this dialog does not appear, skip the next step).

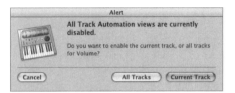

3   Click All Tracks.

The dialog closes, and Track Automation is turned on.

In the Arrange area, each track now has a gray area with a data line through it. This gray area is the *automation track*. The Track column also expands to display a few new areas, including an Automation Parameter menu and an automation fader, which displays the current setting of the parameter displayed in the Automation Parameter menu.

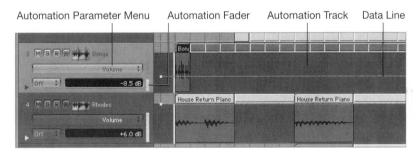

4   If the Bongo track is frozen, click its Freeze button to turn the Freeze mode off.

5   In the Bongo track, grab the automation fader and drag it up or down.

As you drag, the pointer turns into a crosshair, and the automation track's data line moves up or down to follow the automation fader's movements. This automation fader comes in handy when you want to make "set and forget" changes to a track's volume, pan position, or other controller data, because it provides a convenient fader right in the Arrange window. However, set-and-forget changes work only when the track contains no automation data, as the next steps demonstrate.

6   Select the Arrow tool, and then click in the automation track to add nodes in the approximate positions shown in the next figure:

The Automation Parameter menu says Volume, and indeed, volume automation has been added to the track. As you can see, adding automation nodes works exactly the same way as adding nodes to the HyperDraw area (refer to Lesson 6, "Editing MIDI in the Matrix Editor"). This includes creating, copying, deleting, and moving nodes. Of course, automation curves are also available to Logic Pro users, and they work exactly like curves in HyperDraw.

NOTE ► Logic Express users do not have access to automation curves.

Let's play this volume automation to see what it does.

7   Move the SPL to the beginning of the song and start playback.

As the song plays, the Bongo track increases in volume over bars 1 to 4 and decreases in volume over the last two bars. In essence, you've just automated a fade-in and fade-out.

8   If you're using Logic Pro, hold down Ctrl-Option, then drag some curves into the automation track.

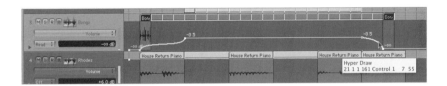

Isn't that a great way to make a fade?

9   Hold down the Shift key, and rubber-band select all of the volume-automation nodes, including the one at the very beginning of the automation track.

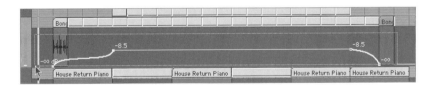

10 Press the Delete key.

All the volume-automation nodes are deleted. Make sure you delete every volume-automation node. You'll know you've done it right when the automation track's data line turns from solid to dashed.

Solid data line indicates that track contains automation data

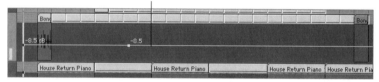

Dashed data line indicates that no automation data exists

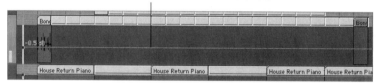

11 Adjust the Bongo track's volume until it plays at an appropriate level.

12 Stop playback.

▶ **When to Use HyperDraw vs. Track Automation**

As you've seen above, Track Automation data belongs to the track, while HyperDraw data belongs to an Object in a track. Your decision to use Track Automation or HyperDraw will depend on your situation and what you are trying to accomplish. In general, though, you'll want to use HyperDraw whenever you are programming control changes that should always affect a particular Region. Use Track Automation for programming control changes that are not necessarily tied to a specific Region, such as a volume fade or a cutoff sweep.

Switching Automation Types

The Automation Parameter menu displays the parameter you are currently editing. In the case of MIDI tracks, this menu shows all 127 MIDI controllers, just as HyperDraw does. For audio tracks and Audio Instruments, these MIDI controllers are replaced by the automation-capable plug-in parameters from the track's inserted plug-ins. And this is Track Automation's greatest virtue, because it allows you to quickly find and automate any plug-in parameter you need!

1   Click and hold the Bongo track's Automation Parameter menu.

Automation Parameter Menu

A hierarchical menu appears. Notice that all the plug-ins inserted into the Bongo channel are listed at the top of the menu.

2   Select 1 ChanEQ > Peak 2 Gain.

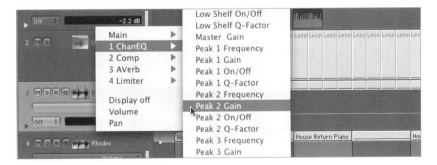

The Automation Parameter menu changes to say Peak 2 Gain instead of Volume.

3   On the Arrange window channel strip, double-click the Channel EQ insert.

Channel EQ   Bongo Track Selected

The Channel EQ opens.

NOTE ▶ If you are using Logic Express, your Channel EQ has four EQ bands, as opposed to the eight bands in the Logic Pro Channel EQ. Nonetheless, the Channel EQ works similarly in both programs, so you will be able to follow along with the steps in this section, even though your Channel EQ looks a bit different.

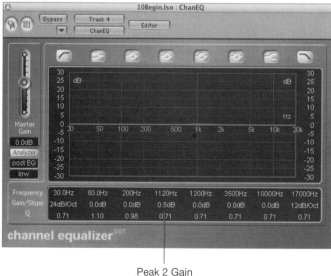

Peak 2 Gain

4   Press the spacebar to play your song.

5   As it plays, drag the Bongo track's automation fader up and down.

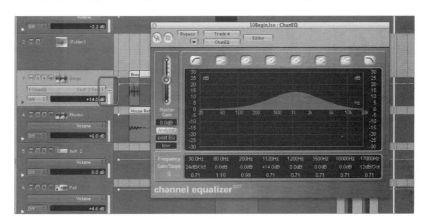

Watch the Channel EQ as you drag the automation fader and listen to the sound of the Bongo track.

Enabling Extra Automation Tracks (Logic Pro Only)

Currently, only one automation track is displayed for each track. If you want to automate a different plug-in parameter, you need to select the parameter from the Automation Parameter menu and then automate. But what if you want to automate or compare the automation of two parameters at once? Logic Pro 7 does not stop you. In fact, you can open as many extra automation tracks as you need for every track in your song.

1   In the Track column, click the small disclosure triangle in the bottom left corner of the Bongo track.

Disclosure Triangle

A new automation track opens.

New Automation Track

2   From the new automation track's Automation Parameter menu, choose 1 ChanEQ > Peak 2 Frequency.

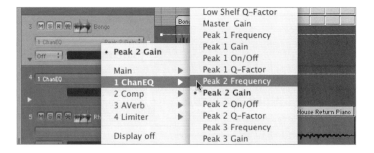

The automation track updates to show the automation data line for the Peak 2 filter's frequency band. You can now adjust and compare both automation parameters at the same time! Furthermore, should the need arise, you can click the disclosure triangle in the bottom left corner of Automation Track 2 to open yet another automation track, and so on.

Automation Track 1

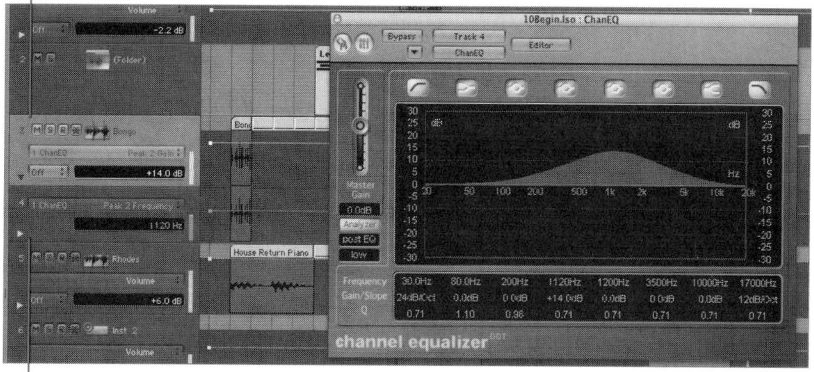

Automation Track 2

Using Live Automation

In the steps above, you've experimented with *offline automation*, a process in which you enter nodes by hand. *Live automation*, on the other hand, records automation data as you move faders and plug-in knobs inside Logic, letting you effectively perform Track Automation in real time.

Track Automation has its own recording system, which functions independently of Logic's other recording features, and the Transport's Record button has nothing to do with it! That's right—Logic can record automation during regular playback. To accomplish this feat, Logic uses Track Automation modes. There are six automation modes available, each with a slightly different purpose:

Off Automation is turned off and Track Automation will be neither sent nor received. In other words, Logic ignores all Track Automation for each track whose Automation mode is set to Off.

Read All existing automation data will be read, but moving any fader or DSP plug-in slider will not result in any new automation data being written to the track.

Touch Logic writes new automation data whenever a fader (or automation parameter) is *touched*. When you stop touching, or moving, the fader, Logic stops writing automation data and the fader returns to the pretouched level.

Latch This is similar to the Touch mode, but Logic continues recording automation data as long as playback continues, even if you stop touching the fader.

Write This mode overwrites all existing data for all the data types selected in the Track Automation Settings window (the Track Automation Settings window is discussed in the next exercise). In general it is better to use the Touch or Latch mode, because those modes overwrite the data only for moved faders, while the Write mode generally overwrites all automation data. Period.

MIDI Track Automation is disconnected from faders and knobs inside Logic, though faders will still send MIDI data.

Well, that's the theory. Now let's put it into practice by automating an EQ curve for the Bongo track.

1   Click and hold the Bongo track's Automation Mode menu.

Automation Mode Menu

2   Choose Latch from the pop-up menu that appears.

The Bongo track is now ready to be automated. All you need to do is play the song while adjusting the Channel EQ's Peak 2 Gain and Frequency parameters.

3   Press the spacebar to start playing the song.

4   Adjust the Channel EQ's Peak 2 Gain and Frequency parameters.

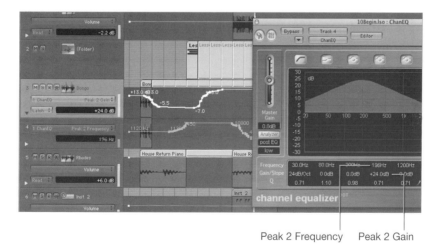

Peak 2 Frequency   Peak 2 Gain

Frequency and gain automation data is recorded into the Bongo track's automation tracks! Note that you did not have to click the Transport's

Record button. To automate this plug-in's settings, all you need to do is set the Automation Mode menu to Latch and adjust the Channel EQ's parameters and sliders as Logic plays. Congratulations—you've just automated a filter sweep!

5   Move the SPL back to the beginning of the song and start playback again.

6   Adjust other settings on the Channel EQ.

Notice that the automation tracks intelligently switch to display the settings as you automate their changes.

7   Click and hold the Bongo track's Automation Parameter menu.

Notice that in the pop-up menu, all automated parameters are listed in bold text at the bottom of the menu. If you need to touch up any of your automation passes, this list lets you quickly select the parameter you're looking for.

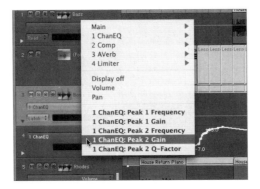

8   Press the spacebar to stop playback.

We're not finished exploring Track Automation, so get this first pass of automation data out of the way. If you are using Logic Pro, skip ahead to the next excercise to learn how to use Logic Pro's Undo History. If you're using Logic Express, proceed to the next step.

9   If you're using Logic Express, press Cmd-Z until you've undone all added automation.

Using the Undo History (Logic Pro Only)

The Undo History keeps a list of the edits you've made, and it provides a great way to undo multiple steps in one fell swoop. On common problem in undoing multiple steps is that you can easily press Cmd-Z too many times, and accidentally undo something you wanted to keep. Using the Undo History, you can see a list of all recent edits, and undo only to the point you intend by choosing the correct edit from the list.

1 Choose Edit > Undo History (Option-Z).

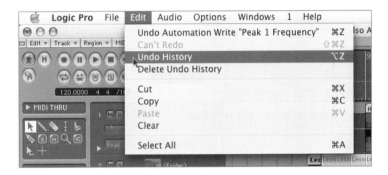

The Undo History window opens.

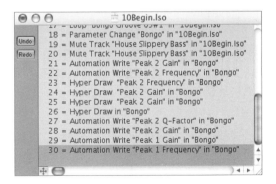

2 Click the step directly before the first instance where the Peak 2 filter was modified.

All of Peak 2's automation is undone.

NOTE ▶ Offline automation is labeled "Hyper Draw" actions in the Undo History.

3   Close the Undo History window.

MORE INFO ▶ By default, Undo History lists 30 undo steps. You can change this by visiting the Global Preferences pane's Editing tab. There you will find a Limit Multiple Undo Steps preference you can adjust as desired.

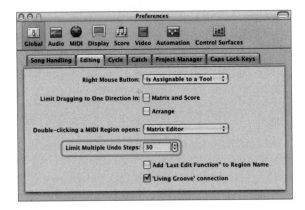

Filtering Automation Types

Logic's automation preferences allow you to specify exactly which type of automation data you want Logic to record. In the Automation Preferences pane there's a line of check boxes labeled Touch/Latch/Write Erase. These check boxes tell Logic which types of automation to record. By default, all the check boxes except Solo are selected, which means that Logic will record automation data for the Volume, Pan, Mute, Send, and Plug-in settings. To avoid accidentally automating something you shouldn't have, it's a good idea to deselect all the check boxes that represent parameters you don't want to automate.

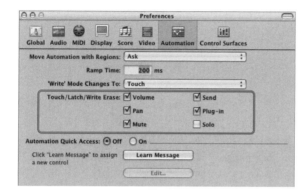

1   To open the automation preferences, choose Options > Track Automation > Track Automation Settings.

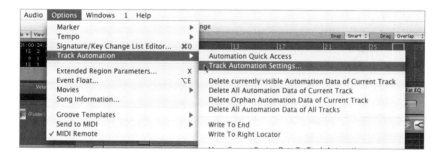

2   For the purpose of demonstration, deselect all the check boxes in the Touch/Latch/Write Erase section of the Automation Preferences pane.

3   Move the SPL to bar 1, and press the spacebar to play your song.

4   Adjust any setting on the Channel EQ.

No automation is recorded, because the Track Automation Settings window's Plug-in check box is currently deselected.

5   Click the Plug-in check box to reselect it, and then adjust the Channel EQ's settings.

Automation is once again recorded.

6   Press the spacebar to stop playback.

In a moment you are going to learn a far better way to automate the Channel EQ, using Automation Quick Access. Let's undo the automation you've just created.

7   Logic Express users, press Cmd-Z until you have undone all added automation. Logic Pro users, use the Undo History to undo the automation.

Using Automation Quick Access

In the previous exercise you adjusted the settings on the Channel EQ to create live automation. Wouldn't it be great to make these automation adjustments using a knob or slider on a hardware MIDI controller, instead of adjusting the relatively nonintuitive knobs and sliders in the plug-in window? Well, you can, using a feature called Automation Quick Access!

Quick Access assigns a slider or knob on your hardware MIDI controller keyboard to modify Track Automation data. The bottom of the Automation Preferences pane has a section dedicated to Quick Access, and here you turn Quick Access on or off. Let's set up Quick Access now and then take it for a test drive.

1   If the Automation Preferences pane is not open, choose Options > Track Automation > Track Automation Settings to open it now.

2   At the bottom of the Automation Preferences pane, click the Automation Quick Access On radio button.

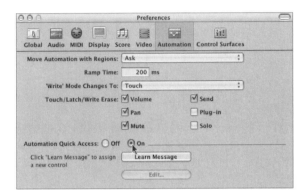

An Alert dialog appears. This dialog informs you that Automation Quick Access is not yet defined. In plain English, this means you need to specify a MIDI controller knob to generate data for automation.

3   Click the Assign button.

The bottom left corner of the Automation Preferences pane updates to say "Slowly move/turn the control up and down you want to assign." At this point you can turn any knob or slider on your MIDI controller—for example, the pitch bend wheel or the modulation wheel—to assign it to Quick Access. (Even better, if you are using a controller keyboard that has several controller knobs on it, such as the Midiman Oxygen 8, you can turn one of those knobs to assign it to Quick Access, leaving the pitch bend and modulation wheels free to do their real jobs.) Let's try it out.

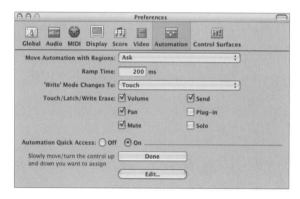

4   On your MIDI controller, move any slider or knob (try the mod wheel).

A help tag pops up to tell you the assignment is complete.

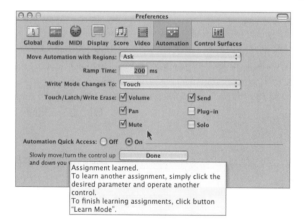

5   Click the Done button to lock in your Automation Quick Access controller assignment.

Quick Access is now turned on and ready to go.

6   On your MIDI controller, move the knob or slider you assigned to Automation Quick Access.

Notice that the parameter displayed in the selected automation track moves, as does the corresponding parameter on the Channel EQ.

They both move as you adjust the modulation wheel! Great—let's record these movements.

7   In the Arrange window, make sure that the Bongo track is selected and the Automation Mode menu says Latch.

8   Position the SPL at the beginning of bar 1.

9   Press the spacebar to play the song.

10 On your MIDI controller, move the modulation wheel as the song plays.

Presto! Automation data is now entered via your MIDI controller's modulation wheel. This provides a much smoother and more intuitive way to enter this data than turning the software knob of the Channel EQ, doesn't it?

11 Select a different automation track, and move your MIDI controller's knob or slider.

Now this automation track's parameter is automated. Indeed, Automation Quick Access can be used to modify the parameter of *any selected automation track*.

12 When you're finished automating, choose Options > Track Automation > Automation Quick Access.

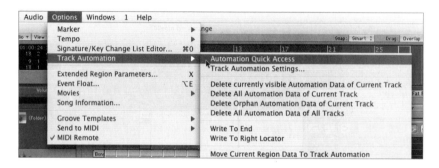

This is a shortcut you can use to toggle Quick Access on or off without having the Track Automation Settings window open.

Assigning Multiple Controllers

Automation Quick Access is a fast way to assign a single MIDI controller for use in automating plug-in parameters. But it is limited by its ability to control only the parameter of the automation track currently selected in the Arrange window. When you adjust the EQ, for example, it's often beneficial to be able to automate both the EQ band and the frequency at the same time, using two controllers.

New to Logic 7, you can assign multiple controllers to automate several plug-in parameters at the same time. You should still have the Automation Preferences pane and the Channel EQ open (if you don't, open them now), so let's explore how this works.

1 At the bottom of the Automation Preferences pane, click the Edit button.

2   The Controller Assignments window opens.

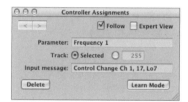

This window lists the controller assigned to Automation Quick Access. Let's remove the Automation Quick Access controller and start with a clean slate.

3   In the bottom left corner of the Controller Assignments window, click the Delete button.

The Controller Assignments window is now empty.

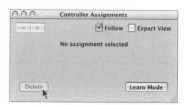

4   In the bottom right corner of the window, click the Learn Mode button.

The Controller Assignments window enters the Learn mode and is ready to accept input from both your MIDI controller *and* a Logic plug-in.

5   On the Channel EQ, adjust the Peak 2 Gain parameter.

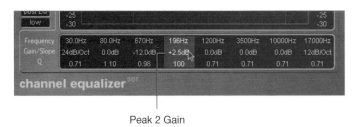

Peak 2 Gain

6   On your MIDI controller, move any knob or slider you wish to assign to this plug-in parameter (if your MIDI controller does not have extra knobs or sliders, move the mod wheel).

The MIDI controller is assigned to the Channel EQ's Peak 2 Gain parameter. To assign a new parameter, keep the Learn mode enabled and move *directly* to the Channel EQ and adjust another parameter.

7   On the Channel EQ, adjust the Peak 2 Frequency parameter.

Peak 2 Frequency

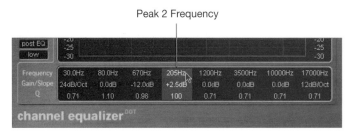

8   On your MIDI controller, move any knob or slider you wish to assign to the Frequency parameter (if your MIDI controller does not have extra knobs or sliders, move the pitch bend wheel).

The MIDI controller is assigned to the Channel EQ's Peak 2 Frequency parameter.

9   On the Controller Assignments window, click the Learn Mode button to disable it.

10 Use the Next and Previous Controller Assignment buttons to make sure you have only one controller assigned to each of the two Channel EQ parameters.

11 Close the Controller Assignments window.

12 Close the Preferences window.

13 In the Arrange window, make sure the Bongo track is selected and in the Latch mode.

14 Move the SPL to bar 1.

15 Press the spacebar to start playback.

16 On your MIDI controller, adjust both assigned knobs.

You are now manipulating two of the Channel EQ parameters at the same time! Now doesn't that put the icing on the automation cake?

17 Press the spacebar to stop playback.

18 Save your song.

What You've Learned

▶ To create a node, click inside the HyperDraw area or the automation track.

▶ To move a node, grab it and drag it to a new position.

▶ To delete a node, click it quickly.

▶ To create an automation curve in Logic Pro, hold down Ctrl-Option and then drag the line between two nodes. The type of automation curve you create is dependent upon whether you drag the line up, down, right, or left.

▶ To enable or disable Track Automation in the Arrange window, choose View > Track Automation.

▶ Automation modes (and not the Transport's Record button) determine how Logic records Track Automation.

▶ In general, it's best to use the Touch or Latch modes to record automation because they do so for only the parameter you are currently moving.

▶ The Write mode overwrites all automation data.

▶ Automation Quick Access is used to assign automation to a slider or knob on a hardware MIDI controller keyboard. Setting up Quick Access is done in the Track Automation Settings window.

Customizing Your Setup

11

Lesson Files	APTS_Logic_7 > Song Files > Lesson 11 Project Files > Autoload
Bonus File	APTS_Logic_7 > Song Files > Lesson 11 Project Files > 11 Extras > MIDIDeviceChart.pdf
Time	This lesson takes approximately 1 hour to 90 minutes to complete, depending on the number of MIDI devices in your studio.
Goals	Learn MIDI signal flow into and out of Logic
	Connect Logic's sequencer to your computer's MIDI ports
	Create and configure MIDI Instrument Objects
	Gain comfort and confidence working with Logic's Environment
	Create a personalized Logic Environment that represents the MIDI devices in your recording studio
	Create a custom Autoload Song

Setting Up the MIDI Environment

Out of the box, Logic is configured to use the default workspace. You can start making music right away using this workspace as the basis for your composition, but chances are the default workspace does not reflect the setup of your studio. The default workspace is configured to support only one General MIDI (GM) synthesizer—a basic setup, indeed. Fortunately, Logic's Environment is extremely customizable, and you can tailor it to exactly reflect the instruments and MIDI devices you use on a daily basis. Are you excited? You should be. You're about to configure Logic so that it melds perfectly with your studio, which will make music production easier and also enhance your creativity.

Getting Started in Logic's Environment Window

Take a moment to look at the studio around you. What do you see? At the very least you must have a MIDI controller (a keyboard or other device that produces MIDI signals), or you will find it difficult to interact with Logic. You may also have other synthesizers, a sampler, and even a few software instruments like Propellerhead Software's Reason or Native Instruments' Absynth. These instruments are your cherished toys, and they are all part of your music production environment.

You can easily look around your studio and see these MIDI devices, but Logic does not have the benefit of eyes—for Logic to "see" your studio, virtual copies of each MIDI device, called *Objects*, must exist inside a special Logic window called the *Environment*.

Exploring the Environment Window

Before we open the Environment window, let's take a moment to look at what you'll find.

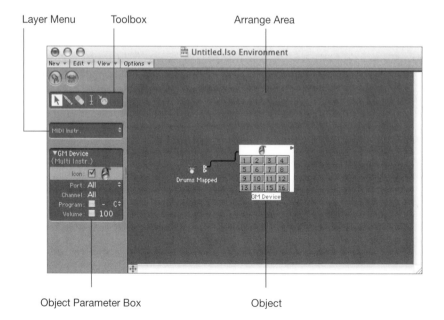

Objects

Dictionary.com defines an object as *the purpose, aim, or goal of a specific action or effort.* The Environment's goal is to create connections between Logic and your studio's MIDI devices, and each connection is represented by an Object. For example, the Instrument Object connects Logic to a synthesizer, while an Audio Object connects Logic to your computer's hardware audio interface, such as an Emagic EMI 2|6 sound card.

The Environment Toolbox

The toolbox is the cornerstone of many Logic windows, and it's no different in the Environment. The tools in this box are used to select, create, erase, and name Objects.

The Layer Box

The Environment can hold many types of Objects, so to keep them all organized and easy to find, Logic lets you divide the Environment into layers that group similar Objects and instruments together.

The Object Parameter Box

The behavior of each Environment Object is controlled by setting its parameters. These parameters are found in the Object Parameter box, which is a context-sensitive display that updates to show you the unique settings of any selected Object.

The Object Parameter box has two homes. It lives along the left edge of both the Environment and Arrange windows. Don't let these dual locations fool you, because it's the same box in both windows, and changing the parameters in one box changes the parameters in the other.

> NOTE ▶ The Logic manual occasionally calls this the Instrument Parameter box, but the Object Parameter box displays the properties of any selected Environment Object—it doesn't have to be an instrument. For the sake of consistency, this book will always call it the Object Parameter box.

Let's open the Environment window.

1   If you don't have an empty song open, press Cmd-N to create a song
(for more information on creating a song, see Lesson 3, "Understanding
Workflow Techniques").

An empty Arrange window appears on your screen.

2   From the main menu bar, choose Windows > Environment (Cmd-8).

The Environment window opens. The Environment window is a very
complex place, indeed. In fact, it can contain so many Objects that it has
to be organized into layers. To switch between Environment layers, you
use the Layer menu.

Layer Menu

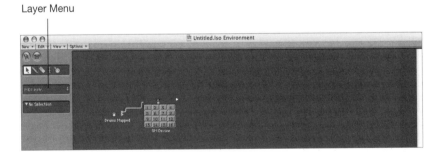

3   From the Layer menu, choose Audio.

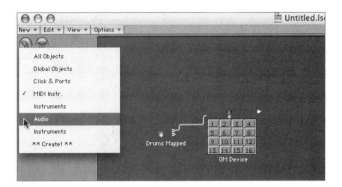

The Audio layer appears. The Audio layer contains a multitude of Audio Objects (Audio Objects are covered in Lesson 12, "Setting Up the Audio Environment"). Indeed, there are more Audio Objects in this layer than you will require for your everyday music making. In the next exercise you will strip the Environment of its default Objects and begin the process of customizing the Environment to match your personal music production studio.

Creating a Plain Vanilla Environment

The most important thing to recognize about the Environment is that it's completely customizable. You can (and should!) alter the Environment to match your work style and make it easier for you to make music. In this exercise you will create a plain vanilla Environment: an empty Environment, devoid of Objects, that's ready for you to customize to suit your particular studio setup.

1   From the Layer menu, choose the second Instruments layer.

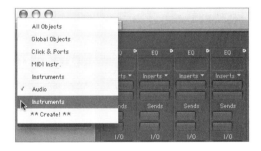

An empty layer fills the Environment.

2 From the Environment's local menu bar, choose Options > Layer > Delete.

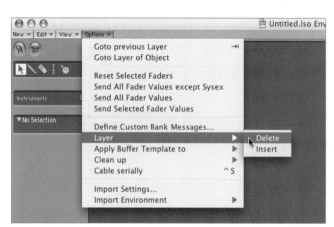

The Instruments layer is deleted, and the Audio layer appears onscreen.

MORE INFO ▶ You can assign a key command to the Delete Layers function. See Lesson 3 for more information.

3 Once again, choose Options > Layer > Delete.

The Audio layer has Objects in it, and an Alert dialog appears to warn you of this fact.

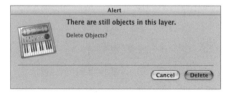

4 In the Alert dialog, click the Delete button.

The Audio layer is deleted.

5 Delete the Instruments, MIDI Instr., and Click & Ports layers.

NOTE ▶ The Global Objects and All Objects layers are reserved layers that cannot be deleted.

The Environment is now empty and ready for customization. But take a quick look at the Arrange window. All of the window's tracks currently say *No Output*. Their track assignments are gone! This raises an important point: *All Arrange window tracks play through Objects in the Environment.* You'll learn a lot more about that as you read through the lesson.

Creating Environment Layers

Now that the Environment is stripped to its bare bones, let's begin building it back up by creating a layer to hold some Objects.

1 From the Layer menu, choose **Create!**

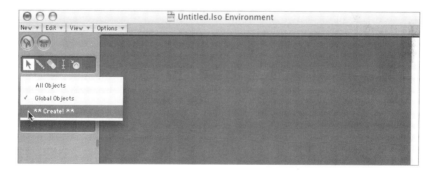

An unnamed Environment layer is created.

2 Double-click the new layer's name in the Layer menu.

A text box opens.

3 Type *Click & Ports,* and press Return.

The layer is named Click & Ports and is now available from the Layer menu anytime you need it.

Creating Objects

Objects process MIDI and audio signals. Most Environment Objects are *channels* that allow MIDI and audio signals to enter and exit Logic. However, some Objects—including the Arpeggiator, Delay Line, and Channel Splitter—are used to process and change signals as they pass through the Environment. Still other Objects, like the Keyboard and Monitor, are helper Objects that graphically display signals as the signals pass through them. Let's create a couple of Objects now.

1 From the Environment's local menu bar, choose New > MIDI Metronome Click.

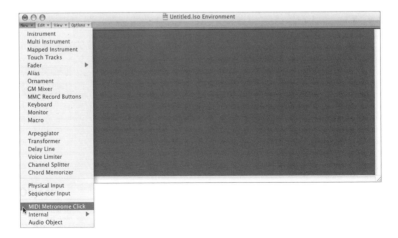

A MIDI Click Object is created in the Click & Ports layer. This Object is responsible for generating the metronome's click, and the metronome will not work if this Object is not present somewhere in your Environment.

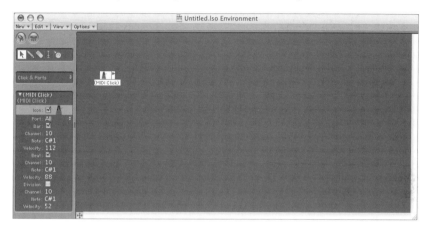

2   Next choose New > Keyboard.

A Keyboard Object is created. The Keyboard is a helper Object that shows you MIDI notes as they are pressed. You'll see just how useful it is a bit later in this lesson. But for now, let's stretch it out so it displays more octaves.

3 Position the pointer over the small box in the bottom right corner of the Keyboard Object, and drag right to make the Keyboard Object bigger.

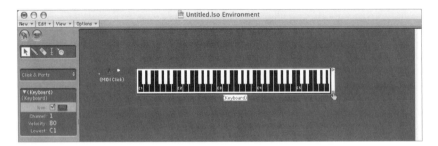

4 Choose New > Monitor.

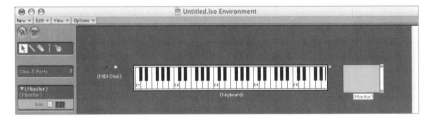

A Monitor Object is created. The Monitor is a helper Object similar to the Keyboard, except it displays the value of any MIDI signal passing through it, and not just notes.

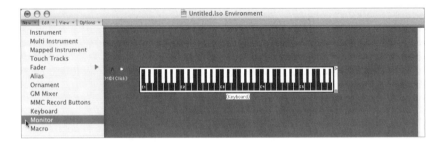

Cabling MIDI Objects Together

Your Environment window currently holds three Objects: a MIDI Click, a Keyboard, and a Monitor. These are all examples of MIDI Objects used to control the flow of MIDI signals. In the top right corner of each Object you'll find a small triangle called the Object's *output*. This output is used to pass the Object's MIDI signals to other Environment Objects through a cable.

In this exercise, you will cable the MIDI Click Object to the Keyboard, and then the Monitor, creating a MIDI signal path that lets you see the MIDI data being produced by the metronome.

1   Click and hold the triangle on the right side of the MIDI Click Object, and drag a cable to the Keyboard Object.

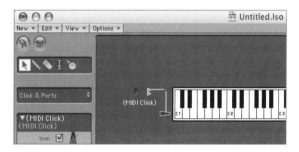

An Alert dialog appears. This dialog tells you that the MIDI Click Object's port is set—in other words, by default the MIDI Click Object is told to send its signal out of your computer's MIDI output ports. You don't need to send the MIDI Click Object's click signal to your external MIDI devices, so let's remove its Port setting.

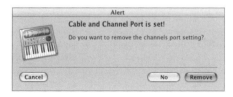

2 On the Alert dialog, click the Remove button.

The MIDI Click Object's Port setting is removed, and the MIDI Click is now cabled to the Keyboard Object.

3 In the Transport, click the Toggle Metronome button to activate the metronome's clicking sound.

4 Press the spacebar to start playback.

Dragging a cable between the MIDI Click and the Keyboard connects these two Objects together. A quick look at the Keyboard shows the MIDI Click is now triggering the Keyboard's C#1 key. This is because the MIDI Click Object is set to transmit a signal on only C#1. A quick look at the Object Parameter box verifies this, and indeed, if you so desire, you can change the notes that the MIDI Click Object transmits.

MIDI Click is set to C#1   C#1 is being triggered

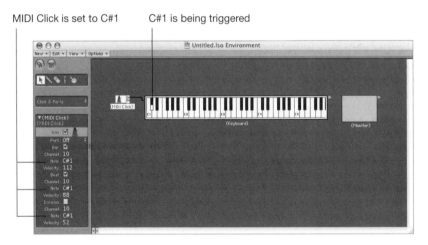

5   Drag a cable from the Keyboard's output to the Monitor Object.

The Monitor Object keeps a list of all MIDI events that enter it. As you've just seen, the MIDI Click is playing the note C#1. These note events are now passing through the Keyboard and into the Monitor Object, which shows a progressing series of C#1 note events.

Because the MIDI Click generates note events, it can also be used to trigger synthesizers.

6   From the Environment's local menu bar, choose New > Internal > Apple QuickTime.

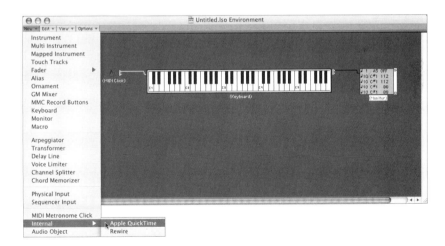

A QuickTime Synth Object appears in the Environment.

NOTE ▶ Apple's QuickTime contains a built-in General MIDI (GM) synthesizer. The Object you've just created is used to trigger that QuickTime synthesizer. The QuickTime Synth provides a convenient way to start making sounds, but it isn't often used for serious music applications. Its audio output is actually outside the Logic program, so you can't bounce its sound as part of your song. In fact, Logic treats the QuickTime Synth Object like an external synthesizer, which for all intents and purposes, it is!

7   Drag a cable from the second arrow on the MIDI Click Object and drop it onto the QuickTime Synth Object.

The QuickTime Synth taps out a rim shot in time with the metronome's click.

8   Select the MIDI Click Object.

9   From the Environment's local menu bar, choose Edit > Clear Cables only (Ctrl-Delete).

The "Clear Cables only" command breaks the selected Object's links to other Environment Objects, so all cables leading from the MIDI Click disappear.

TIP ▶ You can also delete cables by using the Eraser tool, or by dragging a cable back onto the instrument it came from.

10 Press the spacebar to stop playback and halt the clicking sound.

Activating Logic's Sequencer

Logic's Environment is a *virtual representation* of the physical environment in your recording studio. It's the gatekeeper connecting Logic to the outside world, because all data entering or leaving Logic must pass through the Environment. While Logic's Environment does contain some MIDI signal processors that change MIDI data as Logic plays (the Arpeggiator, for example), the Environment primarily listens for incoming MIDI information and also sends MIDI information back out to your synthesizers and samplers.

The Environment you're working in is currently not set up to receive MIDI data. It's missing two important Environment Objects, a Physical Input and a Sequencer Input.

The Physical Input Object   This Object monitors all of your computer's MIDI input ports. If it hears a MIDI signal, the Physical Input grabs that signal and brings it into Logic's Environment.

The Sequencer Input Object   This Object transfers MIDI signals from the Environment to Logic's sequencer. From the sequencer, MIDI signals are directed to the track currently selected in Logic's Arrange window, which allows you to record MIDI Regions or trigger MIDI devices.

NOTE ▶ Logic comes preconfigured to correctly receive MIDI signals, but for the purpose of this exercise, the MIDI input path has been intentionally broken to give you a chance to explore how MIDI passes into Logic from the outside world. Also, please note that you're free to place your Objects anywhere within the Environment window, so your newly created Objects may not appear in the same places as the Objects in the following figures.

Let's create these two Objects and use them to activate the sequencer.

1 From the Environment's local menu bar, choose New > Physical Input.

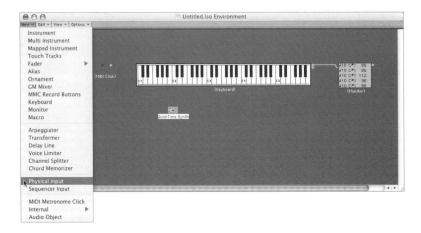

A Physical Input Object appears.

2 Drag the Objects by their names and reorganize the Environment so that it looks like the figure below.

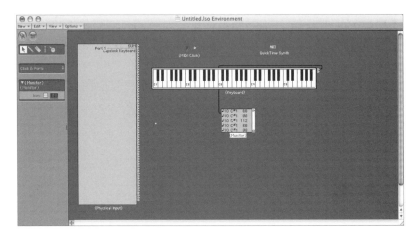

NOTE ▸ In Logic Express, the Physical Input looks like a small rectangle, similar in size to the QuickTime Synth Object.

3 Drag a cable from the Physical Input's SUM output (arrow) and drop it on the QuickTime Synth.

4 Play the controller keyboard connected to your computer.

> **TIP** ▶ If you don't hear sound, try pressing the Caps Lock key to open Logic's Caps Lock Keyboard. If you hear sound when playing the Caps Lock Keyboard but not when playing your MIDI controller, you know the problem is a disrupted MIDI chain outside Logic (try a new MIDI cable, or if you're using a USB keyboard, re-install your keyboard's driver). If you don't hear sound when playing the Caps Lock Keyboard, then the problem is with your audio interface or speakers, because if you've followed these steps correctly, the Caps Lock Keyboard is definitely playing the QuickTime Synth.

MIDI is now passing from the Physical Input straight to the QuickTime Synth, and you hear the sound of a piano. Great! You have just verified that MIDI signals are coming into the Environment through the Physical Input. However, getting MIDI into the Environment is just half the battle; next you need to pass that MIDI into Logic's sequencer.

> **MORE INFO** ▶ The Physical Input's SUM output collects the MIDI signals from all your computer's MIDI ports and combines them. The listings under SUM correspond to the individual MIDI input ports available to your system.

5   From the Environment's local menu bar, choose New > Sequencer Input.

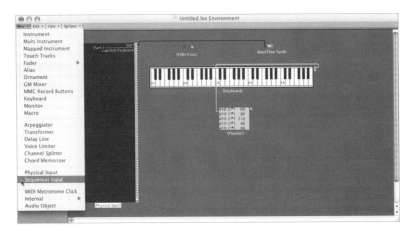

A Sequencer Input Object appears.

6   Drag a cable from the Physical Input's SUM arrow and drop it onto the Sequencer Input.

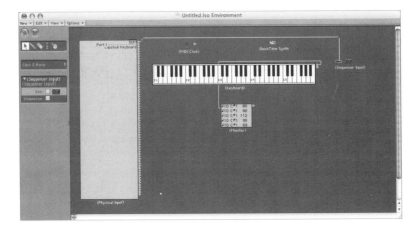

This breaks the connection between the Physical Input and the QuickTime Synth Object, and instead connects the Physical Input to the Sequencer Input. With this cable in place you've just connected Logic's sequencer to the outside world, and Logic can now record MIDI data.

7   Play your keyboard.

Do you hear anything? No. Logic makes no noise, so how do you really know that MIDI data is coming in? The easiest way to find out is to create a quick visual test using the Environment's Keyboard and Monitor Objects.

8   From the Physical Input's SUM arrow, drag a cable to the Keyboard Object.

This breaks the connection between the Physical Input and the Sequencer Input, but only temporarily.

NOTE ▶ The Keyboard Object should still be connected to the Monitor Object. If it isn't, connect it now.

9   Drag a cable from the Monitor to the Sequencer Input.

MIDI events are now coming in through the Physical Input, which sends them down the cable to the Keyboard, Monitor, and finally the Sequencer Input.

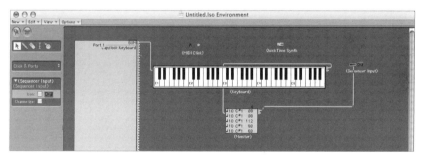

10   Play your controller keyboard.

The keys on the Environment's Keyboard play, and the Monitor updates a list of incoming MIDI events (in this case, notes). But do you hear anything yet? No, because Logic currently has no instruments to play. Let's change that.

Playing an Instrument

With the Sequencer Input connected to the Physical Input, MIDI signals are now passing from the outside world into Logic's Environment, and then through to the sequencer. Using the Arrange window, you can redirect those incoming MIDI signals to any MIDI device connected to your computer, including the QuickTime Synth.

1   Close the Environment window (Cmd-W).

   The Arrange window is now the only one open.

2   In the Arrange window, click and hold the top track on the words *No Output*.

   A hierarchical menu called the Instrument List appears. This list is used to assign Environment Objects to tracks.

3   Choose Click & Ports > QuickTime Synth.

   The track's name changes from MIDI Click to QuickTime Synth.

4   Play your controller keyboard.

   TIP ▶ If you don't hear QuickTime's piano, save your song and quit Logic. Then restart Logic and open the saved song. The QuickTime Synth Object will be re-initialized and should now work properly.

   You hear QuickTime's piano. Great news!

   This experiment reaffirms the important point brought up earlier: *All Arrange window tracks play through Objects in the Environment.* But we'll continue exploring that later. There's a lot more to learn about the Environment, so let's open it back up.

5   To open the Environment window once again, press Cmd-8.

Moving Objects Between Layers

Earlier you saw how the Environment uses layers to hold Objects. How you organize your Environment layers is up to you—any Object can be placed on any layer. But as a general rule of thumb, Objects of the same type are usually placed on the same layer. For example, so far in this lesson you've been working in the Click & Ports layer. This layer holds a MIDI Click Object that clicks and Input Objects that connect Logic's sequencer to your computer's MIDI input ports: Click & Ports!

Earlier in this lesson you created a QuickTime Synth Object on the Click & Ports layer. The QuickTime Synth Object is not a MIDI Click or a port—it's an instrument! So it makes a bit more sense to put the QuickTime Synth on a different layer.

1   Click and hold the Layer menu, and choose **Create!**

> **TIP** You can also create Environment layers by choosing Options > Layer > Insert (from the Environment's local menu bar). And don't forget, if you create too many layers, you can delete the unnecessary ones by choosing Options > Layer > Delete.

An unnamed layer is created. Unnamed layers don't tell you much about the Objects they hold. In a moment you will transfer the QuickTime Synth Object to this layer, so give the layer an appropriate name.

2   Double-click the Layer menu.

A text input field appears. Type *QT Synth,* and press Return.

3 Click and hold the Layer menu, and reselect the Click & Ports layer.

4 In the Click & Ports layer, select the QuickTime Synth Object.

5 Hold down the Option key, then from the Layer menu select the QT Synth layer.

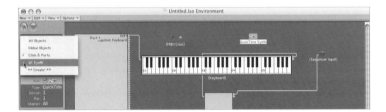

The QuickTime Synth layer appears, and the QuickTime Synth Object automatically jumps to its new home.

TIP You can also cut (Cmd-X) and paste (Cmd-V) Objects between Environment layers.

6 Select the Click & Ports layer one last time.

Notice that the QuickTime Synth Object is now gone from the Click & Ports layer.

Creating a Standard Instrument

Synthesizers have come a long way in the 20 years since MIDI became standard on all keyboards. In the early days of computer music, most synthesizers were *mono-timbral*, which means they could send and receive MIDI data only over a single MIDI channel. By today's standards those early synths were MIDI challenged, to say the least! But even today some digital-effects units use only a single MIDI channel, so to simplify using these MIDI devices in your songs, Logic provides the *Standard Instrument Object.*

The Standard Instrument transmits MIDI data over just one channel, which makes it perfect for connecting to an external mono-timbral MIDI device such as a Lexicon Alex reverb, so this lesson shows you how to set up this reverb in Logic. If you have an external mono-timbral MIDI device, follow this section's steps by substituting your device for the Lexicon Alex reverb used here. Even if you don't have a mono-timbral MIDI device at hand, you should still work through this exercise, because it covers MIDI ports and Object icons, which are important parameters common to all Logic instruments. (When you're finished with this exercise, just delete the newly created Standard Instrument Object.)

1   Create an Environment layer and name it *MIDI Instruments.* Press Return.

By the end of the lesson, this layer will hold Instrument Objects that point to all of your studio's MIDI devices. Begin the process now by creating a Standard Instrument.

2   From the Environment's local menu bar, select New > Instrument.

A Standard Instrument is created.

3   In the Object Parameter box, click the instrument's name to open a text entry box, and type the name of the MIDI device this Instrument Object represents. Press Return.

Setting an Instrument's MIDI Port and Channel

The Instrument Object's Port setting connects it directly to one of your computer's MIDI ports. All MIDI ports are available.

NOTE ▶ By now, your studio's MIDI devices should be connected to your computer. If not, take a moment to connect them. Pay particular attention to which of your computer's MIDI ports you plug each device in to, because you'll need to know this to correctly set up your instruments inside Logic.

1   From the Object Parameter box's Port setting, click and hold the menu option All, and select the MIDI In port connecting this Standard Instrument to its MIDI device.

MIDI data flows through MIDI ports in *channels,* and up to 16 separate MIDI channels can pass through each port at the same time. However, mono-timbral MIDI devices can receive data on only one MIDI channel at a time, so you must set the Standard Instrument Object's MIDI channel to match the MIDI channel of the device it represents.

2   From the Object Parameter box's MIDI Channel setting, double-click the number 1 and enter the MIDI channel that your mono-timbral MIDI device is set to receive on.

NOTE ▶ You can also click and drag the MIDI Channel setting to quickly increase or decrease its value.

Selecting an Object Icon

An Object icon provides a visual reminder of an Object's purpose. Logic contains many high-resolution instrument icons that look great and help you tell at a glance exactly which instrument is which (this Object icon also shows up in the Arrange window's Track column after you assign the Object to a track). You don't have to select an icon for every Object you create, but it's a quick and easy way to make your workspace a little nicer—and more personalized!

1   In the Object Parameter box, click the Instrument icon. Press Return.

An Icon menu appears.

2   Select a graphic to represent your instrument. Press Return.

TIP ▶ Logic's instrument icons are stored inside the Logic application package. If you Ctrl-click the application package in the Finder window and choose Show Package Contents from the pop-up menu that appears, you can tunnel down into the application package contents and find these icons.

MORE INFO ▸ Using Adobe Photoshop, you can create your own custom icons and add them to same folder as the other icons in the application package. Back in Logic, your custom instrument icons will be available from the Instrument Icon menu, just like any of the default icons. All custom icons must be 128-by-128-pixel PNG files, saved with an alpha channel so you can see through the parts around the icon. Additionally, you must name the icons with numbers that are not already taken by one of Logic's default icons (unless you want to replace those icons).

Creating a Multi Instrument

Multi Instrument Objects are designed to represent *multi-timbral* MIDI devices: devices that send and receive MIDI signals over many channels at once. Almost all modern synthesizers and samplers can do this, so unless you collect vintage synthesizers, this is the Instrument Object you'll use most while working with Logic.

To demonstrate how a Multi Instrument works, this exercise sets up a Novation Supernova, but feel free to use any multi-timbral synthesizer connected to your computer.

1 From the Environment's local menu bar, choose New > Multi Instrument.

A Multi Instrument is created.

2   From the Environment's toolbox, select the Text tool.

3   On the Multi Instrument Object, click the Multi Instrument's name and type the name of the MIDI device this Object will transmit MIDI signals to, then press Return.

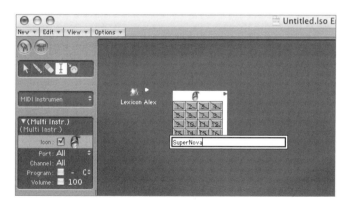

4   In the Object Parameter box, click and hold the word *All* (located directly to the right of the word *Port*), and select the MIDI port that this Multi Instrument will transmit MIDI data through.

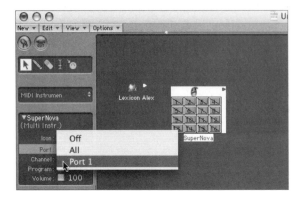

5   In the Object Parameter box, click the Instrument icon and select a graphic to represent your instrument.

A dialog appears asking if you'd like to change the icon for all subchannels.

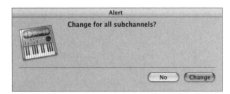

6   You will explore subchannels in the next exercise, so for now click Change.

Logic assigns the selected icon to the Multi Instrument and to all of its subchannels.

Activating Subchannels

Multi-timbral instruments can use several MIDI channels at the same time. To give you access to those multiple channels, the Multi Instrument provides 16 small buttons representing its subchannels. Button 1 equals MIDI channel 1, button 2 equals MIDI channel 2, and so on.

1   In the Object Parameter box, you'll notice the instrument's Channel parameter is currently set to All. Leave this setting untouched.

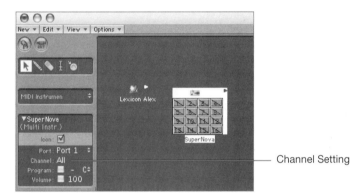

With the Channel parameter set to All, this Multi Instrument will transmit on all 16 MIDI channels—but in a very particular way: Subchannel 1 (button 1 on the Multi Instrument) transmits through MIDI channel 1 of the instrument's port, subchannel 2 transmits through MIDI channel 2 of the instrument's port, and so on.

2   From the toolbox, select the Arrow tool and click the subchannel buttons until you've enabled all the MIDI channels over which your multi-timbral MIDI device is able to receive MIDI signals.

Clicking a subchannel removes the strike through it and enables it. You can now select this subchannel from the Arrange window's Instrument List and assign it to a track.

Using Instruments

This exercise walks you through setting up and playing a Multi Instrument and then finishes by showing you how to use programs to select synthesizer sounds.

If you don't have an external synthesizer, don't worry—the QuickTime Synth you created earlier is a multi-timbral MIDI device! Even though the QuickTime Synth is software on your computer, it works just like any other multi-timbral synthesizer and provides a good example of how to use Multi Instruments. Work through this exercise using the QuickTime Synth, and then apply what you've learned to setting up Multi Instruments for your other multi-timbral MIDI devices.

Setting Up a Multi Instrument

1   In the Environment, select the QT Synth layer.

2   Create a Multi Instrument, and name it *QuickTime GM*.

3   Enable subchannels 1–16 (by clicking all the buttons on the Multi Instrument's surface).

4   From the Output arrow in the Multi Instrument's top right corner, drag a cable to the QuickTime Synth Object.

This arrow represents the Multi Instrument's MIDI output. Dragging a cable from this output to another Environment Object creates a MIDI signal path. All MIDI data passing through the Multi Instrument will now go directly to the QuickTime Synth Object.

5   Logic asks if you want to remove the Port setting. Select Remove.

You want this Multi Instrument to send MIDI data to the QuickTime Synth only. Clicking Remove turns the Multi Instrument's Port setting off, and MIDI data will now transmit only through the virtual cable to the QuickTime Synth Object.

6   Select the QuickTime GM Multi Instrument.

In the Instrument Parameter box, the QuickTime GM Multi Instrument's Port setting is now off. Again, this means the Multi Instrument sends no MIDI data to any of your computer's MIDI ports. Instead, all MIDI data is transferred through the cable to the QuickTime Synth Object.

Port setting is off

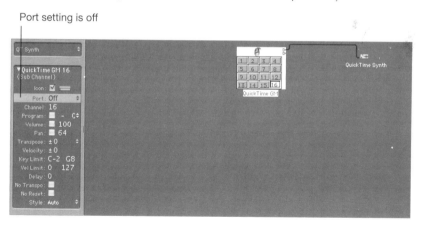

This Multi Instrument is now set to play the QuickTime Synth only. But first, you must assign the Multi Instrument to one of the Arrange window's tracks, using the Instrument List.

Playing an Instrument

Arrange window tracks and Environment Objects are two hands that play together to make sound. In previous exercises you've seen there's a direct relationship between Arrange window tracks and Environment Objects, because double-clicking a track's name in the Arrange window pops open the Environment and automatically selects an Object. This selected Object is called the track's *Output Object*, and you assign it to the track using the Arrange window's Instrument List.

The Instrument List

The Instrument List is a hierarchical menu that determines which Environment Object a track plays through. It operates via several levels: The first level displays your Environment's layers, the second level lists the types of Objects on each layer, and the third level displays each Object's channel(s).

1   Click the Arrange window to make it the active window.

2   Click and hold the left side of the QuickTime Synth track's name to open the Arrange window's Instrument List.

3   From the hierarchical menu that appears, choose QT Synth > QuickTime GM > 1 (Grand Piano).

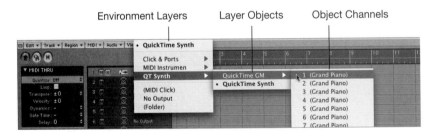

The Instrument List's Objects level shows the QuickTime Synth Object along with the QuickTime GM Multi Instrument. Notice that the QuickTime Synth Object is highlighted in bold letters, which indicates that it's the currently selected Object. From now on you will use the QuickTime GM Multi Instrument to target specific channels in the QuickTime Synth. To avoid clutter and make things easy to find, you will want to remove the QuickTime Synth from the Instrument List.

4   Switch back to the Environment window.

5   Select the QuickTime Synth Object.

6   In the Object Parameter box, deselect the QuickTime Synth's Icon check box.

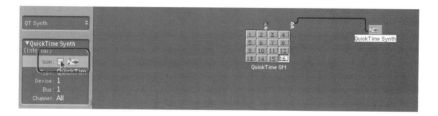

The Arrange window's Instrument List shows only the Objects with ticked check boxes. By deselecting the Icon check box, you tell Logic to remove the QuickTime Synth from the Instrument List.

NOTE ▸ On a Multi Instrument, the slash through each subchannel button is similar to the check box beside the Object icon. Enabling a subchannel makes it available for selection in the Instrument List, while disabling a subchannel removes it from the Instrument List.

7   Make the Arrange window the active window (press the 1 key).

8   Click and hold the left side of the QuickTime Synth track name and check
     out the Instrument List.

The QuickTime Synth Object is no longer displayed on the Instrument
List's Objects level.

9   Play your controller keyboard.

The QuickTime Synth still sounds like a piano—exactly the same as
before! To change this you can select a different instrument sound using
the Object Parameter box's Program setting.

Using Programs to Select Sounds

Programs are sounds on your synthesizer. One of the most creativity-draining
parts of making music is reaching over to select programs on hardware synthesizers, or switching between windows to control your software instruments.
Logic is designed to enhance your creativity by making music production easy,
and it happily lets you select synthesizer programs from right inside its workspace (no need to take your eyes off the screen).

Effectively using instrument programs turns your studio into an extension of
Logic itself, because selected programs are saved into your song. Session after
session, just turn your MIDI devices on, open your song, and Logic automatically sets up your synthesizers by telling them which programs to play.

1   In the Object Parameter box on the left edge of the Arrange window, click
     the Program check box.

Program selection is now enabled.

2   To the right of the Program parameter's check box, click and hold the
number 0.

The Program menu appears.

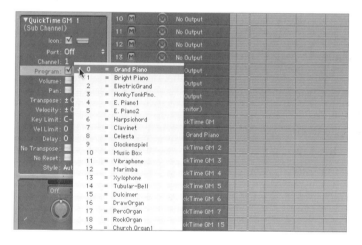

3   Choose program 49 (Slow Strings).

4   Play your controller keyboard.

You now hear a string patch. Choose a few more programs and try out
their sounds.

Automatically Recalling Programs at Song Launch

To make sure that programs are recalled and properly loaded into your synthesizer when the song is opened, you need to make one final setting.

1   Choose File > Song Settings > MIDI.

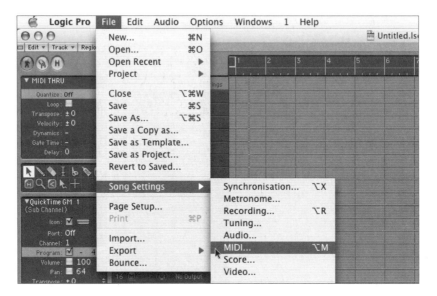

The Song Settings dialog opens to display the MIDI pane's General tab.

2   In the Miscellaneous section of the General tab, select both the "Used
instrument MIDI settings" and the "All fader values" check boxes.

Now, when you open the song, Logic automatically loads the correct programs into your synthesizers and sets their volume and pan positions to
the same levels as when you last saved and closed the song. This sets up
your synths to play the proper patches so that your songs sound the same,
session after session after session.

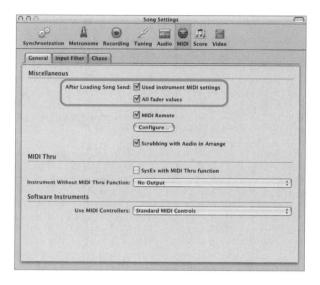

Customizing the Program List

Logic's default program list represents the GM sound set. The QuickTime Synth also uses the GM sound set, and Logic's default program names conveniently match the QuickTime Synth's sounds. That's great for the QuickTime Synth, but the reality is that most synthesizers don't conform to the GM sound set. To make the names in the program list match the names of your synth's programs, you must modify the program list.

1   At the top of the Arrange window's Object Parameter box, click the Object's name.

MORE INFO ▶ Some synthesizer manufacturers have a download section on their Web sites where you can find Logic projects containing preconfigured instruments. When customizing your program lists, these files save you from having to type program names by hand.

A window opens showing the programs in the GM sound set. The program currently used is selected.

NOTE ▶ You can also open this window from the Environment window by double-clicking the small Instrument icon at the top of a Multi Instrument Object.

2   Double-click a program name.

A text box appears around the program's name.

3   Type a new program name into the text box and press Return.

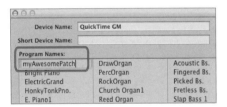

4   Work through the program list until you've changed all programs to the names used by your synthesizer.

5   If your synthesizer has more than one bank of sounds, choose bank 1 from the Bank Select menu.

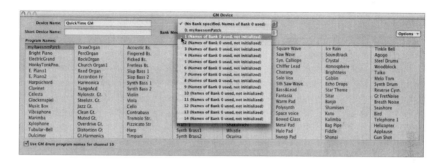

Logic asks if you'd like to initialize the new bank.

6   Choose Initialize.

NOTE ▶ Initialize new banks only when absolutely necessary, as each new bank adds to your project file's size.

7   Follow steps 2 to 4 to enter the program names for this new bank.

8   To select the new bank, choose it by number from the Object Parameter box's Bank Select menu, which currently looks like a hyphen (-) beside the Program parameter's check box.

9   Close the GM Device window.

Finishing Your MIDI Environment

To finish setting up your MIDI Environment, create Standard or Multi Instrument Objects to represent every MIDI device in your studio. If your studio is small and has only a few MIDI devices, you can probably remember which MIDI port and channel(s) each device is connected to. But if your studio is more complex, using many MIDI devices connected to several MIDI ports, you'll benefit from compiling a studio inventory.

MIDI DEVICE CHART

MIDI Device	Port		MIDI Channels															
			1	2	3	4	5	6	7	8	9	10	12	11	13	14	15	16
Novation Supernova	MT4 1	In	X	X	X	X	X	X	X	X								
		Out	X	X	X	X	X	X	X	X								
Yamaha A3000	MT4 2	In	X	X	X	X	X	X	X	X								
		Out	X	X	X	X	X	X	X	X								
Lexicon Alex	MT4 3	In	X															
		Out																
Sequential Multi-Trak	MT4 4	In	X															
		Out																
Unity Session	Internal	In	X	X	X	X	X	X	X	X	X	X	X	X	X	X	X	X
		Out																
		In																
		Out																
		In																
		Out																
		In																
		Out																
		In																
		Out																
		In																
		Out																

Sample of a MIDI device chart to reflect the instruments in a project studio

A studio inventory is simply a chart that lists each of your MIDI devices, the MIDI ports that connect each device to your computer, and the MIDI channel(s) they are set to receive and transmit on. You can find a studio inventory chart on this book's companion DVD-ROM.

1 From the Finder window, navigate to Lesson 11 Project Files > 11 Extras > **MIDIDeviceChart.pdf.** Open and print the file.

2   Fill out the chart.

3   Refer to this studio inventory while creating Instrument Objects for each MIDI device in your studio.

Depending on the complexity of your MIDI setup, this may take some time. But you only need to do it once. In the next exercise you will save this custom Environment as your personal Autoload Song, and it will serve as a template from which you'll begin all new Logic compositions.

Creating an Autoload Song

Over the course of this lesson, you've filled Logic's Environment with Instrument Objects that reflect the MIDI devices in your studio. You've created MIDI Input Objects to channel MIDI signals into Logic, and Instrument Objects to send MIDI signals back out to your MIDI devices, and you've arranged all of the Environment's Objects on their own layers, which makes them easier to find when needed. Only one step remains, and that's saving the "song" you've built as your own personal Autoload Song. Each time you start Logic or create a new project, the Autoload Song will automatically open on your screen, providing you with a blank workspace perfectly configured to get you making music.

1   Make sure the Arrange window is the only window open on your screen.

You'll want to start new songs from the Arrange window, so it's best to save the Autoload Song with only the Arrange window open. This ensures that the Arrange window is the first one to appear onscreen each time you open Logic or create a new song by choosing File > New (Cmd-N).

2   In the Arrange window, delete all of the tracks except for the first eight.

3   Use the vertical zoom control to make the tracks bigger.

The look of the Arrange window is saved with the Autoload Song, so it's important to set up the Arrange window exactly the way you want it.

4   Choose File > Save As.

The Save As dialog opens.

The Autoload file needs to be saved in a very particular place on your hard disk, with the exact name *Autoload,* so follow the next steps carefully.

5   Type *Autoload* into the Save As field.

The file you save *must* be called exactly Autoload, or Logic will not recognize it as the Autoload Song.

6   Navigate to your User > Library > Application Support > Logic > Song Templates folder.

For Logic to recognize the Autoload Song, it must be located in this exact folder. If the Autoload Song is moved out of this folder, new projects will use the default workspace, so make sure you save your Autoload Song in the right place.

NOTE ▶   If you follow the steps above, your Autoload Song will be available only to you. To create a global Autoload Song that is available to all users, save the Autoload Song in the Startup Disk > Library > Application Support > Logic > Song Templates folder.

7   Click Save.

8　Choose File > Close to close the song.

9　Choose File > New to create a new song.

The New dialog appears.

10　Make sure both the Use Song Template and Create Project Folder check boxes are not selected, and click OK.

The Autoload Song opens on your screen. You've now successfully set up the MIDI side of the Autoload Song. In Lesson 12, "Setting Up the Audio Environment," you will configure the audio side. Are you excited?

What You've Learned

▶　To get MIDI data into Logic, the Environment must have a Physical Input cabled to a Sequencer Input.

▶　To make things easier to find, Logic's Environment is organized into layers holding similar Objects.

▶　Standard Instrument Objects point to mono-timbral MIDI devices that use only one MIDI channel.

▶　Multi Instrument Objects point to multi-timbral MIDI devices that use up to 16 MIDI channels. The buttons on the Multi Instrument's surface represent each of the 16 available subchannels.

▶　By using the Instrument Object's Program parameter to select instrument sounds, you ensure that the correct synthesizer programs are saved with your song and then properly recalled every time the song is opened.

▶　The Autoload Song contains customized Instrument Objects that reflect the setup of your personal studio.

▶　For Logic to recognize the Autoload Song, it must be saved in the User > Library > Application Support > Logic > Song Templates folder.

12

Lesson 12

Setting Up the Audio Environment

In Lesson 11, "Setting Up the MIDI Environment," you learned that Objects form the connections between Logic and the rest of your studio. For example, MIDI signals enter and exit Logic through Instrument Objects in Logic's Environment. Audio is handled much the same way, and before Logic will record or play sound, you must populate the Environment with Audio Objects that connect Logic to your computer's audio interface.

Configuring Audio Hardware and Drivers

To get sound into and out of your computer, you must have an *audio interface.* An audio interface is a device that converts digital audio from your computer to analog waves that speakers can broadcast. In the other direction, an audio interface converts analog waves into digital audio you can save and manipulate on your computer. Either way, an audio interface has only one purpose: It converts sound between the digital and analog domains.

> **MORE INFO** ▶ The audio interface that comes with your computer is sufficient for using Logic, but it offers only a stereo eighth-inch input and a stereo eighth-inch output. These connections are usually reserved for attaching headphones to your computer or for basic recording purposes. They do not offer professional sound quality.

To communicate with its audio interface, a computer needs a small software application called a *driver.* All audio interfaces have their own special drivers, and in most cases you'll have to install that driver before Logic will recognize it. But once that driver's installed, there's very little else you need to do. Logic will automatically recognize your audio interface along with all available inputs and outputs (most audio interface manufacturers have a support section on their Web sites where you can download drivers).

However, situations might arise where Logic unexpectedly uses the wrong audio interface. For example, if Logic starts playing from the speaker on your computer, it's using your computer's built-in audio controller instead of your audio interface. Fortunately, this situation is easy to fix—just select your audio interface's driver from Logic's Audio Drivers Preferences pane.

> **NOTE** ▶ Logic's Core Audio represents a massive step forward for audio on the Macintosh. In OS X, several applications can stably share a single audio interface at the same time. For example, you can now play a Logic arrangement, preview a video in QuickTime, and audition Apple Loops in iTunes—all at the same time!

Selecting an Audio Driver

1   Open the Autoload Song you saved at the end of the previous lesson.

> **NOTE** ▶ If you don't have this file, you can follow along using the file
> named **12Begin.lso,** located in the APTS_Logic_7 > Song Files > Lesson
> 12 Project Files folder.

2   Choose Audio > Audio Hardware & Drivers.

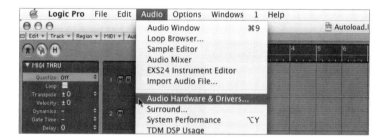

The Audio Drivers Preferences pane opens. The Core Audio tab is automatically selected, and Logic will choose either the built-in audio driver
or your audio interface from the Driver menu.

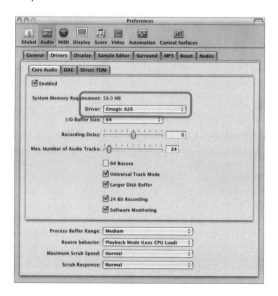

If you have more than one audio interface attached to your system, you can choose a different interface from the one that Logic has automatically selected.

3   From the Driver menu, choose the audio interface you want to use.

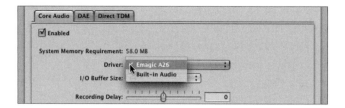

If you selected a different audio interface from the one Logic automatically chose, you will be presented with a new dialog that asks you to reboot Logic.

4   Click Try (Re)Launch.

You do not actually need to reboot Logic, because the audio interfaces can switch in the background while Logic remains open.

Increasing Available Audio Tracks

By default, Logic gives you 24 audio track channels. If you need more, you can increase this number using the Max. Number of Audio Tracks setting in the Audio Drivers Preferences pane.

1   If you closed the Audio Drivers Preferences pane, reopen it now by choosing Audio > Audio Hardware & Drivers.

The Audio Drivers Preferences pane opens. In the middle of the Core Audio tab is a preference that says Max. Number of Audio Tracks.

2   Set this number to the number of audio tracks you'd like to make available.

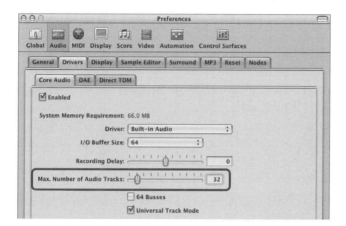

For Logic to lock in this change in the maximum number of audio tracks, you need to relaunch the Core Audio driver.

3   In the top left corner of the Core Audio tab, click the Enabled check box to disable Core Audio.

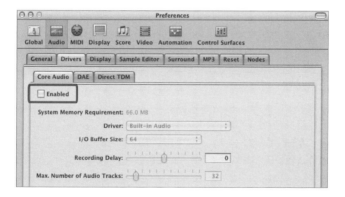

4   Click the Enabled check box a second time to reenable Core Audio.

Once again an Alert pops open to tell you to reboot Logic.

5 Click the Try (Re)Launch button.

Core Audio is reenabled, and you now have access to the number of tracks you specified in the Max. Number of Audio Tracks preference.

6 Close the Preferences window.

Exploring the Audio Configuration Window (Logic Pro Only)

A *channel* is a path used to transport a signal. Lesson 4, "Editing Audio Regions," demonstrated how MIDI channels transport MIDI signals between your studio's MIDI devices and Logic. Audio channels are similar, but instead of sending MIDI messages to a synthesizer, audio channels transport sound to and from your audio interface's outputs and inputs.

Audio channels can also be used to move audio around inside Logic. Busses, which transmit audio from Object to Object inside Logic, are channels. Audio tracks are also channels, but a very special type that reads audio files off the hard disk(s) and sends them to an output or records audio files from an input and saves them on your hard disk(s). To see an overview of the audio channels available on your system, check out the Audio Configuration window.

1 Select Audio > Audio Configuration.

The Audio Configuration window opens.

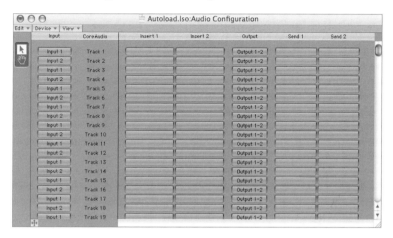

2   Scroll down the Audio Configuration window to see a list of your system's available audio channels. (The audio channels are listed in the Audio Confguration window's CoreAudio column.)

3   Using the descriptions that follow as a reference, check out the types of channels available for your system.

The types of channels that may appear for your system include the following:

Inputs   Input channels represent the physical audio inputs of your audio interface.

Tracks   Track channels record audio to your computer's hard disks and also play back recorded audio files.

Bus   Bus channels move sound from channel to channel inside Logic. For example, you can send sound from several channels into the same bus, then insert a real-time effect (such as a reverb) on that bus. This lets you use a single reverb on several tracks at the same time.

Instruments   Using any of Logic's software instruments, Instrument channels transform MIDI information into audio signals that are transmitted to your audio interface's outputs.

NOTE ▶ Don't modify Instrument channel 128. Logic automatically inserts the Klopfgeist synthesizer on Instrument channel 128 and assigns it to the MIDI Click Object. (*Klopfgeist* is German for "knocking ghost.") If you remove Klopfgeist from Instrument channel 128, your metronome won't make a sound!

Aux Aux channels are similar to inputs but can also receive signals from busses, making them perfect for creating submixes.

Outputs Output channels represent the individual physical outputs of your audio interface.

Stereo Inputs and Outputs Stereo Input and Output channels are stereo versions of the standard inputs and outputs.

Master The Master channel is a global volume control for all output channels.

Working with Plug-ins in the Audio Configuration Window

The Audio Configuration window's primary advantage over other editing windows is that it provides a single page where you can examine the plug-ins inserted into your tracks. But even more important, you can move the plug-ins from insert to insert, either in the same channel or to entirely different channels. This works great in situations where, for example, you realize you need your delay after the compressor, instead of before. Just open the Audio Configuration window and move the inserted plug-ins where you want them.

1 Click and hold the Insert 1 slot on Track 1.

The hierarchical plug-in menu appears.

2 Choose any plug-in you like.

The plug-in is inserted and a plug-in window opens. Interestingly, the plug-in window is empty! The reason? This song currently has no Audio Track 1 Object set up in its Environment, so there's no channel to hold the plug-in. You'll create this Object in a moment, but for now, let's work with this empty plug-in.

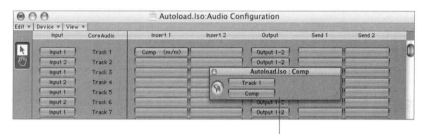

Empty Plug-in Window

3 From the Audio Configuration window's toolbox, select the Move tool.

TIP There are only two tools in the Audio Configuration window. If you select the Arrow tool and then press the Command key, you'll engage the secondary tool, which is the Move tool. Then you can Command-drag plug-ins to move them from insert to insert. And if you press Option-Cmd as you drag, you can copy plug-ins to any new location.

4   Grab the plug-in you've just inserted, and drag it to the second Insert slot in Track 1.

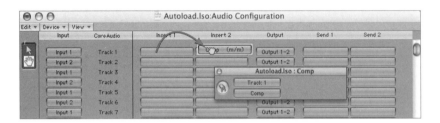

The plug-in jumps to the new slot! Keep this trick in mind when you want to reorder your DSP plug-ins. For now, let's clear this plug-in out of the channel strip and continue exploring audio objects.

5   Click and hold the insert slot containing the plug-in.

A hierarchical Plug-In menu appears.

6   Choose No plug-in.

The plug-in is removed from the insert slot.

7   Close the Audio Configuration window and the empty plug-in window.

Using Audio Objects

The channels listed in the Audio Configuration window are always available and ready for use—but first you have to assign them to Audio Objects. The Audio Object itself initializes the channel and then acts as a virtual channel strip that you can use to control the channel's sound. Audio Objects are the last link that connects Logic to your audio interface, and their primary function is to show Logic where and how to send audio signals.

Creating and Populating an Audio Layer

In Lesson 11 you created a couple of new Environment layers to hold MIDI Instrument Objects. Now, it's time to make a new Environment layer for Audio Objects and create your first one.

1   Press Cmd-8 to open the Environment window.

The Environment window opens and displays the layer that was onscreen the last time you used the Environment.

2   From the Environment's Layer menu, choose **Create!**

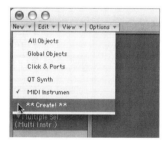

An unnamed layer is created.

3   On the Layer menu, double-click the word *(unnamed)* to open a text box, then name the layer *Audio.*

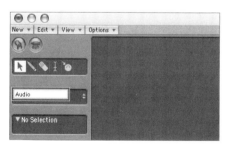

4   From the Environment's local menu bar, choose New > Audio Object.

TIP You can (and should!) assign a key command to create new Audio Objects. Check out the Environment Window section of the Key Commands window. Cmd-Ctrl-A (A for "Audio Object") is a good choice.

An unnamed Audio Object appears in the Environment's Audio layer. This Object looks like a little rectangular icon.

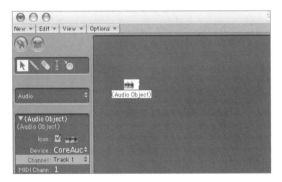

5 Double-click the new Audio Object icon.

The Object expands into a channel strip!

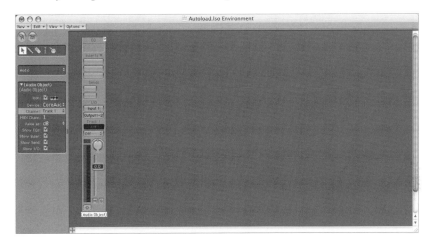

This is called the *channel view,* and it looks just like a channel strip on a standard hardware mixing console. The channel view provides an interface to control and manipulate a channel's sound by boosting or attenuating (lowering) the volume, changing a sound's pan position, and inserting digital signal processing (DSP) effects.

TIP Audio Objects can be reduced by double-clicking the top left corner of an Object that is in channel view.

Exploring Audio Object Parameters

Audio Objects are the chameleons of Logic. An Audio Object can assume the form of any audio channel available to your system—a track channel, an Audio Instrument channel, a bus, or an output. It's up to you to determine what each Audio Object will be, and you do so by specifying which channel the Audio Object will play out of. This is the single most important concept about Audio Objects, so let's create an audio track, an Audio Instrument, a bus, and an Output Object to see how it works.

1   In the Environment's Object Parameter box, click and hold the word *Track 1* (to the right of the Channel parameter).

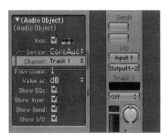

A hierarchical menu opens to display a list of available channels.

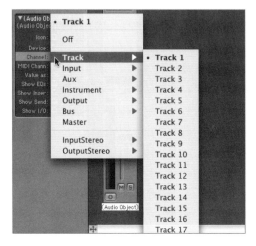

NOTE ▶ Items in boldface indicate that the channel is assigned to an Audio Object in the Environment. In the example, only Track 1 is assigned to an Audio Object, so only Track 1 is bold.

2   Leave the Channel parameter set to Track 1.

The Audio Object has been named *(Audio Object)*. That doesn't tell you very much about its function, and in fact, it's best to give all Objects descriptive names that indicate the type of channel the Audio Object represents, such as *electric guitar* or *lead vocal*.

TIP ▶ Names in parentheses are provided by Logic. If you see such a name, it's a good idea to change it to something more descriptive of the Object's purpose.

3   At the top of the Object Parameter box, click the words *(Audio Object)*, and name the Audio Object *Track 1*.

4   Create a new Audio Object and expand it to the channel view.

5   This time, from the Object Parameter box's Channel menu, choose Instrument > Instrument 1.

The Audio Object becomes an Audio Instrument channel.

6   Name the Object *Inst 1*.

7   Click and hold the channel's Input slot, and assign an Audio Instrument.

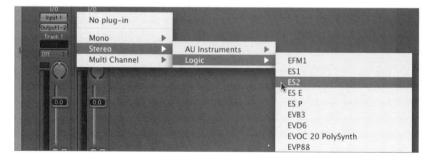

The Audio Instrument opens in a plug-in window.

8   Close the Instrument plug-in window.

9   Create a new Audio Object and expand it to the channel view.

10 From the Object Parameter box's Channel menu, choose Bus > Bus 1.

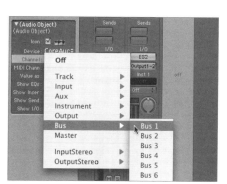

11 Name the Object *Bus 1*.

12 Create a new Audio Object and expand it to the channel view.

13 From the Object Parameter box's Channel menu, choose OutputStereo > Output 1-2.

14 Name the Object *Output 1-2*.

Voilà! You now have four Audio Objects, and each is assigned to a different audio channel. As you can see, it's very easy to create exactly the type and number of Audio Objects you need for your unique way of making music.

Looking at the Channel View

Let's take a moment to check out the channel view and find out what it lets you do.

The Channel View Areas

We'll start with the five areas of the channel view.

> **NOTE ▶** Some audio channels do not have all five of the areas discussed below. For example, the Master channel has only a Fader Area, while Bus channels lack Send slots.

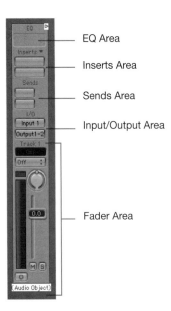

EQ Area

Inserts Area

Sends Area

Input/Output Area

Fader Area

The EQ Area Double-clicking the gray box directly below the word *EQ* reveals an equalizer with spectrum analyzer. With the exception of a Master channel, each channel may have its very own dedicated EQ to boost or attenuate specific frequency ranges in the channel's sound.

The Inserts Area The Inserts area assigns DSP effects such as dynamic range compression and delay to a channel's sound.

The Sends Area The Sends area sends the channel's sound to a system bus, which transports the sound to a different channel in Logic.

The Input/Output Area The I/O area sets the channel's input and output path. Depending on the type of channel assigned to the Audio Object, the input can be an audio interface input, a bus, or one of Logic's software instruments.

The Fader Area The Fader area sets the channel's volume and pan position and also has Mute and Solo buttons. The Mute button turns off the channel's sound, while the Solo button turns off the sound of all channels other than the one being soloed (you will also hear other channels whose Solo function is enabled).

Setting Audio Object Parameters

Now, let's zoom in on the box to the left of the channel view that shows the settings for the Audio Object parameters.

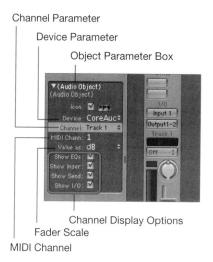

NOTE ► Logic Express users do not have Channel Display Options.

Device (Audio Driver and Interface) The Device parameter selects a driver and, in turn, an audio interface for the audio channel to use. Unless you changed this driver in the exercise at the beginning of this lesson, this parameter will say Core Audio.

Channel (Audio Channel) The Channel parameter sets the Audio Object's channel. By default, new Objects are assigned to the first unused track channel, but you can use this setting to assign the Object to any channel that Logic has available.

MIDI Chann (MIDI Channel) Back in the good old days of Logic, before we had such awesome track automation built into the program, to automate Audio Objects you had to use MIDI. And you can still do so. The MIDI Chann setting determines from which MIDI channel the Object receives controller information such as volume or pan.

Fader Scale (Value as) Value as changes the scale of the Object's fader between decibels (dB) or numbers similar to the volume settings on a MIDI synthesizer (0–127).

Channel Display Options (Logic Pro only) Channel display options show or hide the selected channel's EQ, Insert, Send, and I/O slots.

Finishing the Autoload Song

You're about to save your finished Autoload Song. But first it's important to create enough Audio Objects to get you quickly making music whenever you start a new song. You'll also want to make sure there are a few tracks ready to go in the Arrange window. Let's add three more Audio Track Objects and three more Audio Instrument Objects.

1   Create three Audio Track Objects and three Audio Instrument Objects (you will have a total of four of each Object).

2   Name your Objects appropriately, and arrange them in the order shown in the figure below. Don't worry about placing them in exact positions; you'll use a special command in the next step to clean up the Audio layer and align all the Objects.

3   Press Cmd-A to select all the Objects on the Audio layer.

4   From the Environment's local menu bar, choose Options > Clean up > Align Objects.

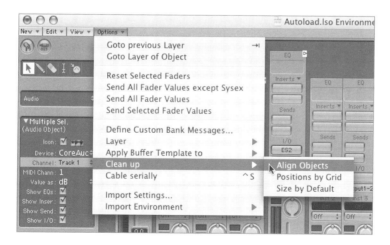

The Audio Objects align in a straight row. Now that the Environment looks pretty and organized, let's turn our focus to the Arrange window.

5   Close the Environment window.

In the Arrange window, assign each of the Environment's Audio Objects to its own individual track.

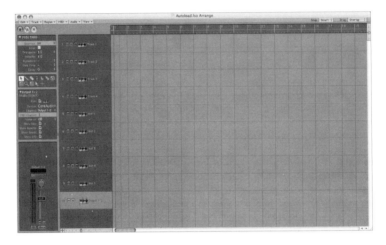

6   If you so desire, assign icon graphics to each channel.

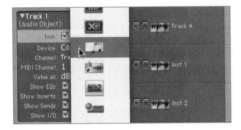

The Autoload Song is done!

7   Save your Autoload Song (Cmd-S).

> **NOTE ▶** If you started this lesson with **12Begin.lso** instead of your own Autoload Song from Lesson 4, you'll need to use the Save As option to save your Autoload Song in the User > Library > Application Support > Logic > Song Templates folder on your hard disk. (See the end of Lesson 11 for details.)

Locking the Autoload Song

Cmd-S! Although OS X is incredibly stable, crashes do happen (particularly when USB audio interfaces are accidentally unplugged). To avoid the sadness of seeing creativity disappear, you are well advised to make Cmd-S your friend, and then visit her often.

However, Cmd-S is no friend to your Autoload Song, and it's easy to accidentally Cmd-S unwanted changes into this very important file. To protect your Autoload Song, lock it instead.

1   In the Finder, navigate to and select your Autoload Song.

> **TIP** The easy way to do this is to hold down the Command key and click the name of the file at the top of the Autoload.lso Arrange window. The entire path to the file will drop down from the title bar; just move the mouse down to Song Templates and release the button, and the Song Templates folder will open.

2   Choose File > Get Info (Cmd-I).

An Info window opens.

3   Select the Locked check box.

Your Autoload Song is now locked and cannot be changed or saved over (if you look closely at the song file, you'll see a little lock attached to its bottom left corner). If you need to change your Autoload Song, you'll have to unlock the song file by deselecting this check box.

What You've Learned

▶ A driver tells Logic how to communicate with your system's audio interfaces, and you select your audio driver from Logic's Audio Drivers Preferences pane (accessed by choosing Audio > Audio Hardware & Drivers).

▶ The Audio Configuration window lists all the audio channels available to Logic (Logic Pro only).

▶ To access an audio channel, you must first assign it to an Audio Object.

▶ Audio Objects provide the graphic interface for audio channels and look like the channel strips on any hardware mixing console.

▶ Audio Objects should be kept on their own Audio layer in the Environment. This makes them easy to locate when needed.

▶ Lock your Autoload Song so that you don't accidentally save unwanted changes.

Logic for Video Editors

13

Lesson Files
APTS_Logic_7 > Song Files > Lesson 13 Project Files >
13Begin.lso

APTS_Logic_7 > Song Files > Lesson 13 Project Files >
13End.lso

Media
APTS_Logic_7 > Song Files > Lesson 13 Project Files

Time
This lesson takes approximately 40 minutes to complete.

Goals
Learn about proxy movies

Open a movie in Logic

Explore the Global Video track

Import audio from a movie

Use the Pickup Clock function

Experiment with Logic's Shuffle modes

Export audio into a movie

Working with Video in Logic Pro

Take a quick peek at the appendix of this book and you'll note that Logic occupies a central position in Apple's digital production platform workflow. Indeed, there's an old saying in the video world: Video is two-thirds audio. This is more than cliché; it's fact. Viewers will tolerate a video that has poor contrast or incorrect color correction, but if your audio peaks to distortion, or if the volume level fluctuates wildly over the course of a program, they will change the channel.

Happily, Logic is an excellent program for scoring video. In this lesson, we will examine Logic's video side by adding a sound effect to a preexisting movie. You'll learn how to open a movie in Logic, choose the video standard appropriate for your country, and also examine a few editing techniques that will help you make those immersive movie scores you've been dreaming about.

Logic Express users should note that most of the features discussed here are available only in Logic Pro. You can still follow the first half of this lesson as we open a movie and work with the Global Video track, but that's about as far as the lesson can take you.

Understanding Video Files and Logic

If a movie will play in QuickTime Player, it'll play in Logic. The movie itself can use any codec (compression/decompression algorithm) that QuickTime understands, and there's no limitation on the movie's dimensions or data rate. Logic is equally adept at scoring standard definition NTSC videos at 720 by 480 pixels as it is at scoring a banner ad movie at 90 by 700 pixels for a Web site. However, there is one important fact to keep in mind: Logic has to read the movie off your hard disk as it plays it. Logic also has to read your audio off the hard disk. Consequently, if you're scoring a video that uses a high-bandwidth codec such as the Animation codec, resources that could be devoted to reading audio off the hard disk will instead be devoted to reading the movie. The result is that Logic will react slower, and you won't be able to work with as many tracks of audio as you would be able to if the movie used a low-bandwidth codec such as Sorenson 3 or MPEG-4.

Because of this, it is common to score to a proxy movie. A *proxy movie* is a low-resolution and tightly compressed version of a high-resolution movie. As long as the frame rate remains unaltered, a proxy movie provides enough of a visual reference that you can still score the video, and you will not place as high a strain on your computer as you would using the uncompressed full-bandwidth version.

> **MORE INFO** ▶ You can create proxy movies using QuickTime Pro Player's export option (Movie to QuickTime Movie). For the codec, use Sorenson 3 or MPEG-4. Both provide exceptional image quality at an extremely reduced data rate, and with a little practice, you may not be able to tell the proxy movie from the original without first looking at its file size.
>
> To reduce a video's file size even further, halve its dimensions. For example, when creating a proxy movie of a 720-by-480-pixel NTSC video, it's very common to reduce the dimensions to 360 by 240 pixels. Your proxy movie will be one-fourth the file size of—and thus use one-fourth of the system resources required by—a full-size version encoded using the same codec.

The "Turtles" movie we'll use in this lesson is just such a proxy movie. (For reference, the uncompressed high-resolution version is included along with the proxy movie so you can open it up and see our turtles in all their swimming glory.) Let's open the proxy movie in QuickTime Player and see what it looks like.

1 Navigate to the APTS_Logic_7 > Song Files > Lesson 13 Project Files > Movie Files folder, and double-click the movie named **Turtles.mp4**.

2 The movie opens in QuickTime Player.

3 Press Cmd-I (Window > Show Movie Info).

QuickTime Player's Movie Info window opens. This window displays several important movie properties, including frame rate, video and audio formats (codec), dimensions, and duration.

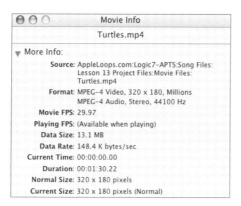

4 Play the movie and familiarize yourself with its content.

As the movie plays, watch the Info window. Notice that the movie uses MPEG-4 video compression, it is 320 by180 pixels, and it plays at 29.97 frames per second.

5 Quit QuickTime Player.

Using the Global Video Track

The Global Video track provides a thumbnail view of the video you're scoring across the top of the Arrange window. The thumbnails let you see at a glance the various scenes in the movie. And you can also use the Global Video track to open or close Logic's internal movie display window. Any way you slice it, the Global Video track is central to scoring video in Logic, so let's dive in.

1 Navigate to the APTS_Logic_7 > Song Files > Lesson 13 Project Files folder, and open the song file named **13Begin.lso**.

2 From the Arrange window's local menu bar, choose View > Global Track Components > Video.

The Global Video track opens at the top of the Arrange area.

Global Video Track

NOTE ▶ A hard cut is a point in the video where a whole scene changes from one frame to the next. In other words, the entire picture must change. The Detect Cuts button scans the movie and places a marker in Logic's Bar Ruler for every hard cut it finds. This function will not identify transitions that blend one scene into the next.

Opening a Movie in Logic

The Track List portion of the Global Video track has an Open Movie button. As its label promises, clicking the button opens a movie in Logic and thumbnail images are displayed in the Global Video track.

1   In the Track List portion of the Global Video track, click the Open Movie button.

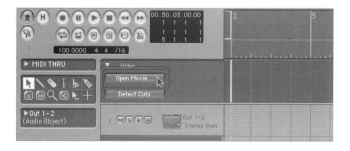

An Open dialog appears.

2   In the Open dialog, navigate to the APTS_Logic_7 > Song Files > Lesson 13
Project Files > Movie Files folder, and double-click the movie named
Turtles.mp4.

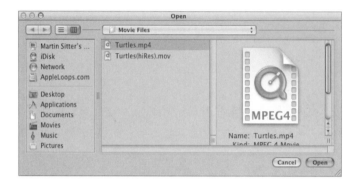

The movie opens in a floating Movie window.

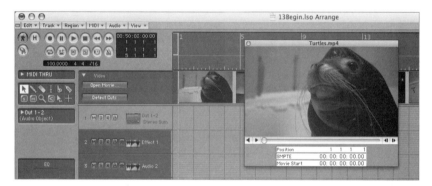

If you close the Movie window, the movie itself does not close; it is still
visible as thumbnail images in the Global Video track.

3   In the top left corner of the Movie window, click the Close button.

The Movie window closes, but the images are still visible as thumbnails.

4   In the Track List portion of the Global Video track, click Open Movie again.

The Movie window reopens.

TIP ▶ You can open movies in either a standard or floating window by visiting the Options > Movies menu. This menu contains options for reopening a closed Movie window similar to toggling the Open Movie button in the Global Video track.

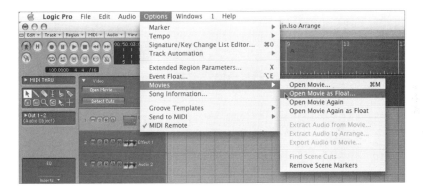

Changing the Movie Window's Display Size

Screen real estate plays an important role in scoring video because you need to see both your video and your arrangement at the same time. Logic provides several options for changing the display size of the Movie window.

1 Click and hold anywhere on the Movie window.

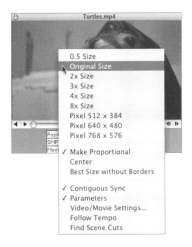

A menu pops open. The top portion of the menu lists several Movie window display sizes.

NOTE ▶ In Logic Express, the Movie window menu has fewer options than shown in the figure.

2 Select a display size.

The Movie window changes to the selected size.

The Movie window also contains a presentation mode you can use while auditioning your score.

3 Logic Pro users, double-click any portion of the Movie window.

The movie expands to fill the screen. Additionally, the Parameter display at the bottom of the Movie window is hidden.

4 To shrink the Movie window to its default size, double-click the expanded movie.

Working with the Movie's Audio

If you were listening a few seconds ago when you opened the Turtles movie in QuickTime, you heard the audio in it. You can choose to have Logic play the movie's audio over the score you're creating, or tell Logic to ignore the movie's audio and just play sound from the Arrange window. (The rest of the tasks in this lesson are for Logic Pro users only.)

1 Press the spacebar to play the song.

As the SPL moves across the Arrange area, the movie plays. However, you do not hear any sound yet.

2 Press the spacebar to stop playback.

3 Click and hold anywhere on the Movie window, and choose Video/Movie Settings from the menu that appears.

The Song Settings window opens with the Video pane showing. At the bottom of this pane is a Sound Output menu.

4   From the Sound Output menu, choose Internal.

5   With the Song Settings window still open, press the spacebar to start playback.

As the song plays, you now hear the movie's audio. However, it's much more useful to have the video's audio in the Arrange area, where you can edit it. In the next section you'll add the movie's audio directly to your Logic song using a single step.

NOTE ▶ If you have your Video Output set to FireWire, the External Sound Output option sends the movie's sound out to the FireWire display device. For more information on using the FireWire Video Output option, see the sidebar below titled "FireWire Video Display."

6   Set the Sound Output menu back to Mute.

7   Close the Song Settings window.

▶ FireWire Video Display

If you have a FireWire video camera or video deck attached to your system, you can set Logic to display the video you're scoring on an external video monitor attached to the FireWire camera or video deck. In this situation, the Movie window is disabled in Logic, freeing up valuable screen real estate for other editing windows. To enable a FireWire display, visit the Song Settings window's Video pane, and choose FireWire from the Video Output menu.

If you use the FireWire Video Output setting, you may notice a slight delay, or latency, in the display of your video. In other words, you'll hear sound playing from Logic before you see the corresponding graphics displayed in the monitor. This occurs because it takes time to send that video down the FireWire pipe, making it very hard to accurately score your video. But all is not lost. You can adjust the offset applied to the video playback by visiting Logic's Video Preferences pane. There you will find an adjustment labeled External Video to Song. Use this setting to

Continues on next page

▶ **FireWire Video Display** (continued)

adjust the playback offset in quarter frames until your video is playing exactly in time with the audio coming out of Logic.

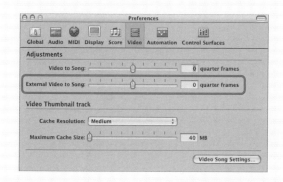

Importing Audio from the Movie

Logic provides a great option for importing the movie's audio directly into your song. When you use this option, Logic provides a dialog that lets you choose which of the movie's sound tracks you wish to extract. Logic then converts all of the audio files in the movie to a stereo AIFF at the sampling rate used for your song.

1   Choose Options > Movies > Extract Audio from Movie.

The "Choose tracks to export" dialog appears. This movie has only a stereo audio track in it, so the stereo track is displayed and selected by default. However, keep in mind that QuickTime is just a media wrapper. You can have several tracks of audio in the same QuickTime movie. Indeed, a QuickTime movie can also have several tracks of video, interactive sprite tracks, and even effect tracks that apply blurs or ripples to the video. QuickTime movies can be very complex creatures.

MORE INFO ▶ To create interactive QuickTime movies, you need a product called LiveStage Professional, by Totally Hip software.

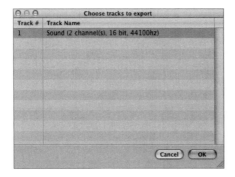

2   Click the "Choose tracks to export" dialog's OK button.

Logic converts the movie's audio and adds it to the Audio window.

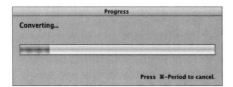

3 Press Cmd-9 to open the Audio window.

There sits the converted movie audio.

4 Drag the movie audio to the track named Audio 2, and drop it at the beginning of bar 1.

5 Close the Audio window.

Working with SMPTE Timecode

When scoring video, you will often reference your song's timeline based on SMPTE time code, which uses hours, minutes, seconds, and frames as a scale, instead of bars, beats, divisions, and ticks. However, the SMPTE time code used in your song depends directly upon the video format you are scoring to. For example, PAL video, the format used in Europe (including Germany, where Logic's designers and programmers reside), plays at 25 frames per second, while the NTSC video format of North America plays at 29.97 frames per second. Consequently, you must synchronize Logic to the correct frame

rate before you begin scoring. To do so, visit the Song Settings dialog's
Synchronization pane.

1   Choose File > Song Settings > Synchronisation (Option-X).

The Song Settings dialog opens to display the Synchronization pane. Near
the top of the Synchronization pane is a Frame Rate menu.

2   From the Frame Rate menu, choose the frame rate of the video you are
scoring, in this case, 29.97.

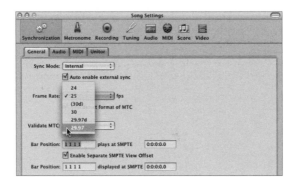

3   Close the Song Settings window.

Enabling the SMPTE Time Ruler

As you score the song, it helps to have the SMPTE time ruler enabled so you can see the SPL's precise SMPTE position within the video.

1 From the Arrange window's local menu bar, choose View > SMPTE Time Ruler (U).

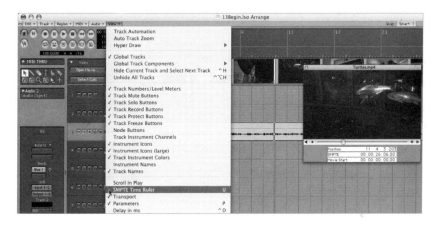

The SMPTE time ruler appears above the Bar Ruler.

SMPTE Time Ruler

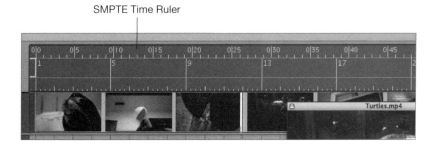

Scoring to Video

The client would like you to add three specific water effects beginning at SMPTE time code 00:00:26.06. In the following section, you'll use some of Logic's scoring features to add these water effects to the score. But first, let's import the effects into the arrangement.

1   In a Finder window, navigate to the APTS_Logic_7 > Song Files > Lesson 13 Project Files > Audio Files folder.

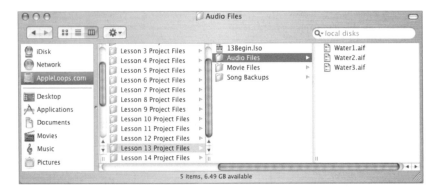

In this folder there are three water effects, named **Water1.aif**, **Water2.aif**, and **Water3.aif**.

2   Select all three of the water effects files, and drag them to bar 1 of the Arrange window's Effect 1 track.

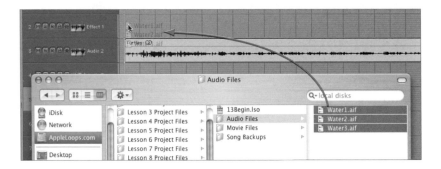

Because you dragged multiple files into the Arrange window, the Add
Selected Files to Arrange dialog appears. These are all water effects that
will be arranged on the Effect 1 track, so let's make sure they all end up
on the track where we want them.

3   Choose the "Place all files on selected track" option, and click the OK
button.

Logic places all three audio files back to back in the Effect 1 track. Don't
worry about their position at the moment. In the following steps you'll
use some of Logic's scoring features to move them exactly where they are
needed.

Using Pickup Clock

The ingeniously named *Pickup Clock* function moves a selected Object to the
SPL's position in the arrangement. In essence, the selected Object *picks up* the
position of the SPL. When you're spotting sound to video, this function comes
in very handy indeed.

However, the Pickup Clock function is available only as a key command. By default this key command is not set, so before you can use it, you have to assign it.

1   Press Option-K to open the Key Commands window.

2   In the Key Commands window's search field, type *pick*.

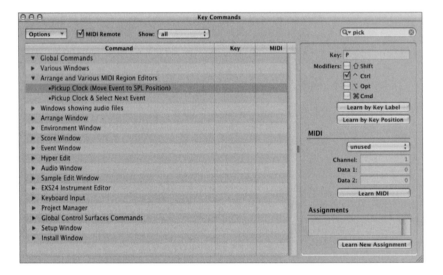

3   Assign Ctrl-P to the Pickup Clock (Move Event to SPL Position) function. (For more information on assigning key commands, see Lesson 3, "Understanding Workflow Techniques.")

4   Close the Key Commands window.

5   In the Arrange area, select the Water1 Region (the first Region in the Effect 1 track).

    As noted above, the client would like you to add the water effects beginning at SMPTE time code 00:00:26.06. Let's move the SPL to exactly that frame.

6 In the Movie window, double-click the SMPTE time code display, type *00:00:26:06*, and press Return.

The SPL moves to the specified time code value.

TIP You can leave some of the 0s out of the entered time code value and replace the colons with periods—Logic will understand exactly what you mean. For example, in the step above you could type 0.0.26.6 into the SMPTE display, and Logic would still move the SPL to 00:00:26:06.

7 Press Ctrl-P.

The Water1 Region jumps to the SPL's position.

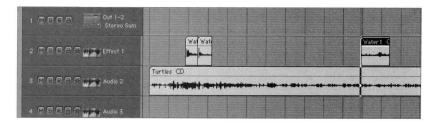

Using Drag Modes

Drag modes (located in the Drag Mode menu in the top right corner of the Arrange window) dictate how Logic moves Regions as you drag them around the Arrange area. By default the Drag Mode menu is set to Overlap, which means that you can drag and drop one Region over the top of another with no problems. This works great for everyday audio editing, but when it comes time to score video, Logic's Shuffle modes are often the Drag mode of choice. The Shuffle mode causes a Region to *shuffle up* to the Region immediately to its left or right, depending on the Shuffle mode selected. This ensures there is no space between the two Regions, so one Region plays smoothly into the next with no drop in the track's audio.

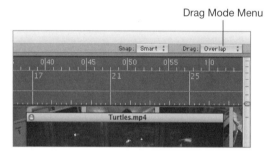

1   From the Drag Mode menu, choose Shuffle R (Shuffle Right).

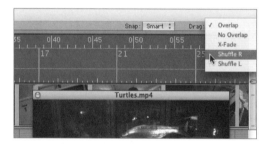

2   In the Effect 1 track, grab the Water3 Region (the one now in the middle of the other two water Regions), and drag it right a little bit, then release it.

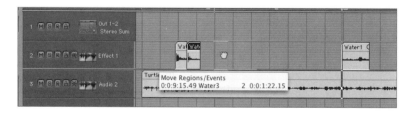

The Region jumps right and shuffles up to the left edge of the Water1 Region at 00:00:26:06.

3 From the Drag Mode menu, choose Shuffle L (Shuffle Left).

4 Drag the Water3 Region back toward the Water2 Region in the beginning of the Effect 1 track, and drop it.

The Water3 Region once again shuffles up to the Water2 Region.

The Shuffle mode in Logic works a bit differently than it does in some other audio editing programs. For example, if you drag both the Water2 and Water3 Regions behind the Water1 Region, you'll notice that *all* of the Regions shuffle forward by the combined duration of the moved Regions.

5 Select both the Water2 and Water3 Regions.

6 Drag them to the right of the Water1 Region.

Notice how the Water1 Region has shifted forward. This isn't exactly where it needs to be—it needs to start at 00:00:26:06. Let's use Pickup Clock to move all of the water Regions to the proper position in the arrangement.

7 Select all three water Regions.

8   Make sure the SPL is at 00:00:26:06.

9   Press Ctrl-P.

The selected Regions jump to the right, and the Water1 Region now begins at exactly 00:00:26:06.

10 Play the song from bar 9 and listen to the water effect.

11 Adjust the volume of the water effect so it sits properly in the mix.

12 Stop playback.

Exporting Audio to Movies

Once you've finished your score, only one thing remains—putting the sound into the movie. And this couldn't be easier using Logic 7, because you can now just export the song's audio straight into a copy of the movie file you've been scoring.

1   From the Arrange window's local menu bar, choose Options > Movies > Export Audio to Movie.

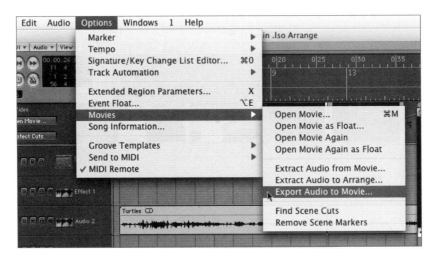

The Sound Settings dialog opens. This dialog assumes the sampling rate used for your song, and it is set to 16-bit stereo audio by default. This is the audio format typically used for video, so there are no further settings to make here.

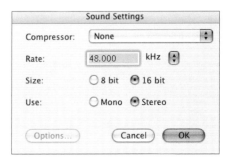

2 Click the Sound Settings window's OK button.

The "Location and name of new movie" dialog opens. By default, it chooses the same directory as the movie you are scoring.

3 Select Desktop as the location to save your movie to, enter a name for the new movie, and click the Save button.

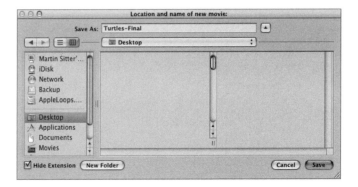

The "Select the audio tracks of movie to keep in new movie" dialog appears. You've already added the source movie's audio tracks to the Arrange window, so there's no need to add them to the new movie.

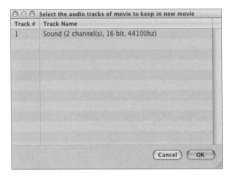

4   Click below the selected track in the dialog to deselect it.

5   Click the OK button.

Logic bounces the song's audio, adds it to a copy of the source movie's video, and saves the finished file on your desktop.

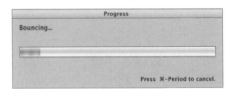

6   Locate the movie on your desktop and double-click it to open it in QuickTime.

7   Play the movie.

Approximately 26 seconds into the movie, you hear the added water sound effect.

What You've Learned

▶ A proxy movie is a low-resolution movie that places less strain on your computer as you score in Logic.

▶ The Global Video track provides a thumbnail view of the scenes in your movie.

▶ To open a movie in Logic's Movie window, click the Open Movie button on the Global Video track.

▶ To adjust the frame rate (frames per second) used in the song, visit File > Song Settings > Synchronisation > General.

▶ To enable the SMPTE time ruler above Logic's Bar Ruler, go to the Arrange window's local menu bar and choose View > SMPTE Time Ruler.

▶ The Pickup Clock function (available only as a user-defined key command) moves a selected Region to the SPL's position.

▶ To export audio into a movie, choose Options > Movie > Export Audio to Movie.

14

Lesson Files   APTS_Logic_7 > Song Files > Lesson 14 Project Files > 14Begin.lso

APTS_Logic_7 > Song Files > Lesson 14 Project Files > 14End.lso

Time   This lesson takes approximately 40 minutes to complete.

Goals   Configure outputs for surround sound mixing

Use the surround sound Pan control to assign tracks to speakers

Control subwoofer sounds with the low-frequency effect channel

Create a final surround mix

Working with Surround Sound

Have you ever noticed that when you watch a movie on a really big screen, you almost start to feel as though you are in the middle of the action? This happens because the screen is so large that it fills your entire field of vision. The screen doesn't need to extend behind you, because your eyes see only what's in front of you. Is that true for sound? Do you hear only what's in front of you? Of course not. So why do people typically listen to music played only through speakers sitting in front of them? These days they can put speakers around them and hear prerecorded sounds from all directions, as they hear other sounds. This is something that the movie industry has done for quite some time, and consumers have begun to follow suit, making surround sound home theater systems hugely popular.

Recent years have seen ever greater activity in surround sound music production. New audio-specific formats such as DVD-Audio and Super Audio CD, and of course DVD-Video are making their way into the market as vehicles to deliver surround sound music to the masses.

Logic Pro has the tools you need for surround sound audio, whether you want to score a movie or produce music only. If you've never experienced surround sound music, then you owe it to yourself to check it out. Here's how you can do it for yourself using Logic!

> **NOTE** ▶ To hear the results of this lesson, you will need an audio interface with six outputs wired to a six-channel surround sound playback system. If you do not have this type of system, you can follow the lesson steps, but you will hear your results only in stereo.

Configuring the Playback System

Of the various surround sound formats introduced over the years, the one that's emerged as most common is called *5.1*. With this format, you typically play your audio through five full-frequency speakers, which are fed by five independent channels (left, right, center, left surround, and right surround), plus one dedicated low-frequency subwoofer, which is fed by a channel referred to as an LFE (low-frequency effect). Many manufacturers package systems that include the speakers and amplifiers to play back 5.1 audio. If you're looking to purchase a system, make sure it has six analog inputs, so that it can receive signals from the outputs of your audio interface.

You can place your speakers in a lot of different ways. The following diagram shows an overview of a common layout designed specifically for monitoring 5.1 music playback. The basic idea is that the speakers are placed at an equal distance from where you (the black dot in the center) typically listen. The numbers indicate degrees of separation. Looking directly ahead, the center speaker is considered to be 0° off center. The right front speaker is 30° to the right of the center speaker, and the right rear speaker is 110° to the right of the center. The left front and left rear speakers are mirrored on the left side. The LFE is not indicated in the diagram because subwoofers tend to sound dramatically different depending on where you put them in the room. Exact placement of the subwoofer will be unique for every room, but typically it is placed on the floor in alignment with one of the front three speakers.

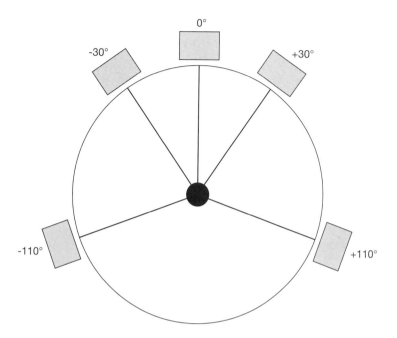

Configuring Logic

You'll need to do a little preliminary work in Logic to get it prepared for surround mixing.

Assigning the Outputs

In order for this to work, you will need not only the speakers but also an audio interface with at least six independently addressable audio outputs. Emagic's EMI 2|6 sound card is a good example of one that will work well. Logic will then need to know which outputs are connected to which speakers. Otherwise, when you tell Logic you want a track to be played out of the center speaker, it may come out of the left rear one.

1 Navigate to APTS_Logic_7 > Song Files > Lesson 14 Project Files, and open the file **14Begin.lso**.

2 From the main menu bar, select Logic Pro > Preferences > Audio.

The Audio Preferences pane opens.

3 On the Audio Preferences pane, choose the Surround tab.

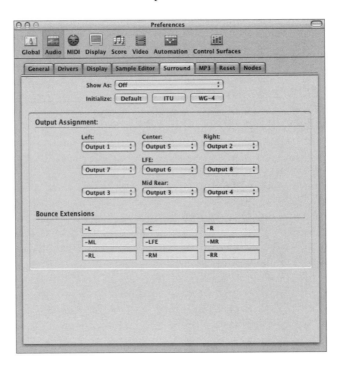

The Surround tab lets you configure various options related to your speaker output. Most important, it shows you which audio interface outputs are designated for which speaker positions. You can assign a hardware output to each surround sound channel by choosing an output from the pop-up menu under each channel, or choose a surround format from the Show As menu. Let's choose 5.1.

4   From the Show As menu, choose 5.1.

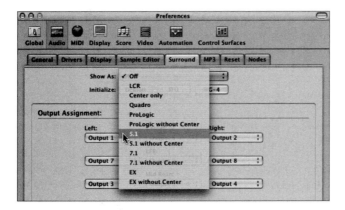

The Output Assignment area updates to show the selected surround format. Pay particular attention to which audio output has been assigned to which channel—this will become important as the lesson progresses.

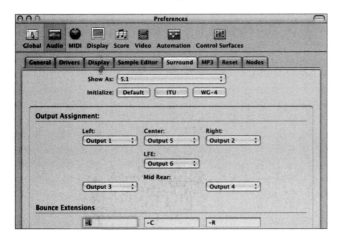

5   Close the Preferences window.

Adding Output Objects

In the exercise above, you set Logic to send signals to six discrete outputs. Logic consequently needs six Output Objects in the Environment to transport the signal to your audio interface. Let's create a Surround Output layer in the Environment and populate it with the appropriate Audio Output Objects.

1 Press Cmd-8 to open the Environment.

2 Switch to the Environment's Audio layer.

3 Create six Audio Objects. (For more information on creating Audio Objects, see Lesson 12, "Setting Up the Audio Environment.")

Logic doesn't have a single surround sound Object, so creating six Output Objects works just the same.

4 Now assign the new Objects to Output channels, and name them to match their speaker positions, as follows:

▶ Assign the first new Output Object to output 1 (in the Object Parameter box), and change the name to *Left*.

▶ Assign the second new Output Object to output 2 (in the Object Parameter box), and change the name to *Right*.

▶ Assign the third new Output Object to output 3 (in the Object Parameter box), and change the name to *Rear Left*.

▶ Assign the fourth new Output Object to output 4 (in the Object Parameter box), and change the name to *Rear Right*.

▶ Assign the fifth new Output Object to output 5 (in the Object Parameter box), and change the name to *Center*.

▶ Assign the sixth new Output Object to output 6 (in the Object Parameter box), and change the name to *LFE*.

5 Select all the new Output Objects, and then deselect the Show EQ, Show Inserts, Show Sends, and Show I/O check boxes.

6 Rearrange the Output Objects so that the meter positions better reflect the actual speaker positions. Compare them with the figure below.

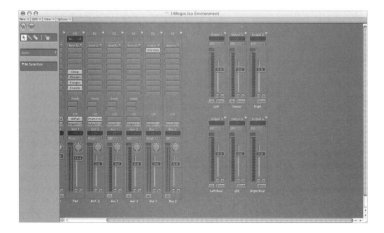

This layout makes it easier to understand at a glance what each meter represents.

7 Close the Environment window.

Using the Surround Control

This is where the real fun begins! By default, tracks in Logic assign themselves to stereo outputs. You will need to redirect them to your surround output. Once you assign them, you will want to control which of the speakers each track is heard from. This is done by way of a Surround control. The concept of the Surround control is similar to that of the Pan control; it's just a little more complex. The Surround control has to distribute sound not only between the left and right positions, but also between the front and back positions. Don't worry—it's pretty simple to understand once you get into it.

Displaying a Surround Control

You've used the stereo Pan control in all the other lessons, but this control is not sufficient for mixing surround sound. Now you'll convert the stereo Pan control in the channel view of each track to a Surround control.

1 In the Arrange window, select the Bass track.

The Arrange window channel strip updates to display the Bass track's properties.

2 On the channel strip, click and hold the output assignment, and select Surround from the pop-up menu.

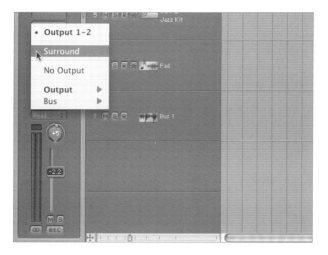

Notice how the channel Pan control changes from a stereo type to a surround type with a dot in the middle of a circle.

Channel set to surround output ⸺

Surround Pan Control ⸺

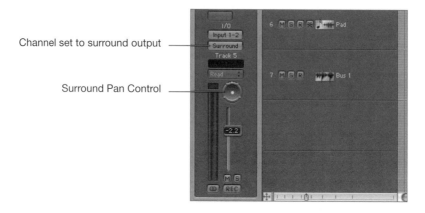

NOTE ▸ The default position is for the dot to be in the center of the circle. This position indicates that the sound for the track will be distributed to all of the speakers shown in the Surround control. Since this is a stereo track, the left channel of the Bass will be played partially from the center speaker and partially from the two left speakers, while the right channel will be played partially from the center and partially from the two right speakers.

3   Repeat steps 1 and 2 for the remaining tracks in the Arrange window. (And don't forget the tracks inside this song's folder—they need to be set to output in surround as well.)

NOTE ▸ In Logic, you can assign some channels to the surround outputs while others remain on the standard stereo output. Those assigned to the standard outputs (1-2) will simply have their audio mixed into the left and right outputs in the surround mix.

4   Play the song.

5   While the song is playing, grab the dot in the Bass Surround control and move it around.

Listen to the movement of the Bass sound as you move the dot. Also notice the output meters and how they reflect your movements. If you want to get a more isolated listen to what's happening, solo the Bass track.

6   Option-click the Bass Surround control.

This is a quick way to return a dot to the center position of a Surround control.

Using the Pan Window

The Pan window is an enlarged view of the Surround control. It allows you to control the pan position with greater accuracy—and gives you access to some very cool features to enhance your panning control.

1   Double-click the Surround Pan control on the Bass channel.

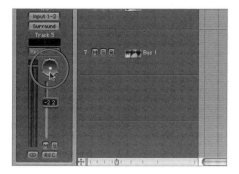

The Surround Pan window opens.

2 Play the song.

3 Move the dot around.

Notice how this moves the Pan control on the Bass channel as well.

4 Click the edges of the Surround Pan control.

The dot to jumps to the position you clicked.

Now that you know the Surround Pan control basics, it's time to learn some tricks with the Command and Control keys.

5 Hold down the Command key.

A line appears across the Pan window.

6 While the Command key is held down, drag the dot in the Pan window.

The dot moves only on the path indicated by the line.

7 Release the Command key. Drag the dot, and hold the Command key again.

Notice that the angle of the line is determined by where the dot is in the Pan control.

8 Release the Command key. Move the dot somewhere other than dead center.

9 Hold down the Control key.

A circle appears in the Pan window.

10 While holding down the Control key, drag the dot around in a circle.

The position of the dot when the Control key is held down changes the size of the circular path. Using the Control key is the way you can create perfect circular pan moves.

11 Option-click the dot to reset it to the exact center of the control.

Changing the Output Assignment

In some cases you may want to intentionally assign the output of a track to something other than the 5.1 setting you have now. An example is when you want to make the track play from the traditional stereo position (playing equally out of the left and right speakers), and not the center speaker. This is often referred to as the *phantom center position*. The problem is that if you position the dot in the front center position, the sound will come from the center speaker. Here's how to get around that.

1　Set the Bass channel to Solo mode.

2　In the Surround Pan window, place the Bass line's dot on the center speaker.

3　Click and hold the surround output assignment in the top left part of the Surround Pan window, and change the output assignment to 5.1 w/o Center.

4　Play the song.

5　Unsolo the Bass track

Notice that the Bass sound no longer plays from the center channel.

Working with the LFE

Sound isn't just something you hear; it's something you can feel as well. Film audio-mix engineers wanted a way to intensify the sound of special effects such as car crashes and explosions, so they came up with the idea of the low-frequency effect channel. It is designed to give you total control over what sounds come out of the subwoofer in your system.

Let's hear what the LFE channel can do.

1   If the Surround Pan window is not open, double-click the Surround control for the Bass track.

2   Play your song back from bar 9. During playback, drag the LFE slider to the right.

You should be able to feel the low-frequency sound increase in your room. Now you can use the LFE as an alternative to equalization to pump up the bass in your mix!

3   Click the small button in the top left corner to close the Pan window.

Finishing a Surround Mix

Working with music in surround sound is new to almost everyone, even veteran musicians, producers, and engineers. There are no rights and wrongs at this point. The picture you paint with a surround mix can be much more varied than with stereo. Do you create the illusion that the listener is watching a band that's up on a stage, or do you put the listener on the stage, in the middle of it all? Now that you know what the controls do, it's time to experiment with them. For this section, there is no formal exercise—simply play with your newfound surround toy and see what happens.

Filtering the LFE

Before bouncing your final mix, it's a good idea to remove frequencies higher than what your subwoofer can produce. The signal being sent to the LFE goes over a full-frequency channel, but the frequency response of the subwoofer generally limits what you hear to a low rumble. However, in some consumer 5.1 playback systems, users can indicate in their equipment configuration options that a subwoofer is not present, causing the LFE channel to be redirected into the main speakers—which means the full-range signal of the LFE channel is heard through the main speakers. If that occurs with your song, the consumer will hear a mix that you never intended, and this could be quite disruptive to the overall sound of your song. By filtering the LFE output in Logic before bouncing, you eliminate any possibility that the full-range signal of the LFE will be heard—regardless of a consumer's configuration.

So, let's go ahead and filter the LFE on your song's output.

1   Open the Environment window and locate your surround Output Objects.

2 Select the LFE Output Object.

3 Click the Show EQs check box in the Object Parameter box.

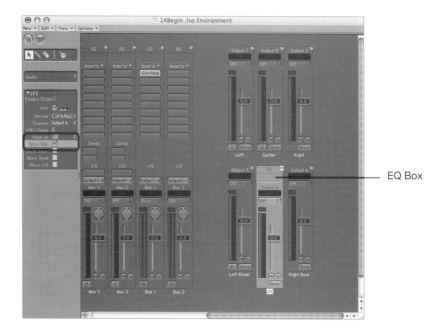

An EQ box appears at the top of the LFE Object.

4 Double-click the LFE Object's EQ box.

A Channel EQ plug-in is inserted into the channel and opens in a plug-in window.

5 Click the Low-Pass Filter button in the top right corner of the Channel Equalizer window.

Low-pass Filter

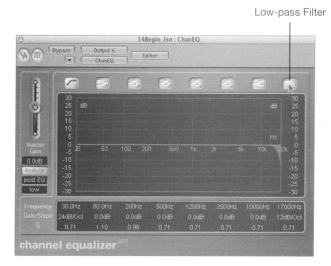

6   By dragging up or down on the setting values as needed, set the Low-Pass Filter setting to 80 Hz, at 48 dB per octave.

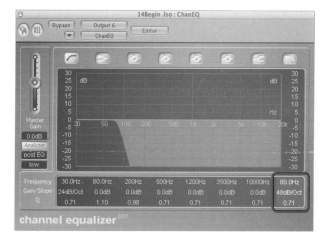

This frequency setting causes sounds with frequencies above 80 Hz to get quieter as their frequencies get higher. The setting of 48 dB per octave specifies how quickly the sounds above 80 Hz die away. You can see this filtering visually represented in the Channel Equalizer display.

The filter point 80 Hz is common for the LFE channel (although some engineers set the LFE cutoff as high as 120 Hz—it's a matter of personal preference). A subwoofer is designed to play only low frequencies anyway, so you don't want frequencies higher than 80 Hz in the LFE signal.

7   Close the Channel Equalizer window.

Adjusting the Surround Mix Level

Currently, you have six Output Objects in the Environment. To raise or lower the volume of your surround mix, you need to raise or lower the volume of all six Output channels together, at the same time. You *could* group the channels and then adjust the volume, but there's an even slicker way. Logic provides a special Master Audio Object that controls the volume level of all outputs simultaneously.

1   In the Environment's Audio layer, create a new Audio Object and position it as shown in the figure below.

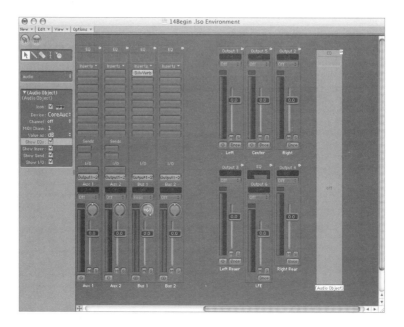

2 Assign the new Audio Object's channel to Master.

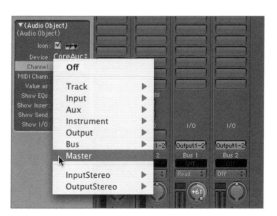

The master fader affects the volume of signals going to any of the Output Objects in a song. If the master fader is turned down low, then the meters in the surround Output Objects will read low. If you raise the fader on the Master Audio Object, the volume of all the surround Output Objects will increase.

3 Play your song.

4 Raise and lower the Master Audio Object's fader.

As you raise or lower the Master Audio Object's fader, the volume sent to the outputs is also raised or lowered.

5 Set the master fader to a level that does not clip any of the Audio Output Objects.

6 Close the Environment window.

> **TIP** ▶ When moving the output faders, select them all first, and then move one of them up or down. This links the faders temporarily to ensure that the relative fader positions remain the same.

Bouncing for Surround Sound

You've already learned in Lesson 1, "Exploring the Workspace," how to bounce a final mix when working in stereo. Bouncing in surround sound is basically the same thing, except you have to pay attention to more meters and change one simple setting.

1 Choose File > Bounce.

The Bounce dialog opens. Everything is properly set up with the exception of the Surround Bounce setting.

2 From the Surround Bounce setting, choose 5.1.

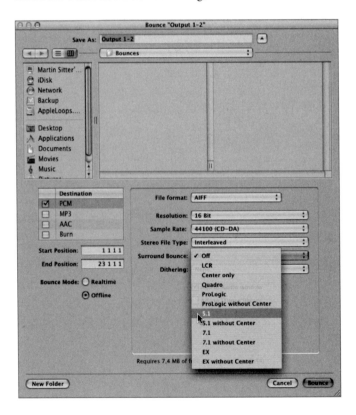

In this song, most channels are assigned to a 5.1 output, and the Bass channel is assigned to 5.1 without Center. When you use 5.1 for the Surround Bounce parameter, all Output channels and groups of Output channels that are part of a 5.1 mix are included in the bounced files.

3   Type *mySurroundStems* into the Save As text box, and bounce the files to your desktop.

> **TIP** ▶ Since six files are going to be created, you may want to create a specific folder to keep them in.

4   Look on your desktop.

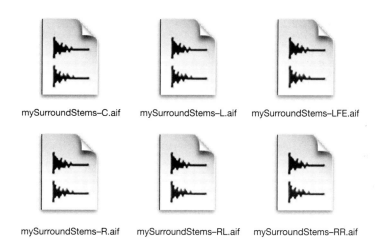

mySurroundStems–C.aif   mySurroundStems–L.aif   mySurroundStems–LFE.aif

mySurroundStems–R.aif   mySurroundStems–RL.aif   mySurroundStems–RR.aif

Logic has created six discrete "Surround Stems" files. Notice the extensions that are added to the end of the filename you chose. They indicate which speaker each audio file represents.

MORE INFO ▶ At this point, the files you have are not capable of being heard by most consumers. They need to be encoded into a format that consumer playback systems understand, such as DTS or Dolby Digital. Logic does not have encoders built into it, but there are third-party programs that do. For example, Apple's DVD Studio Pro comes with a Dolby Digital encoder called A.Pack, which allows you to apply the 5.1 sound track you've created in Logic to your own DVD-Video discs! To learn more about A.Pack, check out *Apple Pro Training Series: DVD Studio Pro 3*, or visit macProVideo.com.

What You've Learned

▶ There are a variety of surround sound formats. The most common is 5.1.

▶ You must pay close attention to the surround configuration of your audio interface and make sure that you've wired your audio interface correctly for your speakers.

▶ Creating additional Output channels is necessary to monitor the master levels of your surround mix.

▶ You can use the Surround Pan control to position tracks into the desired speaker positions.

▶ By changing the output assignment you can achieve a phantom center position (5.1 without a center channel).

▶ To ensure proper playback on consumer surround systems, you need to filter the LFE output.

▶ You can use the Master Audio Object to control the volume level of all outputs simultaneously.

Round-Trip Production

Since the introduction of Final Cut Pro in 1999, Apple's portfolio of content creation software has expanded to include a dozen professional applications that aid the entire production process, including editing, graphics and effects, music and audio, and delivery tools.

Just as there is an unending stream of new video formats, the tools and techniques in postproduction continue to evolve to meet the demands and budgetary requirements of today's sophisticated producers and viewers. Fortunately, there are a few typical production workflows that stand out as standard operating practices.

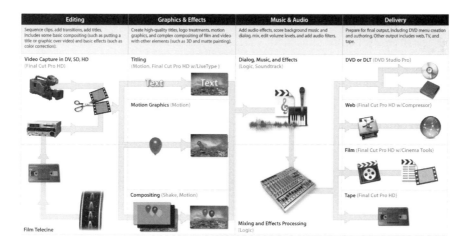

At different stages in the process, these workflows may involve audio (dialog, music, and sound effects), video (whether originated from film or some video format, including high definition), and other elements (text, 2D graphics, and 3D objects and characters). The professional production workflow is the art and science of blending together these separate elements into a single project, hopefully one that is as technically sound to the engineer as it is captivating to the audience.

Content Creation Workflows with Apple's Professional Applications

In this appendix, we'll examine how professionals can leverage the latest genera-tion of Apple applications in a *round-trip production* environment—an environ-ment where media and project files can move seamlessly between the different stages of the creative process, and where changes made at one stage, with one application, are automatically reflected in the other stages, in other applications.

For an individual in a home or project studio, this may involve working with multiple applications on the same computer. For the independent artist collabo-rating with a larger studio, this may include the transfer of media and projects on FireWire drives or a via a wide area network. And for a multi-seat, full-service production facility, this may involve a collective of artists, editors, and engineers accessing terabytes of data on a fiber channel storage area network.

Apple's professional applications have been designed to work in all of these scenarios and are helping to drive the industry in a new direction—one where reasonably priced "off-the-shelf" software can be used effectively to create award-winning content. Just ask the dozens of Academy and Emmy award–winning editors who now cut their films and TV shows on Final Cut Pro, or any one of the hundreds of musical artists whose Grammy award–winning songs were composed on Logic. But enough about them already—let's look at how you can use these tools to create masterpieces of your own.

Editing

After the director shouts "Cut!" the editing process begins. Editing involves logging the best takes, capturing them to the hard drive of the workstation, and trimming and sequencing them in a timeline. Increasingly, this process is taking place on location, with portable systems, during production. Checking for timing, continuity, and performance on location provides an opportunity to get it right before the actors have departed for their trailers.

Apple's wildly popular video-editing application, **Final Cut Pro**, is ideally suited to run on the current generation of PowerBook laptop computers, making effective use of the laptops' FireWire ports to capture a variety of native digital video formats to the hard disk, including DV, DVCAM, DVCPRO, DVCPRO 50, and DVCPRO HD.

While it's entirely possible to complete a DV or offline film project on a Power-Book, higher-resolution formats (SD and HD) require the performance of a dedicated workstation to finish (online) the content. Editing in these formats is best suited to a Power Mac G5, where Final Cut Pro can take full advantage of the desktop's dual processors. Digital video is captured either via FireWire or, for high-bandwidth formats like uncompressed HD, through a PCI-X card installed in the chassis.

> **NOTE ▶** For projects shot on film, Final Cut Pro includes **Cinema Tools**, a relational database that keeps track of the original film negative feet, frames, and audio timecode throughout the entire editorial process. Cinema Tools works in tandem with Final Cut Pro to ensure that every frame of film is properly accounted for during editing.

Today's generation of video producers are comfortable with both the horizontal and vertical nature of the editorial process. In addition to performing cuts and transitions between shots and applying filters and color corrections to clips, they know how to make effective use of multiple video tracks. This routinely involves superimposed titles, split screens, and picture-in-picture effects. It can even involve compositing techniques including travel mattes, blend modes, and keying for blue- and greenscreen effects. Final Cut Pro supports all of these operations.

The latest version of Final Cut Pro includes an architecture called **RT Extreme**, which leverages the power of the host PowerPC processor, the operating system, and the graphics processing unit to calculate transitions and filter effects in real time. This design philosophy—to provide the full creative palette of effects in real time—is at the heart of round-trip production.

Round-trip production also lets you create, import, and revise parts of your project in separate applications, with updates in one application automatically reflected in the others. Apple has leveraged XML (Extensible Markup Language) to make all media metadata and project information accessible to Apple and third-party applications to facilitate this automatic updating process.

Several parts of the production workflow require tools well beyond your basic cut and splice. Those parts include audio (music, dialog, sound effects) and motion graphics (text, illustrations, animations).

Effects and Graphics

Final Cut Pro includes some fairly sophisticated titling tools within the application itself, including the ability to create extruded 3D titles, but **LiveType** (included with the purchase of Final Cut Pro) takes animated titling to another level entirely. The Media Browser of LiveType includes both titling tools and titling content. The content includes LiveFonts, 32-bit animated fonts that dance and draw themselves onscreen. In addition, LiveType includes a massive library of animated textures (atmospheres, liquids, moving canvases) and objects that range from sparkly Particle Effects to organic flames and interstellar explosions. One of the most popular features of LiveType is the ability to apply prebaked animated effects (fades, glows, zooms, caricatures) to otherwise lifeless system fonts.

Motion is to LiveType what the jet engine is to air travel. With it, you can take your titles and graphics much further in less time. Like LiveType, Motion includes a library full of compelling content, including some of the LiveFonts and text animations that come with LiveType, but that's where the similarities end. Motion makes full use of Quartz Extreme (the revolutionary composited windowing system in Apple's operating system, Mac OS X) and Apple's ultra-high-bandwidth hardware architecture to provide a level of real-time performance that needs to be seen to be appreciated. Video clips are played back directly from SDRAM (the computer's internal memory). Text, particles, and filter effects are loaded into the VRAM (video memory) of today's state-of-the-art graphics cards. Finally, natural physical simulations or screen behaviors like wind and gravity are applied to objects and particles and calculated in real time by the CPUs—dual processors in all current Power Macs. In LiveType, text animations and other motion graphics need to be rendered into RAM to be previewed, whereas in Motion all effects can be viewed and manipulated in real time.

Shake is the preeminent application for visual-effects compositing, a highly specialized craft used to create special effects that, when seamlessly composited, are impossible to distinguish from reality. The primary objective of visual-effects compositing is to take dozens, often hundreds, of separate elements—matte paintings, computer-generated 3D models and animated characters, live action photography (whether filmed on location or against a green- or bluescreen), and particles—and weave them all into a series of photorealistic images. Media files are often exported and imported between Final Cut Pro and Shake, a process that has been accelerated with the addition of new QuickTime codecs (compression-decompression algorithms) in Shake 3.5. In addition to QuickTime, Shake supports a variety of file formats that are commonly used by visual-effects artists, including those for animation (IFF, RLA) and film (Cineon, DPX)—over 20 formats in total.

Let's return to titles, motion graphics, and round-trip production integration. In LiveType, Final Cut Pro projects simply appear as a movie background. Text is superimposed over the video, enhanced (with color, outlines, drop shadows, and so on), positioned, and animated when appropriate. Objects, like simple particle effects, and filters, like blurs and glows, may be added to further enhance the animated titles. With **Exposé**, which instantly tiles all open windows, the LiveType document can be dragged from its menu bar directly into the Timeline of Final Cut Pro, where it's superimposed over the original video track. There's no longer a need to first render the titles as a movie from LiveType before importing them into the editing environment. Best of all, with round-trip production it's possible to launch the LiveType application directly from within the Final Cut Pro

Timeline, should it be necessary to make any last-minute changes. Once the changes are made in LiveType, a simple save of the project is all that's required to automatically update the title in Final Cut Pro. XML is used communicate the revisions between the two applications. No need to render out a new title from LiveType, no need to copy and paste files between applications; a simple save automatically updates the information from one app to another.

The interoperability between Final Cut Pro and Motion works in exactly the same manner. In addition, it's possible to export the Final Cut Pro project directly into Motion with all editing, scaling, cropping, positioning, and keyframe information for all layers retained during the exchange. Graphic designs can be roughed out in Final Cut Pro and fine-tuned in Motion. Some of the most impressive technologies found in Motion are its advanced particle engine and natural physical simulations, both of which are often used in tandem to create stunning designs. Motion also accepts Adobe Photoshop files and imports them with the separate layers intact or merged into one. Photoshop users, even those who have never worked with video, can easily convert their 2D designs and images into visually stunning animated motion graphics.

Once the motion graphic design work is completed in Motion, the project file can be imported directly into Final Cut Pro. Round-trip production functions exactly the same with Motion as with LiveType. When a save command is executed, all project revisions in Motion are automatically communicated directly to Final Cut Pro. To the user, the media in the Timeline goes offline for a moment and then returns reflecting the updates.

In addition to the content creation workflow that defines the look of your video, Apple's professional applications provide an incredible level of interoperability between music and audio as it relates to the visuals. We'll examine this aspect of round-trip production in the next section of this appendix.

Music and Audio

A great music score can enhance an otherwise lackluster film or video. Conversely, dialog that is inaudible or distorted can ruin an otherwise well-edited scene. When background audio levels and room acoustic dynamics vary dramatically from shot to shot, viewers unconsciously sense that something is wrong, and their ability to remain connected to the message, story, or characters diminishes exponentially. Well-produced music and audio can't salvage inherently poor footage, but poorly produced music and audio can ruin an otherwise completely enjoyable sequence. Fortunately, Apple's portfolio of professional applications includes some very powerful tools for music composition and audio editing, sweetening, and mixing.

Let's first examine music for music's sake.

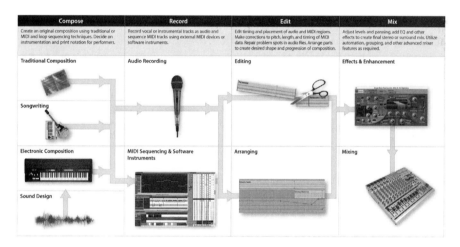

Compose	Record	Edit	Mix
Create an original composition using traditional or MIDI and loop sequencing techniques. Decide on instrumentation and print notation for performers.	Record vocal or instrumental tracks as audio and sequence MIDI tracks using external MIDI devices or software instruments.	Edit timing and placement of audio and MIDI regions. Make corrections to pitch, length, and timing of MIDI data. Repair problem spots in audio files. Arrange parts to create desired shape and progression of composition.	Adjust levels and panning, add EQ and other effects to create final stereo or surround mix. Utilize automation, grouping, and other advanced mixer features as required.

Apple's primary applications for music composition on the computer are GarageBand, Logic Express, and Logic Pro.

GarageBand is an incredibly intuitive application ideally suited for musicians who are composing on a computer for the first time. Songs composed in GarageBand can be exported directly to an iTunes playlist in a single step. These same songs can also be used as music beds for videos in iMovie, Final Cut Express, or Final Cut Pro, or to enhance menus in iDVD or DVD Studio Pro. Because GarageBand does not provide a way to synchronize sound to picture, the job of scoring music to picture is best suited to Logic and Soundtrack, both of which we'll review here.

The production workflow for music consists of four discrete processes that tend to fold back on themselves over and over until either the artist/producer is satisfied with the final song, or the production deadline has elapsed—hopefully the former before the latter. The workflow includes composition, recording, editing, and mixing. Composition can begin with musical notation as supported in Logic, but often it's part of the recording process, roughing out the melody or beat with Logic's built-in MIDI (Musical Instrument Digital Interface) sequencing and software instruments, considered by many to be among the finest ever developed.

Logic Pro includes a collection of vintage instruments that provide near-perfect emulations of classic instruments like the Hammond B3 organ, software synthesizers that can re-create classic analog textures, and a full-featured stereo sampler that provides the songwriter with access to a myriad of sounds from the countless number of sample libraries currently available—from esoteric collections of obscure world instruments to elaborate orchestral libraries. In addition to sound design and electronic composition with MIDI instruments, such as keyboards, Logic is used to record vocals or other real instruments directly to the tracks of each song. Like a multitrack tape recorder, Logic can record multiple audio inputs (vocals, drums, guitars) in real time, whereas GarageBand can only record one input at a time.

Editing involves trimming, timing, and placement of the audio and MIDI tracks in the song. Logic also provides the ability to repair spots in recorded audio files, as well as tools to correct the pitch, length, and timing of MIDI.

The final step in the songwriter's workflow is mixing, and it allows the composer to enhance or "sweeten" the acoustics of each track with a selection of digital signal processing plug-ins including EQ, dynamic compressors, and reverb. The **Space Designer** reverb plug-in that comes with Logic Pro is based on state-of-the-art convolution technology that actually models the physical characteristics of a room so that the exact acoustics of that room (or any room that's been modeled) can be applied to one or more tracks of audio at any time during the mix. During mixing the producer will adjust individual track levels and pan positions in relation to one another (for example, "cowbell louder and to the left side of the stereo image"). This often involves mixing in a surround sound environment to support the increasingly popular multichannel playback capabilities of DVD and high-definition television.

It's important to note that more and more musicians are finding Logic perfectly suited for live performance as well. Mac OS X includes a number of features that have been specifically designed to please musicians and audio engineers. Chief among them is Core Audio, which essentially removes any cap on the number of audio tracks that the computer can support. Core Audio also supports high-definition audio sampling rates and bit rates up to 96 kHz and beyond. For live performance, Core Audio provides the lowest levels of audio latency in the industry. Latency can best be described as the time it takes to move audio from the input (recording) stage through digital signal processing (DSP) and back out again to be monitored. Any significant delays, and it's like hearing yourself talk to yourself, talk to yourself…you get the idea. Mac OS X now provides levels of audio latency well below 1 millisecond in duration, which has helped Apple to retain its dominant position as the preferred platform for live venues. Musical artists can perform in perfect sync with Logic—vocals enhanced with DSP and all tracks mixed in real time on to the waiting ears of the audience.

Soundtrack is a music composition application developed by Apple for musicians and non-musicians alike. Included in Soundtrack is a massive library of over 4,000 audio samples (loops) of sound effects and musical instruments—everything from the aforementioned cowbell to Motown's finest drum riffs. Apple calls these samples Apple Loops because they offer far more functionality than your standard audio samples. Soundtrack takes advantage of the Velocity Engine of Apple's PowerPC processors by providing the unique ability to preview new loops while simultaneously auditioning other tracks in the timeline. The unparalleled power of this feature becomes evident when you realize that loops are originally sampled (recorded to hard disk) in any number of keys and tempos. To help keep your tracks in tune, Soundtrack can restrict the selection of Apple loops to only those that will work best with other tracks already in the song—within two semitones of the project key. While it's still possible to combine instruments into something that sounds like it was just dragged in by the cat, Soundtrack provides the necessary tools and technologies to help keep you from going down that path.

Round-trip production between Final Cut Pro and Soundtrack is accomplished primarily through the use of Scoring Markers. The markers are positioned in the Timeline of Final Cut Pro as a reference between the music score and the visual activity (such as a crescendo at a car crash). When a sequence is exported from Final Cut Pro, the scoring markers appear in the timeline of Soundtrack alongside the QuickTime movie—construction cones on the highway to musical bliss. Apple Loops can be positioned to coincide or snap directly to the markers, but that's not all. Soundtrack allows you to effectively re-time musical cues to the scoring markers by simply dragging the marks to new positions in the timeline to match any additional trim edits made in Final Cut Pro.

Round-trip production between the visual applications in Apple's portfolio and Logic is accomplished primarily through the use of the QuickTime media format. Video movies are exported from Final Cut Pro and Motion and are imported into Logic, where they appear in the audio Timeline as video thumbnails. Perfect sync between picture and sound is maintained via timecode—that dependable timepiece under the hood of QuickTime assets, to keep track of hours, minutes, seconds, and frames. Music is exported from Logic either as discrete tracks or stems (groups of discrete tracks), or as a final mix (stereo or surround) and is imported into Final Cut Pro, where it can be mixed further with location audio and other tracks, like sound effects, replacement dialog, or background ambience.

Producers who recognize the importance of a well-engineered audio mix often ask to be a part of the creative review process—enter DVD, the first mass distribution format to dramatically raise the bar on audio quality, with support for Dolby Digital, DTS, even uncompressed PCM audio, with sample rates up to 92 kHz and dynamic range up to 24 bits in length.

Delivery

Finished audio and video programs are distributed to their audience in a variety of formats, some no bigger than a postage stamp (as viewed on the latest generation of 3GPP mobile phones) and some that span screen projection dimensions bigger than the side of a barn (IMAX theaters).

Apple's production applications are completely scalable—designed to support the creation of content in these formats and every resolution in between. In some workflows, **Compressor**, included with Final Cut Pro, Motion, and DVD Studio Pro, is used to encode the completed project into a small form factor more suitable for mass distribution. In other workflows, **Cinema Tools** acts as the intermediary, forwarding a list of instructions to another application or person that uses the information as a roadmap. Quite often, the finished project is simply printed to videotape. In the case of visual-effects shots and other digital intermediate formats, the high-resolution frames are recorded directly to film via what is essentially a high-resolution printer, referred to as a *film recorder*.

Final Cut Pro has revolutionized the world of broadcast news journalism. Hundreds upon hundreds of reporters take to the streets each day armed with camcorders and PowerBooks. Final Cut Pro was the first generation of nonlinear digital editing applications to embrace the mobile tape formats for DV, DVCAM, and DVCPRO. Video that is acquired in these formats is captured with Final Cut Pro via FireWire. The 21st century video journalist is fully capable of editing in the field—shuttling to find the best takes to edit them together into a finished news story. In news, the first to air the story wins, which is why journalists can no longer wait for the van to make it back to the studio before they can edit their content.

MPEG-4 and MPEG-2 are common file formats used to transfer and transmit news stories from the field back to the news bureau. Video journalists, especially those with tight deadlines and bigger capital expenditure budgets, often transmit edited stories directly to the studio via mobile satellite phone systems. Video journalists, especially those with a bit more lead time between deadlines, modest cap ex budgets, and a hankering for double-tall lattes, will often waltz into the nearest Starbucks, connect to the bureau via AirPort Extreme (Wi-Fi), and transfer their finished stories via FTP, while patiently waiting for their next assignment.

Another popular content distribution format is DVD. Since the launch of DVD in 1997, the format has become a favorite of consumers, surpassing VHS tapes in both rentals and sales for a number of obvious reasons. DVDs provide superior image and audio quality. DVDs are digital, and since the laser-reading mechanism never actually comes in contact with the physical disc, the quality does not degrade even after thousands of viewings. DVDs are multilingual, with support for up to nine different audio mixes and 32 different subtitle tracks synchronized to the same video content. Most important, DVDs are both interactive and nonlinear. A few clicks of the remote and you have instant random access to any segment within the program. With all these attributes going for it, DVD makes an ideal distribution format for all forms of video content—feature films, television series, concert films, training videos, product promotions, and client show reels.

iDVD is Apple's consumer DVD authoring application that comes bundled with every Apple computer. Many Final Cut Pro users may consider iDVD to be more than sufficient for their authoring requirements. It's important to know that Apple's DVD Studio Pro application is to iDVD what Final Cut Pro is to iMovie. While it's true that iMovie is a powerful and intuitive consumer video-editing application, there isn't a competent Final Cut Pro editor alive that would trade down to iMovie, because Final Cut Pro offers a level of creative control well beyond anything the iLife application has been designed to deliver.

Likewise, **DVD Studio Pro** provides a level of creative control that goes well beyond the beautiful themes of iDVD. The real-time menu design capabilities of DVD Studio Pro provide the ability to change…well, everything: buttons, shapes behind buttons, movies in buttons, text, motion menu backgrounds, audio beds behind menus, and much more. More important, DVD Studio Pro is engineered to work with still and motion menu templates that have been created by the user.

Audio mixes created in Logic and Soundtrack can be encoded (faster than real time) in **A.Pack**, the Dolby Digital encoding application that is included with DVD Studio Pro. All manner of Dolby mixes, from stereo to 5.1 surround, are supported. For musicians and audio engineers, DVD Studio Pro's Timeline can support multiple audio mixes, which means they can author audio-only DVDs that producers can use to audition different versions of the mix (stereo, surround, music without vocals for karaoke, and so on). Buttons and menus can be created directly within DVD Studio Pro, which has integrated menu design tools to greatly simplify the authoring process.

Round-trip production in DVD Studio Pro perfectly complements still menus created in Photoshop. In DVD Studio Pro, it's possible to select a menu and open-in-editor directly into Photoshop, with all layers intact. You can make any revisions you like within Photoshop, and saving the file communicates the revision update directly back to DVD Studio Pro.

Motion should be considered the ultimate DVD motion menu design application. In the menu-creation workflow, video elements from the originating program are imported into Motion, where filter effects and motion paths are added to convert them into vibrant video montages. Text for buttons, like "play all" and "chapter selection," can be created and animated directly within Motion. For added effect, particles from Motion's built-in particle engine can be incorporated into menu designs. Exporting menus from Motion for use in DVD Studio Pro is as simple as saving the project to the user's Movies folder.

Round-trip production is tightly integrated between Motion and DVD Studio Pro. From the authoring asset bin of DVD Studio Pro it's possible to open-in-editor, launching the application for direct access to those elements originally crafted in Motion. Any changes made to motion menus in Motion are automatically updated to DVD Studio Pro upon saving. This kind of revisionist functionality is perfectly suited to the design of DVD menus, many of which are recycled from project to project—different movies and slideshows in the same overall DVD menu theme.

Workgroup Collaboration

As stated at the introduction to this appendix, round-trip production can range from a single user working with multiple applications on the same computer, all the way up to a large group of editors and engineers accessing vast amounts of data in a shared storage environment. Any facility with two or more artists creating content under the same roof is perfect for workgroup collaboration of this sort because productivity increases exponentially when multiple users can access the very same media. No time wasted copying files; less chance of errors from revision-naming conventions. Investments in hardware can be recouped sooner when the storage is centralized, simply because the storage can be dynamically allocated wherever it is needed most.

A *storage area network*, or *SAN*, is designed for exactly this type of collaboration. A SAN is a network whose primary function is to link multiple storage systems to multiple desktop workstations. Typical SANs today operate on 2-gigabit-per-second fiber channel cabling connected through one or more multiport fiber channel switches. One of the best features of a properly designed SAN is that the storage volume can be scaled dynamically as the production workload increases, without users' ever having to take the network offline or reboot administrative systems. **Xsan** is in this class. It is what's referred to as an enterprise-class (that is, large-facilities-that-can't-afford-the-slightest-bit-of-downtime), high-performance SAN file system. It runs on Mac OS X and is compatible with systems running on a selection of qualified non-Apple SAN client seats.

Like the best enterprise-class SANs, Xsan includes a *metadata controller* that acts like a network traffic cop. Whenever any user on the network wants to read or write to a file, the user's computer asks the SAN traffic cop for permission to proceed. Xsan's metadata controller software includes a "failover" provision, which means that these traffic cop duties are automatically handed over to another computer in the event the first controller should fail for whatever reason. The whole point of built-in protections like failover and multi-pathing (where a second cable is used if the first is cut) is to ensure that the network is operational and the media and project files on the SAN volumes are available to all users all the time.

Storage area networks offer the promise of tremendous increases in creativity and productivity not unlike those of the networked office environment where multiple users have simultaneous access to the Internet and printers. Apple's pro apps, and the level of round-trip production they provide, are ideally suited for use in a centralized storage, collaborative workgroup environment supported by Xsan.

Summary

Professional production involves a number of creative disciplines, including capture and editing of digital video; design of complex motion graphics and photo-realistic visual effects; composition of well-crafted music scores; and editing, sweetening, and mixing all the audio tracks, including dialog and sound effects. Depending on the intended audience, finished projects are either printed directly to videotape, recorded to motion picture film, or compressed for distribution via FTP, satellite transmission, or some other streaming-media format. Thanks to the proliferation of DVD, the creative process doesn't end when songs, videos, or films are mastered. Instead, elements from programs are used to create compelling, interactive DVD menus, the majority of which now include motion graphics and seamless motion menu–to–motion menu transitions.

Apple's round-trip production paradigm heralds a new era in content creation workflows. In the same way that you can save spreadsheets in Microsoft Excel and have them automatically update in Microsoft Word, designers can now save their motion graphics in Motion and have them update automatically in Final Cut Pro and DVD Studio Pro. Xsan's storage area network brings all these apps together in a collaborative workgroup environment. The accompanying increase in productivity is incalculable, with benefits that go well beyond financial measures. The quality of design improves dramatically, simply because there's more time to experiment; more time to try the best filter, behavior, text animation, or particle effect; more time to try various cuts and transitions; more time to create custom DVD menu transitions and designs. And because Apple's system architecture takes full advantage of the stability of Unix and the increased performance of 64-bit processors, powerful graphics cards, and fast SDRAM, new combinations of effects, transitions, filters, behaviors, and particles can be previewed in real time.

Real-time performance and round-trip production, on a single system or in a collaborative workgroup—that's how the creative work *flows* between Apple's professional applications.

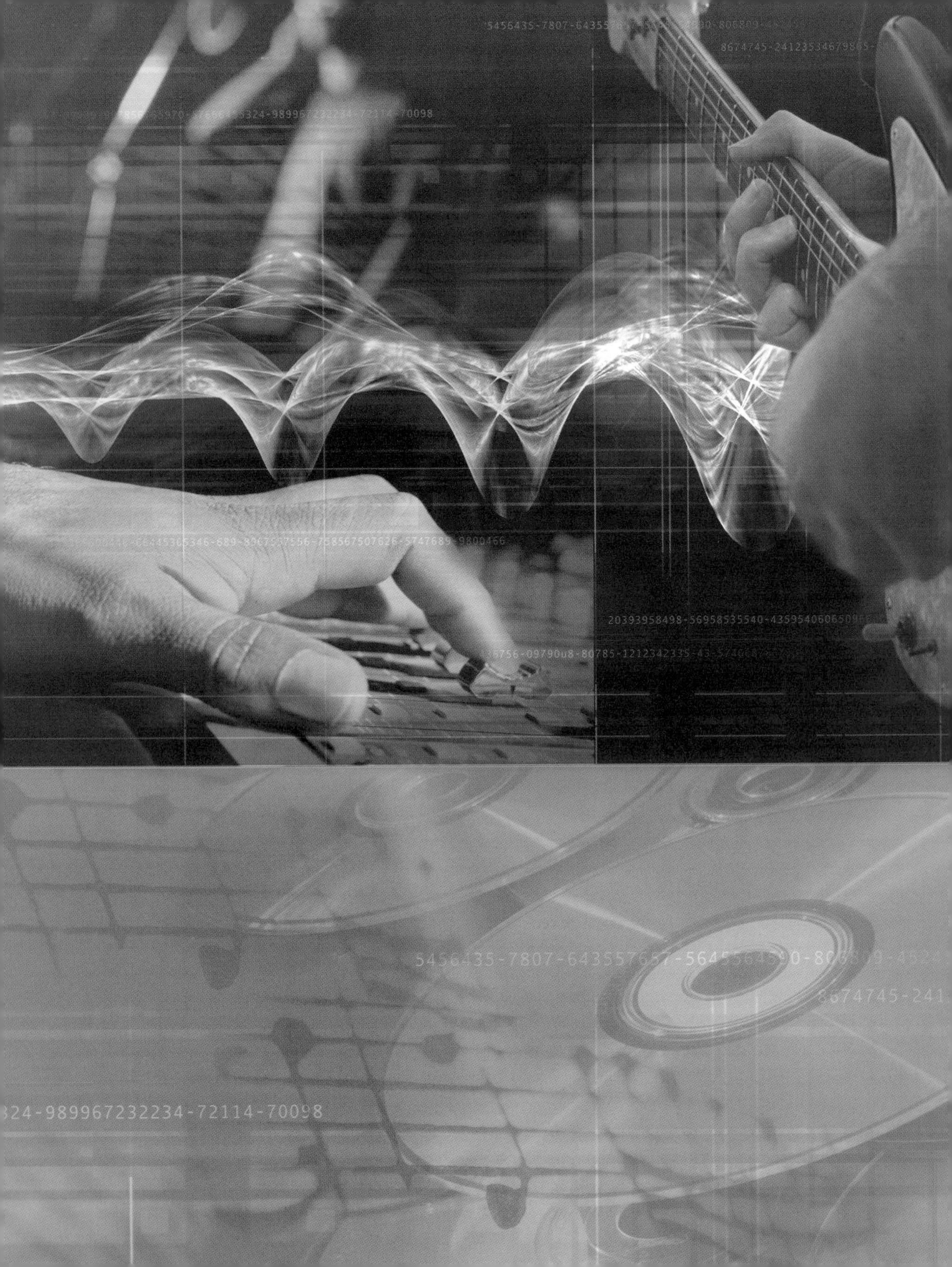

Glossary

aftertouch MIDI data-type generated by pressure on keys after they have been struck. Aftertouch is also known as pressure.

AIFF Audio Interchange File Format. A cross-platform file format supported by a large number of digital video and audio editing applications. AIFF audio can use a variety of bit depths, but the two most commonly used are 16 bit and 24 bit.

alias An object in the Arrange window that mirrors a MIDI Region someplace else. You cannot edit an alias, only a real Region, but any change to the Region will be reflected in the alias. To create an alias, Shift-Option-drag the original MIDI Region to a new location.

Anchor point A temporal reference point, or the point Logic uses to snap a Region to the Arrange window's time grid. In the Audio window and Sample Editor, the Anchor is represented by a small triangle under the Region.

Apple Loops An audio file in which recurring rhythmic musical elements or elements suitable for repetition are recorded. Apple Loops have tags that allow Logic to perform time stretching and pitch shifting. These tags also allow you to quickly locate files by instrument, genre, or mood in the Loop Browser.

arming Enabling a track to be recorded.

Arrange window The heart of Logic. The primary working window of the program where Audio and MIDI Regions are edited and moved to create a song arrangement.

Arrow tool The default selection tool, shaped like an arrow. It is in every window's toolbox. In the Logic Reference Manual it is sometimes called the Pointer tool.

audio file Any digital audio recording stored on your hard disk. The default storage format for audio files in Logic is AIFF, but you can store audio files in the Sound Designer II and WAV formats as well.

Audio Instrument A software instrument. In Logic, software instrument plug-ins are inserted into Audio Instrument Objects. Software instrument recording takes place on Audio Instrument tracks in the Arrange window. Playback of these tracks is routed via the Audio Instrument Object.

audio interface A device that converts sound between the digital and analog domains.

Audio Object An Object found in Logic's Environment that shows Logic where to send audio signals. It can assume the form of any audio channel available to your system—a track channel, an Audio Instrument channel, a bus, or an output. When it's expanded, an Audio Object looks like a channel strip on a standard hardware mixing console.

Audio Region Chosen area of an audio file that is registered in the Audio window for use in the song and that can be placed on audio tracks in the Arrange window, just as a MIDI Region can be placed on MIDI tracks. Audio Regions are pointers to portions of audio files. You can use all of Logic's tools to edit Audio Regions. Editing is nondestructive to the original audio file. See also *Region* and *MIDI Region.*

audio track A track in Logic's Arrange window used for the playback, recording, and editing of Audio Regions.

Audio window Logic window used to add audio files from your hard disks to your song. You can use this window to rename audio files and Regions, to optimize files, and to change your song's sampling rate.

Autodrop mode A mode that forces Logic to automatically start and stop recording at predefined positions. Typically, it's used to re-record a badly played passage in a recording that's fine otherwise. This technique is also called punching in or out (see *punch in/out*).

Autoload Song A song with your favorite settings and preferred window layouts. It loads automatically when you launch Logic and serves as a starting point for your songs and projects.

automation The ability to record, edit, and play back the movements of all knobs and switches, including volume faders and Pan, EQ, and Aux Send controls.

Automation Quick Access A Logic feature that assigns a slider or knob on your hardware MIDI controller keyboard to modify Track Automation data.

Aux An Auxiliary Object, either mono or stereo, in the Audio layer of the Environment. The Aux Object serves as a way to monitor an audio signal in Logic without recording it.

B

bar A measure of music, containing a specified number of beats, that establishes the rhythmic structure of the composition.

Bar Ruler The timeline that runs the length of the song, divided into bars, beats, and even finer divisions. It contains the Song Position Line (SPL), the cycle and autodrop locators, and markers. It is found at the top of the Arrange, Matrix, Hyper, and Score windows.

bit resolution A representation of the dynamic accuracy of a recording.

bounce To combine several tracks of audio into one file.

bus A send/return routing scheme for audio channels. In Logic, effects can be sent to and from Bus Objects for processing or submixing tasks.

Bus Audio Object in the Environment's Audio layer. Usually used to route the signal of an individual send bus to Output Objects.

bypass To temporarily deactivate a plug-in.

C

Caps Lock Keyboard A small MIDI controller on your screen, activated by pressing the Caps Lock key on your computer keyboard.

Catch A window function that enables you to see the positions of recorded events in a song as it plays. The Catch button shows a man running.

CD-Audio Short for *Compact Disc–Audio;* the current standard for stereo music CDs: 44.1 kHz sampling rate and 16-bit depth.

channel A path used to transport a signal.

channel strip A virtual representation of a channel strip on a mixing console. Each channel strip contains a number of controls, such as a Mute button, volume fader, pan/balance knob, output selector, and Bus or Insert slots.

Channel Strip settings Plug-ins that combine to make a certain sound.

clip To feed too much signal through a channel, producing a distorted sound. Audio Objects have a clip detector.

continuous control number (cc#) The number assigned by the MIDI specification regarding audio events or software functions such as volume, modulation, or sustain.

Core Audio The standardized audio driver for a computer running Mac OS X 10.2 or higher. Allows the connection of all audio interfaces that are Core Audio compatible.

Core MIDI The standardized MIDI driver for a computer running Mac OS X 10.2 or higher. Allows the connection of all MIDI devices that are Core MIDI compatible.

cross-fade To bring the volume of one audio file up while simultaneously lowering the volume of another file in a smooth transition.

Crosshair tool A crosshair-shaped tool used in the Hyper Editor to select and adjust MIDI events.

Cycle mode A mode in Logic in which you can repeat a section of a song. To turn on the Cycle mode, click the Cycle button in the Transport window. Two locators define a cycle Region.

D

dB Short for *decibels,* a measurement that relates the relative change in the volume of audio. Audio Objects have level meters that display playback or input monitor levels in decibels.

digital audio workstation (DAW) A computer that records, mixes, and produces audio files.

Digital Factory A suite of digital signal processors in the Sample Editor. It can time-compress or time-expand an Audio Region, change its pitch, add groove or swing to a machinelike audio loop, or alter its sampling rate. The Digital Factory functions are destructive, permanently changing the source audio file.

digital signal processing (DSP) In Logic, the mathematical process of manipulating digital information to modify sound. An example is in the Inserts area, which assigns DSP effects such as dynamic range compression and delay to a channel's sound.

dithering A process of reducing an audio signal from a higher-bit resolution to a lower one.

driver A software program that allows your computer to communicate with another piece of hardware.

E

editor In Logic, one of a multitude of editors to help you compose music. All of them alter the raw input in some way. The primary MIDI editors in Logic are the Hyper Editor and the Event List, and the Matrix, Sample, and Score Editors. You can edit Audio Regions in the Arrange window, Audio window, and Sample Editor.

Environment A section of Logic that graphically reflects the relationship between hardware devices outside your computer and virtual devices within your computer.

Environment layer A place to organize the Objects in the Environment for easy access. As a general rule, Objects of the same type are usually placed on the same layer.

Eraser tool A tool for deleting items. When you click a selected item, all other currently selected items are also deleted.

event A MIDI message. The main events in Logic are note, control-change, pitch bend, aftertouch, and SysEx events. MIDI events can be edited in a number of ways.

Event List A list of events and Objects that gives you access to all recorded event data. Thus, you can directly manipulate events and Objects and make precise alterations.

F

fader Generally thought of as a volume control found on audio channels. In Logic, a fader can also be an Object that sends out and responds to MIDI events. In this context a fader can be a knob, slider, numerical display, or button.

Fade tool One of the tools in the Arrange window toolbox. The Fade tool creates a cross-fade when you click and hold the mouse button as you drag across a section where two Audio Regions meet. You can also drag it over the beginning or end of a Region to create a fade-in or fade-out, respectively.

Finger tool A tool that looks like a hand with an extended index finger. The selection tool changes from the Arrow tool to the Finger tool to enable you to manipulate events or change window parameters. Different mouse and key commands activate the Finger tool in different windows.

5.1 A common surround sound format, typically comprising five full-frequency speakers, which are fed by five independent channels, plus one dedicated low-frequency subwoofer.

floating A term that describes a window that's always visible on your Desktop. You can open a window as a floating window by holding down the Option key while selecting from the Windows menu.

folder An Object in Logic's Arrange window that contains MIDI Regions, Audio Regions, or other folders.

Freeze function A function that freezes a track and its plug-ins into a file and then plays back the frozen file instead of the original one, saving your computer's processing power.

G

General MIDI (GM) A specification designed to ensure compatibility between MIDI devices. A musical sequence generated by a GM instrument should play correctly on any other GM synthesizer or sound module.

Global Tempo track A way to view and edit all the tempo changes of a song. The track displays tempo changes as nodes.

Global Video track A track displaying frames of a QuickTime movie as "thumbnails" that are perfectly synchronized with the music, making it ideal for film scoring. Cuts in the movie can be automatically detected and marked.

Glue tool A dedicated tool for merging Regions or Objects.

grid Vertical lines used to map the positions of measures, beats, and sub-beats in various editors.

H

Hand tool A tool that appears when you click and hold an Object with the Arrow tool. It is used to move Objects or events in the editors.

headroom Refers to how may decibels are available before *clipping,* or distortion, occurs.

help tag A small text window that appears when the mouse cursor is placed over an interface element, indicating its name or value.

HyperDraw A function that lets you create and edit automation data in the Arrange window by graphically inserting a set of points or nodes, which are automatically connected. Using HyperDraw, you can also make volume and panning changes in the Matrix and Score Editors.

Hyper Editor One of Logic's four editors for MIDI data. It is used mainly for creating and editing drum sequences and control-change data.

hyper set A layer in the Hyper Editor containing a user-defined collection of MIDI events.

I

input filtering Preventing MIDI information such as pitch bend or after-touch events from reaching a track. The Input Filter tab is in the Song Settings window's MIDI pane.

input monitoring A way to determine which signal to listen to on record-enabled tracks. You can use Auto Input Monitoring to hear a track even when Logic is not recording.

Input Object Audio Object in the Environment's Audio Layer. It represents the physical inputs of your audio interface and helps manage audio from your audio interface into Logic.

insert A way to enhance the sound passing through an Audio Object with a plug-in.

Instrument An Object in Logic's Environment that represents a physical or virtual device that reacts to MIDI information.

I/O buffer size How big a bite a computer tries to chew at one time when working with audio. The larger the buffer, the more recorded channels of audio can be played at the same time. Larger buffers make your system react more slowly when recording, however. The buffer size is set in the Audio Hardware & Drivers preferences.

K

key command An instruction to Logic that triggers an action, done by pressing a key or a combination of keys. All of Logic's main functions can be activated by key commands.

L

latency The delay between, say, playing your keyboard and hearing the sound. One factor contributing to latency is the I/O buffer size.

Link mode A mode that determines the relationship of one window to another. Clicking the Link button toggles the Link mode.

local menu The place where the functions of the currently active window can be found.

locators Indicators displayed to the right of the Transport buttons in the Transport window. You can define locator points for the cycle (on the left-hand side) and autodrop zones (on the right-hand side). Cycle locators themselves are referred to as *left* and *right locators.* The left cycle locator is on the top; the right cycle locator is on the bottom.

Loop A Region parameter. When the Loop function is on, the Region will repeat until it encounters another Object on the same track in the Arrange window, the end marker of a folder, or the end marker of a song.

M

Magnifying Glass tool A tool that enables you to zoom in on any part of the display. Pressing the Control key while rubber-band selecting a part of the window section enlarges the area. You can also activate the Magnifying Glass from other tools by holding down the Control key.

marker Used for indicating and quickly moving to sections of your song.

Marquee tool A crosshair-shaped tool in the Arrange window with which you can select and edit Regions, or even portions of Regions.

Matrix Editor The main MIDI editing environment in Logic. It displays note events as horizontal beams. Events can be cut, copied, moved, and resized in a similar fashion to Regions in the Arrange window.

menu bar The bar extending along the top of the computer screen that gives options for global functions like opening windows and saving and loading songs. The local menu bars in the individual editing windows provide access to most of Logic's functions.

metronome In Logic, a component that produces a sound measuring the beat. It can be set with a button in the Transport. A MIDI Metronome Click Object must be present in the Environment to activate the metronome.

MIDI Musical instrument digital interface. It's an industry standard that allows devices like synthesizers and computers to communicate with each other. It controls a musical note's pitch, length, and volume, among other characteristics.

MIDI channel A conduit for MIDI data. MIDI data flows through MIDI ports in channels, and up to 16 MIDI channels can pass through each port at the same time.

MIDI Region Data container for MIDI events, shown in the Arrange window as a named horizontal beam. It does not contain sounds, but rather contains MIDI events that tell a synthesizer how to produce sounds. In earlier Logic versions MIDI Regions were called sequences.

mixing The process of shaping the overall sound of a song by adjusting the volume levels and pan positions, adding EQ and other effects, and using automation to dynamically alter aspects of the song.

MP3 A digital coding standard used to compress audio files and distribute them over the Internet.

Multi Instrument An Object in the Environment that represents a multi-timbral device.

multi-timbral Describes an instrument or other device that can use several MIDI channels simultaneously.

mute To silence the output of a Region or track.

Mute tool A tool that enables you to stop an Object from playing by clicking the Object with it.

N

nodes Positions in HyperDraw and automation tracks that mark the positions where data manipulation begins or ends. Occasionally referred to as points.

nondestructive Said of an audio editor that does not change your source audio files in the course of editing. Logic is generally a nondestructive editing application.

O

Object In Logic, a general term that refers to the graphical representations of elements in the Environment. Each connection between Logic and your studio's MIDI devices is represented by an Object, and Objects can be used to create and process MIDI and audio data. Audio Objects (see separate entry) reside in the Environment's Audio layer.

Object Parameter box A box that displays the properties of an Object in the Environment or of a selected track's Object in the Arrange window.

Output Object Audio Object in Logic's Environment controlling the output level and pan/balance for each output on your audio interface. It is assigned to a specific hardware output in the Object Parameter box.

P

PCM Pulse-code modulated audio. This is simply uncompressed digital audio, including AIFFs, WAVs, and SDII files.

Pencil tool A tool used to draw various types of information in an editor.

plug-in A small software application that adds functions to a main program (in this case, Logic). Logic's plug-ins are typically audio effects processors.

pointer A general term for the mouse pointer. (Logic documentation sometimes refers to the Arrow tool as *the Pointer tool*.)

points The positions in HyperDraw and in the automation editors that demarcate the spots where data manipulation begins or ends.

preferences User settings that are applied to all Logic songs.

programs Synthesizer sounds.

proxy movie A low-resolution and tightly compressed version of a high-resolution movie that places less strain on your computer as you score.

punch in/out A technique that allows you to interrupt playback and record audio as the sound is playing. It can be automated in Logic.

Q

quantize To correct the rhythm of notes so that they conform to a specific time grid.

QuickTime Apple's cross-platform standard for digitized media. You can run QuickTime movies in a Logic window or on a Global Video track, in sync with the song. Whenever you move the Song Position Line, the video follows, and vice versa.

R

Region A rectangular beam that represents a container for audio or MIDI data. Regions can be found in the tracks of the Arrange window. There are three types: Audio Regions, MIDI Regions, and Folder Regions.

Region Parameter box Box in the top left corner of the Arrange window, used to nondestructively set the individual Regions' playback parameters, including quantization, transposition, velocity, and delay. These parameters do not alter the stored data. Rather, they affect how the events are played back.

Replace mode An operating state you can activate in the Transport window. The Replace button is next to the Cycle and Autodrop buttons. In Replace mode, newly recorded information takes the place of the old information.

rubber-band select A method of selecting multiple items at once. With the Arrow tool, click, hold, and drag the mouse on a window's background. Any item that the rubber band encloses or touches is selected.

S

sample accurate Describes editors (such as the Sample Editor or Arrange window) that display or allow you to edit individual samples in an Audio Region.

Sample Editor An editor in Logic in which stereo or mono audio files are destructively cut, reversed, shortened, changed in gain, and processed in a number of other ways. The Sample Editor allows sample-accurate editing of an audio file.

sampling rate Refers to the number of times per second a digital audio file is sampled. When audio comes in through your sound card, analog-to-digital converters *sample*, or check, the signal's voltage level. Logic can record and edit audio at sampling rates ranging from 44.1 kHz (44,100 times per second) to 192 kHz.

Scissors tool A tool with which you divide Regions. It offers different options for dividing Audio Regions from those for MIDI Regions.

Score Editor Logic editor that deals with standard musical notation.

screenset An onscreen layout of windows that you can save. Each window retains its position, size, and zoom settings. You can save up to 90 screensets for each song.

Scroll in Play A function similar to the Catch function, but instead of the SPL playing across the Arrange area's Regions, the Arrange area's Regions scroll past a stationary SPL, like tape scrolling past a playhead.

scrubbing Moving the pointer back and forth (in a scrubbing motion) while playing back an Audio Region to locate a specific section.

Send An output on an audio channel that splits a portion of a channel's sound out and *sends* it through a system bus to another Audio Object.

sequencer A computer application that allows you to record both digital audio and MIDI data and blend the sounds together in a software mixing console.

Shuffle A Drag mode that causes a Region to *shuffle up* to the Region immediately to its left or right, depending on the Shuffle mode selected. This ensures that one Region plays smoothly into the next with no drop in the track's audio.

SMPTE Society of Motion Picture and Television Engineers. These folks set up a synchronization system that divides time into hours, minutes, seconds, frames, and subframes.

solo A way to temporarily allow you to hear one or more selected tracks, events, or Regions without hearing others that aren't soloed.

Solo tool A tool that enables you to listen to selected Objects by themselves (click and hold the Object to do so).

song A main Logic file that contains all references necessary to produce a final audio output.

Song Position Line (SPL) A vertical gray line on the Bar Ruler and in other horizontal time-based windows that indicates where you are in a song. In Play mode the SPL lets you hear that section of your song. You can position the SPL with the mouse, by clicking the Bar Ruler, or by entering bar numbers in a dialog.

song template   An empty song file that is preconfigured with a set of empty Arrange window tracks designed for a specific purpose such as mastering, 24-track recording, or surround mixing.

Standard Instrument   The simplest track playback Object. It transmits MIDI data over just one channel, which makes it perfect for connecting to an external mono-timbral MIDI device such as a digital effects unit.

Standard MIDI file   A common file type that almost any MIDI sequencer can read. In Logic you can export selected MIDI Regions as Standard MIDI files.

step-time   Recording notes one at a time in a MIDI Region.

synthesizer   A hardware or software device used to generate sounds. Logic features several software synthesizers, including the ES1, ES2, EFM 1, ES E, ES P, and ES M.

SysEx   System Exclusive data.

T

tempo   The speed at which a piece of music is played, measured in beats per minute. You can create and edit tempo changes in the Global Tempo track.

Text tool   A tool for naming Audio and MIDI Regions.

time signature   Two numerals separated by a diagonal bar that appear at the beginning of a song. Common time signatures are 4/4 and 2/4. The first number denotes the number of notes in a measure, or bar. The second number denotes a unit of time for each beat. With a 2/4 signature, each bar has two beats; each beat is a quarter note long.

time-stretch   To change the length of an Audio Region without changing its pitch. You can do this in the Arrange window or Sample Editor by using menu or key commands.

toolbox   The box on the left edge of Logic's editing windows that holds editing tools.

track A row in the Arrange window that contains a collection of MIDI or Audio Regions that can be played back. Each track has a specified destination where the data will go.

Track Automation Used for programming control changes that are not necessarily tied to a specific Region, such as a volume fade or a cutoff sweep. Track Automation allows you to quickly find and automate any plug-in parameter. It has its own recording system, which functions independently of Logic's other recording features.

Track List A list to the left of the Arrange window's Arrange area that displays the Objects assigned to various tracks as well as the Track buttons. Sometimes called the Track column.

Track Mixer A virtual mixing console used to position Logic's tracks. It mirrors the number and order of tracks in the Arrange window. Using this window, you can also change a track's volume or panorama (pan) position, insert DSP effects, or mute and solo channels.

Transform window An editor used to select and modify various aspects of MIDI events according to user-defined parameters.

Transport panel An area in the top left of the Arrange window that holds buttons used to control Logic's playback and recording functions. These buttons (Record, Pause, Play, Stop, Rewind, Forward) work the same way as the control buttons on a cassette deck or recordable audio CD player.

Transport window A window that contains controls for recording and playback functions. It contains the same settings as the Transport panel as well as other settings.

V

velocity The force with which a MIDI note is struck.

virtual instrument A software element that mimics a traditional hardware sound module.

W

WAV, WAVE The primary audio file format used by Windows-compatible computers. In Logic, all recorded and bounced WAV files are in Broadcast Wave format.

waveform A visual representation of an audio signal; it fluctuates according to the signal's volume over time.

X

x/y scroll element A feature of every window that enables you to move horizontally and vertically at the same time.

Z

zero crossing A point in an audio file where the waveform crosses the zero amplitude axis. If you cut an audio file at a zero crossing there will be no click at the cut point.

zoom An action that enlarges (zooms in on) or reduces (zooms out from) a viewing area in any window. The Zoom controls found in the bottom left and top right corners of windows and the Magnifying Glass in the toolbox are zoom tools.

Index